I LIKE IKE

D0864163

American Presidential Elections

MICHAEL NELSON

JOHN M. MCCARDELL, JR.

I LIKE IKE

THE PRESIDENTIAL
ELECTION OF 1952
JOHN ROBERT GREENE

UNIVERSITY PRESS OF KANSAS

Published by the University Press of Kansas (Lawrence, Kansas 66045), which was organized by the Kansas Board of Regents and is operated and funded by Emporia State University, Fort Hays State University, Kansas State University, Pittsburg State University, the University of Kansas, and Wichita State University.

Library of Congress Cataloging-in-Publication Data

Names: Greene, John Robert, 1955– author.

Title: I like Ike : the presidential election of 1952 / John Robert Greene.

Description: Lawrence, Kansas : University Press of Kansas, 2017. | Series: American presidential elections | Includes bibliographical references and index.

Identifiers: LCCN 2016047603 | ISBN 9780700624041 (hardback) | ISBN 9780700624058 (paperback) | ISBN 9780700624065 (ebook)

Subjects: LCSH: Presidents—United States—Election—1952. | BISAC: HISTORY / United States / 20th Century. | BIOGRAPHY & AUTOBIOGRAPHY / Presidents & Heads of State. | POLITICAL SCIENCE / Political Process / Elections.

Classification: LCC JK526 1952 .G74 2017 | DDC 324.973/0918—dc23

LC record available at https://lccn.loc.gov/2016047603.

British Library Cataloguing-in-Publication Data is available.

Printed in the United States of America

10 9 8 7 6 5 4 3 2 1

The paper used in this publication is recycled and contains 30 percent postconsumer waste. It is acid free and meets the minimum requirements of the American National Standard for Permanence of Paper for Printed Library Materials Z39.48-1992.

For Patty, T. J., Kate, Chris, Jenny, Mary Rose, and Luna

CONTENTS

I have been writing books now for thirty-five years, and from that experience and the writing of this book in particular, I have learned a very valuable lesson—one that leads me to make a modest proposal to the publishing industry. I have come to believe that it should be required of authors of every nonfiction book that they agree to revisit that same topic twenty years later and write another book on the same topic. I float this proposal with tongue only mildly in cheek; the book that follows sprang from just such a revisitation, and it was a career-changing experience.

In 1985, I published my first book, *The Crusade: The Presidential Election of 1952*.[1] It was a(n ever so slightly) revised dissertation, which meant two things. First, while it was the best I could do at the time, the writing wasn't great. And two, I was trying to break into the business by defending a revisionist thesis that would make me stand out from the academic crowd. My archival research was strong—I vaguely remember driving all over the country in a well-dented Ford Pinto and consulting every document I could find. I looked at the documents with the eye of a youthful skeptic. I argued that in 1952, Dwight D. Eisenhower and Adlai E. Stevenson II, both of whom repeatedly told their supporters and the world that they did not want to be candidates or to campaign for the presidency of the United States, were little more than Machiavellian dissemblers. Indeed, I came within a hairbreadth of calling both of them liars. Instead, I settled for a new term (dissertations and first books are full of new, catchy terms)—"Non-Participant Politics"—arguing that while they consistently said that they didn't want to run, in reality they did want to run. But saying that they didn't want to run was part of a calculated strategy designed to make both men more appealing to a public that was sick of politics as usual, particularly during the Korean War phase of the Truman administration. I liked what I wrote, and I was proud of the output. I moved on to other things.

For whatever reason, I have remained the only writer to have produced a book-length monograph on the whole of the presidential election of 1952. Thus, while I was toiling in different historical vineyards, I continued to be called upon to speak on the subject, which I gladly did, without revising the conclusions I had come to in 1985. My "Non-Participant Politics" argument was great fodder for audiences that loved either Eisenhower or Stevenson, and during the question-and-answer session they would often come at me with a vengeance, charging that I had characterized their hero as a liar. My thesis was like red meat thrown at angry lions, and the resulting give-and-take was always fun.

That is, until I was asked by Daniel Holt, then the director of the Dwight D. Eisenhower Library in Abilene, Kansas, to deliver the keynote address at a daylong conference, titled "The Great Crusade: The Road to the White House, 1952," held in November 1992 on the fortieth anniversary of Eisenhower's victory. My job was to set the table, so to speak, for the alumni of the era who had joined the panel—including Abbott and Wanda Washburn of the Citizens for Eisenhower, former governor of Minnesota Harold Stassen, *NBC News* correspondent Ray Scherer, and Herbert Brownell, Eisenhower's political Yoda in 1952 and ultimately his attorney general. When I spoke, I laid it on thick about Eisenhower and Stevenson and their political deceit. Polite applause followed my talk, and then we adjourned. As I moved away from the podium, I saw the panelists huddling. I started to walk toward them, but Scherer intercepted me. With a wide grin, he quietly mumbled, "Dr. Greene, you don't want to go over there." I froze and took my seat at the table onstage. Sitting next to me was Brownell, who, as was his wont, immediately began to make small talk with me while we reset for the next session. But I could not help myself. "General Brownell," I quietly pleaded, "what were you folks discussing over there?" He smiled but did not look me in the eye as he slowly intoned, "Oh, we liked your speech. But you know, don't you, that you are dead wrong?" Believe me when I tell you that no negative book review can hit you quite as hard as that. They were gentlemen all; none of them—not Brownell, not Abbott Washburn (who quietly took me to task on another break)—said anything remotely critical about my work in public during the conference, and they continued to be polite with my lame attempts to wheedle into their conversation with the audience about the campaign (I mean, for a bit, I was shaking). But my notes for that day's conference belie a bit of an epiphany; on the back of a program, in big block letters, I scribbled: "Was I wrong?"

That question would dog me for the next two decades. Although given the opportunity to speak on the election on several more occasions, I found myself backing off from the stridency of my thesis. I used words that had not been in my younger lexicon—words like "might" and "perhaps." I began to consider revisiting the election, but the opportunity to rethink *The Crusade* was buried in a host of other projects and responsibilities: that is, until 2013, when I first spoke with Fred Woodward, then the director of the University Press of Kansas and now the emeritus director of that press, about writing a book on 1952—a new book—for its American Presidential Elections series. Fred always reminded me of what I like to think the editors of the great trade houses in New York City were like: nurturing their authors' ideas, tolerating their peculiarities, and, in general, being shepherds who help the author move a good book from his or her mind to the printed page. Thus, he didn't shoot me down when I said that I wanted to "fix" (I think I used that word—if I didn't, I should have) *The Crusade*. After finishing a few books that I had been working on, including one for Kansas, where, for the first time, I revised and expanded a previous work, I was ready to begin on 1952.

So I read. There was much to read. I reread each of the major sources used for *The Crusade*, as well as the wealth of new writing on Eisenhower and Stevenson. I revisited the Eisenhower Library and the Seeley G. Mudd Manuscript Library at Princeton University, repository of the Stevenson papers. I revisited Walter Johnson's edition of Stevenson's papers, which was available to me in 1985, but which I found I had simply glossed over. I read Clarence E. Wunderlin's new edition of the papers of Ohio senator Robert A. Taft, Eisenhower's chief opponent for the Republican nomination, as well as the magnificent editing job done by Louis Galambos and others on Eisenhower's papers (as I claim in my bibliographical essay, the epitome of manuscript publication projects). I read them as carefully as I could, with a patience that I do not believe is inherent in a doctoral student and is rarely present in anyone writing his or her first book. I tried to practice what I have preached in more than thirty years of the teaching of historical methodology to eager undergraduates: let the sources come to you. Don't read into them. Let them talk to you. And *then* judge them.

Finally, I felt it was time to reread *The Crusade*. I had not read it in three decades, and as I did so, I continually heard Brownell whispering in my ear that I had been wrong. What I found were two things, both of which ultimately informed this volume. The first was that I had, indeed, made very few factual errors in 1985. Several sections of *The Crusade*, I humbly believed, were still pretty good. With some fine-tuning, they are included herein as parts of *I Like Ike* (for which I am grateful to the Rowman and Littlefield Publishing Group). But the second thing was the unmistakable, unalterable revelation that Brownell had been absolutely right. After reading the sources with patience and context, I had come to a completely different conclusion than I had thirty years ago. This present volume will argue that both Dwight Eisenhower and Adlai Stevenson were absolutely sincere in their desire not to run for the presidency in 1952. However, for myriad reasons that were different for each man, they ultimately changed their minds. While they never lost their disdain for the process and never lost their hope that somehow, in Stevenson's borrowed words at the Democratic Convention in July 1952, the cup would pass from them, they both eventually decided that they had to run. Neither man was drafted—on that point I was clear in *The Crusade*, and I have held to that point even more emphatically in *I Like Ike*. But there was nothing Machiavellian or dissembling about their efforts. "Non-Participant Politics" was a great catchphrase, but it is no longer how I see the evidence.

Quite aside from recasting my basic thesis, I found myself reintroducing myself to the protagonists in the story. I found a new, deeper role for Bob Taft. I found a much less important role for Richard M. Nixon, Eisenhower's running mate, than most scholars have assigned him, and I now see his famous "Checkers Speech" in the full light of this revelation. I brought Harry Truman into the narrative—loudly and earthily, of course—in a manner that had eluded me before. Most important, I found a deeper respect for the political skills and the intellectual sincerity of both Dwight Eisenhower and Adlai Stevenson. If the reader continues to believe, as did I thirty years ago, that Ike and Adlai were Machiavellians who coyly sold Americans on their reticence, when in fact they wanted to be sought out for the job, I continue to respect that point of view. It has many strong and worthy adherents, many of whom I have referenced when relevant. But I would ask the reader to reconsider the election of 1952, as I hope I have done, on its own terms, without straining the evidence. Should he or she persist in supporting "Non-Participant Politics," I might well smile and softly mumble, "But you're wrong."

My biggest debt of gratitude goes to two directors of the University Press of Kansas: first, Emeritus Director Fred Woodward, who let me read and reflect on this material in a timely fashion; second, Charles Myers, who showed patience with this project and possesses the wit of a writer (writers know what I am talking about). I am proud to claim Kansas as my publishing home; my thanks to Mike Kehoe, Karl Janssen,

Andrea Laws, Larisa Martin, and Sara Henderson White for their efforts and skill. Special thanks to Kelly Chrisman Jacques, who guided this project from start to finish, and copy editor Susan Ecklund, who improved this book with every query. My friend and colleague Professor Roxana Spano read the entire manuscript, offering many thoughtful and probing insights.

Cazenovia College has been my intellectual home for almost four decades. I cannot imagine teaching anywhere else, and teaching there has no doubt helped me evolve into a better writer. I particularly thank Interim President Margery A. Pinet, Vice President of Academic Affairs Sharon Dettmer, and Division Chair Stewart A. Weisman for their daily support. I also thank Sarah Diederich and Anna Marchant, late of the Academic Affairs Office at Cazenovia, and Michele Tesch and Rebekah Beckwith, presently of that office, for their cheery goodwill and professional expertise. Money can often be tight at a small school, but at Cazenovia College, there has long been a true commitment to the fostering of innovative scholarship throughout the faculty. The institution as a whole must be thanked for its financial support, both through a yearly professional development grant and through other research and travel grants, such as the Margery A. Pinet Fund. I would also like to thank my friend Paul J. Schupf, who not only lends his name to my title—one that I have worn with pride for many years now—but whose largesse has also allowed me to expand my travel and research opportunities to a higher level. The Cazenovia College librarians are par excellence—ask, and the researcher shall receive. I thank Library Director Heather Whalen-Smith and librarians Judy Azzotto, Nanette Bailey, and Lauren Michel. I was particularly well served by the research efforts of three notable undergraduates: Lydia Dorward, Yvette Fall, and Joanna Stach.

Traveling to archives is one of the perks of the writing game. Working with these materials not only can lead to the discovery of new historical theses but also is a royal good time. This project benefited from two of the best archival repositories in the nation. I thank the staff at the Dwight D. Eisenhower Presidential Library (Abilene, Kansas), particularly Timothy Rives, Valoise Armstrong, and Kathy Struss. I also thank the staff at the Seeley G. Mudd Manuscript Library at Princeton University, holder of the Adlai E. Stevenson Papers as well as several other collections of note—particularly Dan Linke, university archivist and curator of public policy papers, April Armstrong, and Crista Cleeton. I am beyond grateful to the Eisenhower Foundation, particularly to Meredith Sleichter, for its generosity in granting me a research and travel grant in 2014. At the Harry S. Truman Library in Independence, Missouri, I was helped by archivists David Clark, Janice Davis, Randy Sowell, and Tammy Williams; at the Richard M. Nixon Presidential Library I was aided by Jon Fletcher. I also appreciate the help of Cooper Hawley in securing the permission of the Republican National Committee to include several of the photos found in this volume.

I noted above the many conferences and other speaking opportunities over the years where I was fortunate enough to have had the opportunity to speak on 1952. I learned from each of them, but two stand out. The first was the aforementioned "The Great Crusade: The Road to the White House, 1952," held at the Eisenhower Library in November 1992. Once again, I would like to thank Dan Holt, then director of the Eisenhower Library, for inviting me to attend. The other was held at Gettysburg College in October 2002. This conference on the 1952 election, directed by my friend Shirley Anne Warshaw of Gettysburg's Department of Political Science, was particularly helpful.

All works of modern history are somewhat parasitic. I thank each of the scholars and writers enumerated in my bibliographical essay, whose work has affected my own thinking.

I like to write in diners. I don't really know why. But to everyone who has brought me coffee, scrambled eggs, and wheat toast, and then watched me read with a pen in my hand—particularly Darlene's Kitchen in Chittenango, New York, and Dave's Diner in Cazenovia, New York— my thanks for the hard work of personal service that you do. Special thanks are also due the Kibby family for their generosity during my research travels.

And to my family, by whom all things are made possible, once again, my gratitude for the help you give in allowing me to be both a teacher and a writer.

Chittenango, New York
April 2017

Congress sent the Twenty-Second Amendment, imposing a two-term limit on presidents, to the states for ratification on March 21, 1947. Although the amendment stated that "this article shall not apply to any person holding the office of President when this article was proposed by the Congress"—namely, President Harry S. Truman—Truman wrote in his diary on April 16, 1950: "Eight years as President is enough and sometimes too much for any man." Looking ahead to the next election in 1952, he added: "I am not a candidate and will not accept the nomination for another term."

If not Truman, whose popularity steadily sank in any event throughout the remainder of his tenure, then who? The Democrats had become the nation's majority party during Franklin D. Roosevelt's tenure, winning five presidential elections in a row. This made the Democratic nomination obviously worth having, and several nationally prominent politicians lined up to seek it, including Senator Estes Kefauver of Tennessee, Vice President Alben W. Barkley of Kentucky, and diplomat W. Averell Harriman of New York. The candidate who eventually got the nomination, after repeatedly eschewing any ambition other than reelection as governor of Illinois, was Adlai E. Stevenson II, the grandson of a former vice president and, in the end, Truman's favorite.

Looking at recent electoral history through different lenses, ambitious Republicans also coveted their party's 1952 nomination. Five defeats in a row was the most for any competitive major party in American history, meaning the GOP's fortunes were surely about to change. Senate Republican leader Robert A. Taft of Ohio—the son of a former president and, to many of his fellow partisans, "Mr. Republican"—emerged as the leading candidate for the party's nomination in a field that also included Governor Earl Warren of California, the party's vice presidential nominee in 1948.

Standing offstage was the preferred nominee of both parties, and the only near-sure winner on the national scene: Dwight D. Eisenhower. The wildly popular supreme allied commander in World War II, now serving in Brussels as supreme commander of the North American Treaty Organization (NATO) while on leave from the presidency of Columbia

University, was Truman's first choice for the Democratic nomination and most eastern Republicans' first choice to lead their party as well. As John Robert Greene argues, "Eisenhower's coming to terms with his own political future is, in many ways, the most important story of the presidential election of 1952."

Eisenhower first declared himself a Republican and then decided not to run but—an important consideration, in his mind—to allow himself to be put forward as a candidate for the party's nomination. "There is a vast difference between responding to a duty imposed by a national convention and the seeking of a nomination," Ike wrote to his chief advocate, Senator Henry Cabot Lodge of Massachusetts. Referring to his current NATO post, he wrote to his friend Swede Hazlett, "A man cannot desert a duty, but it would seem that he could lay one down in order to pick up a heavier and more responsible burden." Facing defeat by Taft, however, Eisenhower eventually left Europe and started running hard, barely edging out his rival at the convention.

In the end, Greene shows that the 1952 election was fought between two avowedly reluctant warriors in a campaign marked by television news coverage and televised political commercials, the first such election in history. Eisenhower won in a landslide, breaking the GOP's losing streak and extending sufficiently long coattails to bring in a narrowly Republican Congress. But as Greene argues, Ike's victory came less as a partisan mandate and more as a manifestation of his being "clearly the most popular American of the post–World War II period," a person "who was somehow above politics."

I LIKE IKE

INTRODUCTION

On 2 November 1948, Harry S. Truman was ecstatic. He had just been elected to his own term as president of the United States, and in so doing, he had confounded the politicos, the pundits, and the American people— virtually all of whom had declared his defeat. Every poll had him dead and buried, so one can only smile and forgive the feisty Missourian for his moment of gloat as he waved aloft a copy of the *Chicago Tribune*, which had predicted with premature certainty that his opponent had beaten him.

Yet as early as the summer of 1949, Truman was threatening to quit. In a note to his wife on 29 June, Truman wistfully remembered past vacations: "Remember the Blackstone, the first visit, not the last, Port Huron, Detroit Statler and the trip home? Maybe in 1953 we will be able to take that trip over again."[1] Within a year's time, he was making plans. The first sentence of Truman's diary entry for 16 April 1950 read simply: "I am not a candidate for nomination by the Democratic Convention." After rambling a bit about the electoral history of George Washington, James Madison, Woodrow Wilson, and others, Truman mused, "Eight years as President is enough and sometimes too much for any man." Although he had not served eight years, and he was not bound by the terms of the Twenty-Second Amendment to the Constitution (passed in 1951, limiting the president to two terms), Truman was adamant to himself: "To reestablish the [two-term] custom, although by a quibble I could say I've had only one term, I am not a candidate and will not accept the nomination for another term."[2]

Nothing happened over the next two years that made Truman regret his decision. Failure to pass his legislative packages; a series of scandals; a failure of policy in China; a war in Korea; and attacks on the loyalty of both him and his administration served to harden his resolve. In mid-November 1951, at his Key West retreat, Truman got his staff together and read to them his April diary entry, telling them that while for the present he required their secrecy, he would release that entry as a public statement in the spring of 1952.[3] Truman began crafting that statement in his diary on 30 January 1952, an entry that he labeled as a "revision" of the 16 April 1950 entry. In a detailed, formal tone, Truman penned what was clearly a future public announcement. Once again, he began his entry with the phrase "I am not a candidate for re-election." But then he crossed out that phrase as he began to think about his life: "When January comes [1953] I will have been in elective public office for thirty years, less two from January 1, 1925 to January 1, 1927. . . . I've given the country and the world everything I am capable of giving." After engaging in a bit of legacy creation ("We've whipped the Communists at every turn. We've saved the free world. We've succeeded in maintaining a balanced economy at home"), he closed with finality: "I am not a candidate for re-election in 1952. I'll say to you what Sherman said, 'If nominated I won't run. If elected I won't serve.'"[4]

It is easy to understand why.

TRUMAN DEFEATS DEWEY: 1948

Truman had won his own term in 1948 despite the fact that his policies had led to significant defections from the political coalition of disparate and often oppositional interest groups—laborers, labor unions, racial and ethnic minorities, liberal intellectuals, urban dwellers, urban bosses, farmers, Catholics, Jews—that Franklin Roosevelt had forged. Truman's antipathy toward the Soviet Union and its leadership, as well as his unyielding opposition to its policies, led to protests from Henry A. Wallace, his secretary of commerce and former vice president under Roosevelt. Along with a sizable portion of the party's more liberal wing, Wallace believed that Americans must negotiate with the Soviets, lest both sides find themselves on a path toward nuclear Armageddon. He also believed that Truman's concentration on the foreign policy of the

Cold War was distracting the nation from a discussion of social welfare policy issues. When Wallace took his criticisms to the public, Truman fired him, and his party's left wing exploded in opposition. Truman professed disinterest—in a letter to his mother and his sister, he quipped: "[Wallace is] out and the crackpots are having conniption fits."[5] But by the end of 1947, Wallace had agreed to run for the presidency in 1948 at the head of the United States Progressive Party ticket.

Truman also suffered defections on his party's right flank. Truman had proved to be the most activist president on civil rights since Abraham Lincoln. On 28 June 1947, he joined Eleanor Roosevelt at the Lincoln Memorial, becoming the first president to address the annual convention of the National Association for the Advancement of Colored People: "We must keep moving forward with new concepts of civil rights . . . each man must be guaranteed freedom of opportunity." And Truman would not stop with mere rhetorical flourishes. On 2 February 1948, he became the first president to send a civil rights message to Congress, presenting legislators with a ten-point plan that included an antilynch law, a repeal of the poll tax, a permanent commission on civil rights, the prohibition of segregation on interstate transportation, and the end of discrimination in the armed forces. Most significant was Truman's call for a permanent Fair Employment Practices Commission (FEPC), which he had supported publicly since a 5 June 1945 speech to black leaders. In his address, Truman argued that "the federal government has a clear duty to see that the constitutional guarantees of individual liberties . . . are not denied or abridged anywhere in our nation."[6]

Southern Democrats were furious at the progressive nature of Truman's civil rights policies. This anger was only augmented by his stand over their oil. At the turn of the century, immense amounts of oil in submerged lands—the Tidelands—were discovered just off the shores of Louisiana, Texas, and California. As soon as the oil was tapped, the states laid claim to the black gold; just as immediately, the federal government began to apply for federal drilling leases. Immediately prior to World War II, the Interior Department put a halt to the federal applications, preferring to wait until the courts ruled on the ownership of the Tidelands. However, in September 1945, Truman stayed that order, issuing an executive order proclaiming that the Tidelands belonged to the federal government and putting the control of those lands under the auspices of the secretary of the interior. Congress balked immediately, passing a law in 1946 that gave control of the Tidelands back to the states; but Truman vetoed the bill, and his veto was sustained. Moreover, the Supreme Court ruled in both 1947 and 1950 that the Tidelands belonged to the federal government.[7] But this did not quell the controversy, as southern Democrats from Louisiana and Texas attacked both the Court and the Truman administration on the issue. One reason for not letting the issue go was, of course, the money; according to the *New York Times*, there was $40 billion in oil in the Tidelands waiting to be added to either the state or the federal Treasury.[8] When mixed with the civil rights issue, the Tidelands oil controversy was but one more dispute in the growing states' rights crisis. Indeed, a biographer of Speaker of the House Sam Rayburn observes that Truman's vetoes and the Supreme Court's decisions moved Texas Democrats "to hysterical behavior."[9]

Talk began to circulate of a southern walkout at the upcoming Democratic Convention. Southern Democrats had been, at best, fickle members of the Roosevelt coalition, often voting against New Deal legislation that they felt encroached on the prerogative of the states. But they and their local machines had supported Roosevelt for president since 1932—it was a stretch to believe that Truman, or any other Democratic candidate, could win without the South. Accordingly, Truman tried to salve southern wounds by opposing a strong civil rights plank in the party's platform, proposed by Minneapolis mayor Hubert H. Humphrey, that read in part, "We again state our belief that racial and religious minorities must have the right to live, the right to work, the right to vote, the full and equal protection of the laws, on a basis of equality with all citizens as guaranteed by the Constitution."[10] Truman tried for compromise, but Humphrey ("there will be no hedging, and there will be no watering down") and most of the northern delegates would have none of it. Against his better judgment, Truman backed the plank, which passed.[11] Most of the southern delegates walked out of the convention in protest, waving Confederate flags and singing "Dixie" as they left the hall. They would reconvene later in Birmingham to form the States' Rights Democratic Party, which would be derisively nicknamed the "Dixiecrats" in the press, and would be led by South Carolina governor J. Strom Thurmond. Because the Dixiecrats controlled the Democratic Party machinery in the South, Truman would have to face the election knowing that his name would not even appear on the ballot in at least ten states.

Yet Truman would win the election on his own terms despite these defections.[12] In the fall of 1948, the feisty president was in his element, his bombastic temperament perfectly suited to his underdog status.

He attacked the Republican front-runner, New York governor Thomas E. Dewey, head-on, employing a shrewd use of the incumbency, good old-fashioned name-calling, and the endurance of a man half his age. First, he called a special session of Congress for August, before which he placed several pieces of semi-important legislation. The Republicans in Congress were busy with their own campaigns and—literally, in some cases—planning for a transition to the expected Dewey administration. When, as he knew it would, the Congress balked at the proposals and passed nothing of substance, Truman lambasted it as the "Do-Nothing Eightieth Congress." From that point on, he refused to take his foot off the accelerator, organizing an impressive whistle-stop campaign of mammoth proportions. That fall, he traveled 31,000 miles, speaking to some 6 million people. On the other hand, Dewey's lethargic campaign, as well as his monotonous call for a bipartisan foreign policy, was just plain boring.

In a result that confounded everyone (except, of course, Truman), Truman won 49.5 percent of the popular vote and 303 electoral votes, to Dewey's 45.1 percent and 189 electoral votes. Thurmond and Wallace combined for 4.8 percent and 39 electoral votes—all in the South, and all for Thurmond. Dewey won the entire industrial Northeast and still lost the election. Truman won the election by winning in the heartland. He captured Wisconsin and Ohio, two states that had gone for Dewey in 1944. He then won all states west of the Mississippi River, save the Dakotas, Nebraska, Kansas, and Oregon (a total of 28 Dewey electoral votes). Moreover, Truman reversed the results of the 1946 off-year elections, winning back both the Senate (54–42) and the House (263–171) for the Democrats.

Truman won the labor vote, the farm vote, and the black vote—all groups that were part of the Roosevelt coalition. There was never any doubt that Truman would carry those in the lower-income stratum—indeed, Dewey's share of that vote dropped by 50 percent between 1944 and 1948. There was equal certainty that Dewey would carry the upper-income stratum of voters—the Republican percentage of the top income earners jumped from 57.4 percent in 1944 to 61.6 percent in 1948. But no one was prepared for the shellacking that the Republicans took among those voters who could be called "middle-class"; the Republican share of middle-class voters shrank by one-fifth between 1944 and 1948, and their share of the rapidly growing "upper middle class" shrank by one-tenth between the two elections.[13]

Harry S. Truman and Thomas E. Dewey, Oval Office, 13 September 1951
(National Park Service, Abbie Rowe, courtesy of Harry S. Truman Library)

FAIR DEAL FAILURES

Truman's victory gave him a more unified party, in that one revolt—that
of the Progressive Party—had been discredited. The party's liberal wing,
satisfied for a moment that it had legislative control and looking forward
to the passage of new, liberal legislation, buried the hatchet and momentarily embraced its president. Not so, however, the southerners. Thurmond's victories in the South showed the depth of the party split over
civil rights, one that could easily flare up in time for the next election.
Those southern Democrats went back to their alliance with conservative
Republicans, and their rekindled coalition was strong enough to stall or
defeat Truman's policies on the Hill.

This they did. While not as liberal as the progressive wing would have
liked, Truman's second-term domestic policies, christened his "Fair
Deal," certainly addressed issues that the New Deal had not been too
terribly concerned about. Over the voices of southern protest, Truman
sent Congress a far-reaching civil rights package, featuring a permanent
FEPC. Despite the protests of conservative Democrats, Republicans, and
medical lobbies, he proposed sweeping health-care legislation that featured a plan for national health insurance. Despite the cries of those who

protested both its cost and its federal overreach, Truman proposed an ambitious plan for stabilizing farm income (the Brannan Plan) that supported prices at 90 percent of parity. Truman also called for the repeal of the Taft-Hartley Act (1947), which had placed significant limitations on the powers of organized labor. All these bills, and more, were defeated by the Eighty-First and Eighty-Second Congresses.[14]

SCANDALS

Along with his lack of success on the Hill, Truman had to deal with the revelation of scandal within his administration. In 1949, the antics of the "Five Percenters"—Truman appointees who obtained government contracts for their friends—were revealed. Later that year, General Harry H. Vaughan, Truman's closest personal confidant, went to jail for influence peddling. Senator J. William Fulbright (D-AR) convened a congressional committee to investigate reports of misdeeds in the Reconstruction Finance Corporation. There was also documentation of income tax fraud from within the administration. The fastidious, basically honest Truman was never personally implicated in any of these scandals, and, as pointed out by Andrew J. Dunar, the most thoughtful student of the Truman scandals, no evidence to the contrary has yet been unearthed by historians.[15] But Truman badly mishandled the investigation of those scandals (he appointed Republican lawyer Newbold Morris to head a federal investigation; for his part, Morris poisoned the well by interrupting a senator who was questioning him before a committee, telling all present that they had "diseased minds").[16] Nevertheless, Truman found himself tainted by a rather broad brush, seen by his growing list of opponents as having an administration that harbored incompetents and crooks. In February 1952, 52 percent of those asked in a Roper poll believed that "there [was] lots of corruption in [the] federal government."[17]

THE "LOSS OF CHINA"

The brutal repression of the Czechoslovakia Coup of February 1948 and the ongoing response to the Berlin Blockade (the American-led airlift of goods ran from 24 June 1948 to 12 May 1949) offered ample evidence to Truman that the Soviet Union was a legitimate threat. As a result, Truman and his new secretary of state, Dean Acheson, believed that a mutual defense treaty with Western Europe was a primary necessity. On 4

April 1949, the North Atlantic Treaty Organization (NATO) was signed, binding together the United States, Great Britain, France, Canada, and eight other Western European nations.

In the debate over ratification, Senate Republicans, led by Taft, were particularly incensed at Article 5 of the treaty: "An armed attack against one or more (members) shall be considered an armed attack against them all." But their cries were for naught; the Democrats controlled the Senate, and in June 1949, NATO was ratified by a wide margin. In response, the Warsaw Pact was immediately formed, binding together the Soviet Union and seven of its Eastern European satellites. In February 1951, Truman sent General Dwight D. Eisenhower, then serving as president of Columbia University, to Paris with the task of converting the alliance into a fully functional European command.

However, the Far East threatened to become even more of a Cold War flash point than had Europe. The Chinese civil war, pitting the Nationalist forces of Chiang Kai-shek against the Yan'an Communists of Mao Zedong (Mao Tse-tung), began in 1927 and ran through World War II. The United States had thrown its lot in with Chiang's Nationalists despite the fact that his government was notoriously corrupt and his military force was hapless and inefficient. By 1945, Mao controlled much of northwest and north central China. While many felt that Chiang had spent more time fighting Mao during World War II than he had spent fighting a rearguard action against the Japanese, a desire to maintain a wall against the encroachment of communism in the Far East led to Chiang's being given an increase in American aid as well as one of five permanent seats on the United Nations Security Council. This, along with $700 million in lend-lease funds to Chiang's government (which promptly swallowed it up in graft), led the Truman administration to believe initially that it had steadied the Nationalists against Mao's advancing forces.

Such beliefs were ill-founded. By 1947, China found itself in full-scale civil war, and Truman's advisers were torn. Some, led by General Albert Wedermeyer, the commander of American forces in China, argued that Truman should send more aid to Chiang; others, led by Truman's secretary of state George Marshall, argued that Truman should abandon China to its own devices and concentrate on directing more aid to Japan to stabilize the region. Truman sided with Marshall. Chiang had been abandoned by the United States. On 1 October 1949, Mao proclaimed the creation of the People's Republic of China (PRC); in December 1949, Chiang took what was left of his army and government and fled to

Formosa, an island off the shore of mainland China. Republicans excoriated Truman for his "loss of China," a cry they would keep up for the better part of the next decade.

KOREA

On 25 June 1950, the forces of North Korea poured over the thirty-eighth parallel, which formed the border between itself and its sister nation to the south. From the very beginning of the crisis, Truman assumed that it was a Soviet-sponsored attack. This goes a long way toward explaining why his initial response to the invasion was a measured one—he firmly believed that one false move would bring the Soviets and possibly their nearby client, the PRC, directly into the war.[18] To meet the initial attack, Truman ordered General Douglas MacArthur, then in Tokyo, to send supplies to the South Korean forces and to order the American Seventh Fleet to position itself between China and Formosa.

But such steps were short-lived. On 27 June—the same day that the United Nations (UN) formally condemned the North Koreans for the attack—Truman committed both American ground and naval troops to action. Despite the fact that American troops would soon be joined in Korea by troops from other UN nations, the Korean War was an American war. At any given point in the war, 50 percent of all ground and air troops would be American, as would 95 percent of all naval forces. By August, the front had stabilized enough so that MacArthur could attempt a courageous rearguard action. On 15 September, in what would become the greatest amphibious operation in military history, MacArthur's X Corps landed behind North Korean lines at Inchon. Catching the enemy completely off guard, MacArthur began to push the North Koreans back toward the thirty-eighth parallel.

The decision to cross the thirty-eighth parallel and take the war into North Korea was the most ill-advised move of the Truman administration. Truman found himself buoyed by advice such as that from Acheson, who told the president, "I should think it would be sheer madness for the Chinese to intervene" in the conflict.[19] In retrospect, it seems foolish to have assumed, as Truman clearly did, that the PRC would stay out of the fight when they began to see the North Korean army being pushed northward to the Yalu River, which formed the border between North Korea and the PRC. Yet the possibility of eradicating communism from the Korean Peninsula proved to be too much temptation for Truman. In a complete refutation of his own containment policy, Truman ordered MacArthur to cross the border into North Korea, to liberate that nation from the yoke of communism. MacArthur's forces sliced through the retreating North Koreans, and by November his troops were literally yards away from the Chinese border; American troops could see Chinese troops on the other side of the Yalu. Truman's confidence that the Chinese would stay out of the conflict was shattered on the morning of 25 November when thousands of PRC "volunteers" poured across the Yalu, forcing thousands of U.S. Marines into a bloody retreat. By early January 1952, the UN front had stabilized below the thirty-eighth parallel. The war soon settled into a stalemate of unknown duration.

Truman believed that American might would ultimately prevail, no matter what the conditions or circumstances. All Truman's advisers, including MacArthur, agreed with that assessment. After the Chinese entered the war, Truman began to hear from those who now believed that a negotiated settlement was necessary. But from MacArthur, Truman got pleas for a full-scale counterattack against the PRC, including an economic and military blockade, approval of previously restricted reconnaissance flights over the Chinese mainland, the unleashing of Chiang Kai-shek's tiny army against the PRC, and the use of nuclear weapons. Stunned by the ferocity of the Chinese counterattack, and justifiably concerned with any action that would draw the Soviet Union directly into the conflict, Truman refused to order the third atomic attack of his presidency.

Believing in the power of American exceptionalism to the point where he viewed American military power as ultimately invincible, MacArthur refused to accept Truman's orders as final. Displaying a rather rare form of overt insubordination, MacArthur directly lobbied Capitol Hill in favor of tactical advice that had been rejected by his commander in chief. On 11 April 1951, Truman relieved MacArthur of his command. Truman's reasoning for the dismissal was absolutely clear. In the first sentence of his address that purported to explain his decision to the American people Truman said: "In the simplest terms, what we are doing in Korea is this: We are trying to prevent a Third World War." But Truman had fired an icon, and the reaction against his decision was both immediate and severe. In May 1951, Taft wrote a soldier fighting in Korea, "I believe that General MacArthur is right in almost every proposal that he makes."[20] House Minority Leader Joseph Martin (R-MA) called for Truman's impeachment.

Wake Island, 14 October 1950, Harry S. Truman and General Douglas MacArthur (U.S. Navy, courtesy Harry S. Truman Library)

A majority of Americans, now saddled with a bloody quagmire that promised no end in sight, now saw Truman as an ineffectual wartime leader, and many began to look forward to his possible replacement in the next election. Historian Elmo Richardson neatly summarized the prevalent feeling: "Instead of making Americans distrust military men, the war made them view the prospect of a soldier in the White House as desirable."[21]

THE STEEL STRIKE

The Korean War also had a profound impact on Truman's domestic policies. Still feeling the sting of the postwar inflation, and with memories of World War II sacrifices still fresh in their minds, the American people were loath to sacrifice too much in order to pay for war in Korea. Truman's attempts to mobilize the American economy for war thus met with continued resistance. Although, in September 1950, Congress passed the Defense Production Act (DPA), giving the president wide-ranging authority over the economy and the power to enact wage and price controls, Truman would not dare to exercise that authority until the Chinese counteroffensive of November 1950. In an attempt to stabilize the American economy as it settled in for a lengthy siege in Korea, Truman used his new powers under the DPA to create the Wage Stabilization Board (WSB), which attempted to limit wage increases to a cap of 10 percent. The outcry against this decision was inevitable and loud.[22]

The crisis of mobilization came to a head over the demands of the steel industry. The major steel companies wanted a price increase; the United Steelworkers of America wanted a wage increase. Truman decided to send their dispute to the WSB and asked both labor and management for patience. On 20 March 1952, the WSB recommended an eighteen-month contract with a wage increase of 12.5 cents per hour, retroactive to 1 January 1952, an additional 2.5-cent increase effective on 30 June 1952, and some fringes. This satisfied no one.

Described by biographer Alonzo L. Hamby as "drawn by his lifelong belief in strong executive authority to something more dramatic and more dangerous,"[23] Truman preferred the seizure of the steel mills by the federal government to what would surely be a prolonged negotiation.[24] Under Section 18 of the Selective Service Act of 1948, the president was allowed to place an offer for goods needed by the armed forces with a manufacturer; if the company failed to deliver, the president could take possession of the property. Thus, on 8 April 1952, Truman signed an executive order announcing that to prevent a strike, the federal government was seizing eighty-seven steel mills, all owned by companies that were involved in the dispute with the union.[25] Truman argued that his Article II powers as commander in chief gave him the authority to seize the mills. This led to an immediate showdown. On 26 May, Senator Pat McCarran (D-NV) announced that he intended to propose an amendment to the Constitution to deny the president any power to seize private property except under processes prescribed by law;[26] the next day a House Judiciary subcommittee decided to hold public hearings on the issue of either censuring or impeaching the president.[27]

The steel strike dragged on until the early part of the summer, as did a series of lawsuits in which the steel companies sued for return of their property, providing both a backdrop to the entirety of the preconvention campaigns and a constant reminder of the innumerable problems that faced the administration. Robert Taft, by then an announced candidate for the Republican nomination, would continually remind his audiences that the seizure of the mills was a "valid case" for impeachment and that "the president once again is usurping power which is not conferred upon him . . . [and] is showing the same disregard of the Constitution and the laws of the United States which he has shown in many other cases."[28] Earl Warren, governor of California and also a candidate for the Republican nomination, said that he would go before Congress and ask for a law to be passed giving him the authority to seize private property before he would have seized the steel mills.[29] As a whole, the American people disapproved, too, in numbers that approximated their disapproval of the war in general.[30] It would not be until 2 June that the Supreme Court, in *Youngstown Sheet and Tube Company v. Sawyer*,[31] ruled 6–3 that the president's actions were unconstitutional.

DOMESTIC COMMUNISM

The events of the Cold War had led many Americans to the conclusion that the Soviet Union was capable of inflicting great destruction on the United States with a nuclear attack. In September 1949, the Soviet Union announced that it possessed the atomic bomb. Any questions as to how the Soviets might have procured the secrets of its construction seemed to be answered with the January 1950 arrest of Klaus Fuchs, a British scientist who had worked on the Manhattan Project. Fuchs confessed in London that he had been part of a spy ring that had supplied nuclear research to the Soviets. That confession also implicated four Americans, two of whom, Julius and Ethel Rosenberg, would be executed for espionage in 1953. The Fuchs and Rosenberg arrests, along with the surprise invasion of Korea, elevated an already present fear of communism—both domestic and foreign—to a fever pitch. In September 1950, Congress hastily passed the McCarran-Walter Internal Security Act, which required any communist organization to register with the federal government, and created a board empowered to investigate any organization deemed to be subversive. Truman vetoed it, but his veto was overridden. The "Second Red Scare" was on; any Americans—college professors, high school teachers of Russian history, intellectual critics of government, Hollywood screenwriters, obscure street corner organizers—could be placed under suspicion of being communists or communist sympathizers. Careers and reputations were destroyed beyond any hope of repair. Even the Constitution itself could not be used as a defense. In *Dennis v. U.S.* (1951), the Supreme Court ruled that an American Communist Party leader did not have the right to disseminate his beliefs and then claim that he had a First Amendment right of freedom of speech.[32]

The most celebrated case was that of Alger Hiss, a former State Department official. In 1948, *Time* magazine editor Whittaker Chambers testified before the House Un-American Activities Committee (HUAC) that Hiss had passed him classified documents between 1937 and 1938. Hiss denied the charge, and in October 1948 he sued Chambers for slander. At Hiss's slander trial, Chambers produced microfilm that had been hidden inside a pumpkin on his Maryland farm that he said proved the charge of espionage. While the statute of limitations kept Hiss from being tried for treason, he was ultimately convicted of perjury before HUAC. Quite aside from their national security implications—implications that continue to be debated hotly by historians to the present day—the Hiss trials were important for the role they played in the developing careers of two politicians who were about to see their stars rise into the stratosphere. As a member of HUAC, Republican senator Richard Nixon of California was relentless in his pursuit both of Hiss and of the attendant publicity; he got both and was instantly on everyone's list of possible vice presidential nominees, no matter who the presidential nominee was. And Illinois governor Adlai E. Stevenson would quietly, by deposition and not by personal appearance, give a statement to the court of personal support of Hiss's character—an act of some bravery but one that would have serious political consequences in the fall of 1952.

The Second Red Scare also jump-started the career of Senator Joseph McCarthy (R-WI). On 9 February 1950, in a Lincoln Day address in Wheeling, West Virginia, McCarthy claimed to "have in my hand 57 cases of individuals who would appear to be either card-carrying members or certainly loyal to the communist party, but who nevertheless are still helping to shape our foreign policy." The claim was wildly exaggerated—right after the speech, McCarthy joked with reporters: "Look, you guys. That was a political speech to a bunch of Republicans. Don't take it seriously."[33] But Americans took it absolutely seriously. McCarthy had many supporters, and the numbers were growing. The leadership of his party, recognizing quickly that despite McCarthy's histrionics (when Truman fired MacArthur, McCarthy called the president a "sonofabitch" who had acted while he was drunk on "bourbon and Benedictine"),[34] the issue of domestic communism could easily be used as a bludgeon against Truman, left the senator to his own malfeasant devices. There were precious few who joined the protest of Maine senator Margaret Chase Smith when, on 1 June 1950, she publicly denounced McCarthy on the floor of the Senate. The issue of domestic communism figured prominently in the fall 1950 elections, which saw the Republicans gain twenty-eight House seats and five Senate seats. Four of the Democratic senators went down to defeat in elections where the issue of domestic communism played a key part.

By mid-1951, Harry Truman, his administration, and his party were damaged goods—little wonder that Truman would tell his staff that he didn't want another term. He was at the helm of an administration that was tainted by scandal, had a floundering domestic policy, was being besieged by McCarthy and his ilk, and was fighting an unpopular and stalemated war in Korea.

But the Republicans did not yet know that Truman was planning on quitting. They were planning to face him once again for the presidency and, given his upset victory in 1948, that was a less than appealing prospect. Moreover, the Republicans themselves were beset with divisions, divisions that might stand in the way of the party's first presidential victory in two decades.

THE REPUBLICAN
PRECONVENTION CAMPAIGNS

Since the Gilded Age, the Republican Party had been identified as the party of big business and of economic prosperity. Unified around conservative platforms that emphasized the value of the gold standard and the desirability of high tariffs, the Republicans controlled the White House, with the exception of the two Cleveland administrations, from the end of the Civil War to the second decade of the twentieth century. However, in 1912 the Republican Party was rent asunder by the ambitions of Theodore Roosevelt. The former president challenged sitting president William Howard Taft for the party's nomination. When he lost in that effort, Roosevelt bolted the Republican Party and formed the Progressive ("Bull Moose") Party, whose platform called for a national health insurance program, a minimum wage for women workers, an eight-hour day for all workers, a federal income tax, and suffrage for women. The new party split the Republican vote and handed the election to Democrat Woodrow Wilson. While the Bull Moose Party eventually met the fate of all third parties, a progressive wing of the Republican Party had been born. Robert La Follette of Wisconsin and George Norris of Nebraska offered that wing both intellectual and political leadership throughout the 1920s. But it was still largely a conservative party, with its power bases located in the farms of the Midwest and the boardrooms of the Northeast, celebrated by Calvin Coolidge as the party that understood "the business of government is business" and adhered to a strict policy of isolating the nation from the travails of postwar Europe.

Following the crash and the onset of the Depression, Republican conservatives were outflanked and outnumbered by supporters of Franklin Roosevelt, who deftly blamed big business for the crash and then proceeded to save capitalism with his New Deal. Thanks to the alliance of his coalition of voters, Roosevelt's landslide victories in 1932 and 1936 consigned the Republicans to a minority status not only in presidential politics but also in the overwhelmingly Democratic Congress. Republicans did not help their cause with a Depression-weary electorate by following their titular leader, former president Herbert Hoover, in opposing every step that the New Deal took. Their demand to keep the country isolated from the oncoming war in Europe was, for a while, fashionable, particularly in the party's midwestern base, but soon seemed unrealistic in the face of the aggrandizement of Nazi Germany and nationalist Japan.

By the 1940s, tired of political defeat and no longer wishing to be seen as obstructionist to progress, the progressive wing of the Republican Party began to re-assert itself. Now labeling themselves "Republican Moderates" and largely members of the eastern establishment, they continued to criticize the economic programs of the New Deal (particularly after the recession of 1937), but they now professed to a more internationalist foreign policy, more in tune with Roosevelt's drift away from neutrality in the face of a new world conflict. Historian John Fousek has labeled this development as "American nationalist globalism . . . the notion that the entire world was now the proper sphere of concern for U.S. foreign policy."[1] The moderates seized control of the party in 1940, led by Thomas E. Dewey of New York, a thirty-eight-year-old lawyer who had become a national celebrity as a result of his role as New York's special prosecutor of organized crime. By 1940, even with an unsuccessful run for New York governor behind him (he had been narrowly defeated for governor of New York in 1938 by Herbert Lehman, who was running for his fourth term in Albany), the now district attorney for Manhattan was being mentioned as a possible presidential candidate. Never a blind critic of New Deal policies, Dewey won every Republican primary in 1940. However, conservative senator Robert Taft of Ohio stopped the Dewey momentum at the convention; the nomination eventually went to Wendell Willkie, a moderate Wall Street industrialist. Willkie promised to make Roosevelt's New Deal bureaucracy more efficient and called for a bigger buildup of forces to make the nation more prepared for war; Roosevelt defeated him narrowly and only after promising that no American soldiers would be sent to fight in another overseas war.

Pearl Harbor made that promise a moot one, but Dewey's hold over the moderate wing of the party was still strong. In 1942, he was elected governor of New York, and in his gubernatorial address he pronounced that "anybody who thinks that an attack on the fundamental idea of security and welfare is appealing to people generally is living in the Middle Ages."[2] Dewey followed this up by giving New York a remarkably progressive administration that included unemployment insurance, old-age pensions, slum clearance, and antidiscrimination legislation.[3] He also argued that after the war America should accept a world role and not retreat into the postwar isolation that Taft advocated. In 1944, Dewey and the moderate wing of the party once again held off a challenge from Taft's conservative faction, only to find it impossible to defeat a popular president in wartime.

Following the war, the split between the moderate and conservative wings of the party grew even wider, particularly over the issue of postwar foreign policy, with the conservatives railing against all types of European aid (centering their wrath on the Marshall Plan) and refusing their support for the United Nations, and the moderates largely supporting Truman's foreign program, in terms of both aid to Europe and collective security. As noted in the introduction, the two wings fought for control of the party in 1948, with Taft and his conservatives once again being defeated by northeastern moderates. Dewey's tacit support of much of Truman's foreign policy was off-putting to many embittered Taftians, who sat out the election rather than vote for Dewey. Dewey's humiliating defeat ended any hope of his ever being renominated for the presidency by the Republican Party. In 1952, it seemed as if it would finally be Bob Taft's turn.

"MR. REPUBLICAN"

Robert Alphonso Taft was bred for the political arena. His father, William Howard Taft, had served as governor of the Philippine Islands, a member of Theodore Roosevelt's cabinet, president of the United States, and chief justice of the Supreme Court. The elder Taft prodded his son to excel, and excel he did, graduating first in his class at prep school, entering Yale at age sixteen, and graduating first in his class from Harvard Law School in 1913. After spending three terms in the Ohio legislature, Taft formed his own law firm in Cincinnati just before the stock market crashed. His own personal frugality, as well as wise investment practices, allowed him to escape the crash unscathed.

Much has been written about Taft's conservatism, and he has largely been presented as an unshakable denizen of his party's far-right wing, longing for a return to an America of the 1920s—freed from the yoke of deficit spending and the intrusion of the federal government into the lives of Americans and the laws of the states, and freed from international commitments of any kind. Much of this is true. On economic issues, Taft was a rock-solid Hooverian conservative. He had worked for Herbert Hoover during World War I at the Food Administration Program, and following that employ, he never once abandoned Hoover—whom, in his correspondence, he addressed as "Chief"—personally, politically, or philosophically.[4] Taft blamed the Great Depression, as did Hoover, on excessive lending abroad. Like Hoover, he was also fundamentally opposed to tinkering with the economy in a time of economic crisis, referring to the New Dealers as "meddlers."[5] Both men refused to accept large-scale public spending as a cure for the Depression. Elected to the Ohio Senate in 1930, Taft opposed state-supported unemployment insurance not only because it was expensive but because his "inclination [was] very much opposed to any system which provides for the payment of money to men for doing nothing."[6] Elected to the U.S. Senate in 1938, he became the leader of what came to be known as the "Conservative Coalition" between the Republican right and southern conservative Democrats. The coalition pushed for lower taxes, more restrictions on labor unions, and reduced government spending across the board. It also blocked Roosevelt's trifling attempts at civil rights legislation as a sop to the southern Democrats.[7] Nor could Taft accept any raise in taxes, which, to him, "would be just as inflationary as borrowing the money." He claimed, "There is no cure for inflation that I know, except to reduce the government spending to a point where the private economy can carry it."[8] However, Taft was not a fiscal troglodyte. In the postwar period, he had come to favor federal aid to education as well as public housing.[9] He could see areas where federal subsidies might be necessary—his correspondence shows that while he felt that federal support for medical schools was fundamentally wrong, "the necessity of increased medical education . . . is so great that unless [private funding] succeeds, I see no alternative, except to provide federal aid to try to protect ourselves against the dangers which might result."[10]

In foreign policy, however, Taft would not be budged. An unabashed isolationist, he called Franklin Roosevelt the "greatest menace to peace in this country," strongly opposing the Destroyer-Bases Deal and the Lend-Lease Act.[11] He went so far as to claim that Roosevelt and Truman had actually created the Soviet threat out of whole cloth.[12] On the issue of postwar economic aid to Europe, Taft argued that such spending would do irreparable damage to the American economy. However, Taft was bested by Senator Arthur Vandenberg of Michigan, a Republican convert to internationalism who helped Truman pass what would become known as the Marshall Plan—which funneled $13 billion to Western European nations before it was halted in 1952. On Truman and the Korean War, Taft firmly believed that, in his words, "the administration's weak policy invited the Communist attack."[13] He wrote a constituent, "We never should have withdrawn our troops. If we had kept the troops there, there would have been no attack."[14] Moreover, Taft—and virtually every other Republican—believed that the president had no right to commit any troops, anywhere, without a formal declaration of war. He was opposed to Truman's argument that the United States had to enter the war because of our UN treaties, writing to a Hearst editorial writer: "It seems clear that the President as Commander in Chief cannot delegate his power to a general chosen by ten nations having no relation to the United States."[15] Aligning himself with the beliefs of General Douglas MacArthur, Taft wrote, "If the atom bomb is made usable for military field operations, I see no reason why it should not be used in any war such as the Korean War."[16]

On the subject of Joseph McCarthy, Taft tried to sound statesmanlike. But like the vast majority of his colleagues, he too gave McCarthy his general endorsement, writing in a letter to a constituent: "I think [McCarthy] performed a great service in arousing the people to the danger of Communist influence in the government. Before he spoke out so vigorously, they simply didn't believe it. Unfortunately he doesn't check his statements very carefully and is not disposed to take any advice so that makes him a hard man for somebody to work with, or restrain. On net results, I think he has done the country a real service."[17] His longevity in Congress earned for Taft the nickname "Mr. Republican." But Truman was not so honorific. Looking at the whole of foreign and domestic policy, the president understated the case when he told an interviewer that "there wasn't anybody who was more against what I stood for as Taft was."[18]

The Republican Party as a whole—moderate and conservative wings alike—was united in its understanding that Dewey would not be granted a third chance at the presidency. Republicans wanted to nominate someone who would attack Truman, much as he had attacked them four years earlier. But at first glance, there seemed to be no fiscal and international moderates available, at least those with a solid enough base either to win the nomination or to win in the fall. This left Taft. But campaigning never came easy for Bob Taft. His record on the national scene was even less stellar than Dewey's—he had already run for the Republican nomination in 1940, 1944, and 1948 and had lost all three times. Moreover, Taft was hardly a glad-hander. Naturally reticent, achingly contemplative, often described as sullen, Taft possessed none of the personal characteristics that one would immediately equate with being successful on the national political scene. One example from the 1940 campaign will suffice: Taft was at a meeting with several key leaders. Listening behind a door was Taft's cousin and political confidant, David Ingalls. For a few moments, Ingalls heard Taft's expert answers to the questions being posed. Then he suddenly heard nothing. Looking in, Ingalls found Taft reading the newspaper, with his guests angrily waiting for more. Later, Taft told Ingalls that he had taken out his newspaper "because I had learned all that I could."[19]

Nevertheless, Taft had a very workable strategy. Guaranteed the support of midwestern delegates, Taft would cede the Northeast to favorite sons and concentrate his efforts on the South, emphasizing his opposition to federal control of Tidelands Oil, his opposition to a permanent FEPC, and his support of the doctrine of "separate but equal." (He shared with a constituent in October 1951: "We have a very difficult problem with the Negro vote. Fundamentally I feel that the Republican Party must oppose excessive government regulation, and excessive federal interference with states. Nearly every measure on which the Negroes have made an issue raises these two questions. . . . I doubt we can satisfy Mr. Walter White and the NAACP, who always demand still more when concessions are made.")[20] As 1951 came to a close, Taft had all but locked up the support of the South, and he was making strides toward capturing delegates in the nation's heartland.[21]

Taft exaggerated the case when, in his announcement of his candidacy on 16 October 1951, he boasted, "I can conduct the only kind of campaign which will elect a Republican to office."[22] But he was itching for a fight with Truman, and he was thoroughly convinced not only that he would win the nomination but that he would defeat Truman in the fall. The day after Taft announced, Truman sent him a note, slyly noting, "I suppose you will have all the fun that goes with that sort of decision." Taft replied with a direct challenge: "Whether my recent decision will involve any fun is doubtful, but perhaps if you feel that way about it you might consider joining the merry throng before many months."[23]

Taft, then, operated on the assumption that he would be facing off against Truman in the fall of 1952. But even Taft's supporters continued to worry about his electability. Congressman Walter Judd of Minnesota, a vocal critic of Truman's China policy and a close friend of Taft, observed: "You're the King, Bob, but Ike's the ace as far as getting votes is concerned."[24]

IKE

Dwight David Eisenhower was born in 1890 in Denison, Texas, but his family did not stay there long. His father moved to Abilene, Kansas, in 1892 to take a job at the Belle Springs Creamery. Young Dwight, who was athletic and precocious, grew up in the outdoors. His personality reminds the casual observer of Tom Sawyer. Pictures of young Ike (a nickname that stood as an abbreviation of his last name) and his buddies camping by the Smoky Hill River lend an air of small-town innocence to his background.

For a young man of meager means, the fastest way out of Abilene was through the military. However, Dwight's mother had put a premium on education, so the youngster tried for an appointment to a service academy. In 1910, after placing as an alternate for admission, he was finally accepted to the U.S. Military Academy when the young man who had placed first in the competitive examination failed his physical. Through his first years at West Point, it seemed that Eisenhower was the classic collegiate jock—average grades but above average on the football field, where he was ranked by many as one of the top pro prospects in the East. However, a freak accident wrecked his knee and ended his football career. Despite these developments (or because of them), Eisenhower graduated in the middle of his class in 1915. There was little of the flaming promise that one would expect from a member of a class that would produce fifty-nine general officers and would be dubbed "The Class the Stars Fell On."

Assigned to the Nineteenth Infantry, stationed near San Antonio at Fort Sam Houston, Lieutenant Eisenhower settled into the life of a career soldier. Two years after his July 1916 marriage to Denver's Mamie Doud, the country was again at war. Eisenhower's pleas for overseas duty went unheeded; in fact, he put in so many applications that he received an official reprimand for his efforts.[25] He was instead assigned to Camp Colt in Gettysburg, Pennsylvania—a tank training school that had no tanks. Following the war, Eisenhower was transferred to Camp Meade, where he developed a close relationship with the flamboyant Major George S. Patton. Together the two men began to develop some rather radical ideas about tank warfare—a lightning-quick offensive strategy that replaced a good portion of infantry with tanks.

Eisenhower's career did a sharp turnaround in 1920 when Patton introduced him to Brigadier General Fox Conner. An aristocratic Mississippian with wide contacts, Conner was immediately taken with Eisenhower. Assigning to himself the task of becoming Eisenhower's mentor, in January 1922, he asked Eisenhower to follow him to his new station in Panama and serve as his executive officer. Conner broadened Eisenhower's horizons by guiding him through a strict regimen of military reading.[26] He also helped Eisenhower procure admission to the Command and General Staff School at Fort Leavenworth, as well as the National War College in Washington. Conner also introduced Eisenhower to the internal politics of the military, helping him procure a position as assistant executive in the office of the assistant secretary of state. There, Eisenhower not only became fluent in the bureaucratic labyrinth of Washington but also met many individuals whom he would come to count as lifelong friends. Of these, none would be more important than Colonel George C. Marshall, whom Conner strongly suggested that Eisenhower befriend.

The assignment at State also led to Eisenhower's introduction to Army Chief of Staff Douglas MacArthur. The brilliantly provocative MacArthur helped hone Eisenhower's developing skill in dealing with the often antagonistic relationship between civilian political authority and military authority. Despite their later falling-out, the two men developed a close bond after their 1930 introduction, and Eisenhower would become MacArthur's chief of staff. When President Herbert Hoover placed MacArthur in command of the troops who would rout the pathetic Bonus Army marchers on 28 July 1932, Eisenhower literally stood by MacArthur's side as they watched the burning of the camps. In 1935, when MacArthur's tenure as chief of staff was completed, Eisenhower followed him to his next assignment, that of military adviser to the Philippine government. Through his close contact with Manuel Quezon, the president of the Philippines, Eisenhower further refined his diplomatic and political skills. When war again came to the world in 1939, Eisenhower returned home, hoping once again for a combat assignment.

Despite his constant entreaties to be given a combat assignment, George Marshall, who had become army chief of staff in 1939, knew that there was little of the field commander in Dwight Eisenhower. Indeed, since 1920, Eisenhower had spent only six months with troops, and between 1930 and 1939, he had spent no time at all.[27] But Marshall saw in Eisenhower the traits of a good military tactician and a superb military politician. The often reticent, always formal Marshall brought Eisenhower again to Washington and began to groom him for advancement. Immediately after the attack on Pearl Harbor, Eisenhower was assigned to the General Staff; in June 1942, Marshall made him assistant chief of the War Plans Department, where Eisenhower began to draft plans for the European theater as well as meet with Allied leaders such as British prime minister Winston S. Churchill. In November 1942, Eisenhower was given command of the North Africa force; in December 1943, Roosevelt promoted Eisenhower over men of vastly superior tactical skills—including MacArthur—to the command of the European theater.

Eisenhower's role in London as supreme Allied commander of Europe reminds one of the role of an ambassador-at-large. His gift was not just in developing Operation Overlord (D-Day), a complexity of the first order, but in keeping it on track once approved. Eisenhower had to balance the demands of three civilian commanders—Josef Stalin, who demanded the immediate invasion of France so as to take pressure off his forces on the Eastern Front; Winston Churchill, who seemed to harbor a secret hope that if he stalled long enough on opening a second front in France, Hitler would destroy the Soviet Union for him; and Franklin Roosevelt, who while probably sympathetic to Churchill, had to strike a balance among the Allies so as to keep Stalin in the alliance. Eisenhower also had to contend with other irritants, such as now General George S. Patton, the irascible warrior whose histrionics and bad manners were a constant distraction. Yet Eisenhower dealt with these disruptions with unmatched skill and political finesse, and he eventually piecemealed Overlord to success. While Eisenhower was quick to laud his field commanders—most notably Patton and General Omar Bradley—for their role in leading the breakout through France, into Belgium, and ultimately into Germany, the public gave Eisenhower the lion's share of the credit.

The first assignment given Eisenhower after the war was as army chief of staff, where he would serve until 1947. In June 1947, he accepted the presidency of Columbia University.[28] In his usual self-deprecating style, Eisenhower told the *New York Times*, "I hope to talk to various officials . . . and possibly get some advance inkling of what a college president is up against. I know nothing about it."[29] Eisenhower never saw his university presidency in administrative terms; indeed, he soon became disenchanted with the goals of Columbia. To his mind, there was at Columbia an overemphasis on scholarship and research and an underemphasis on the teaching of undergraduates, particularly the teaching of civics. Thus, Eisenhower sought to create a forum where great minds from all walks of life would meet to discuss issues facing the American citizenry. A quasi think tank that met in a house provided to the university by then special assistant to the president W. Averell Harriman, the American Assembly hoped to, in the words of a press release, "throw impartial light on the major problems which confront America." Administered by the Graduate School of Business, the Assembly would invite "leading representatives of business, labor, the professions and government" to meet in conferences throughout the year. The immediate fund-raising objective for the Assembly was half a million dollars.[30] Eisenhower would take many hits in the press for the Assembly. For Eisenhower, his time at Columbia *was* the American Assembly—he put more time and effort into it than any other venture. Many on Columbia's faculty criticized his single-mindedness, which led to the ignoring of other fund-raising needs;[31] others attacked his naive belief that talking about the nation's problems, in bursts of patriotic fervor, would ultimately solve those problems.[32] But Eisenhower brushed off the criticisms. His correspondence shows him to be in constant fund-raising mode for the Assembly; indeed, his interest in the Assembly, as well as his active participation in fund-raising for the project, continued well into his next military assignment in Europe.[33]

The American Assembly also offered Eisenhower some significant political rewards. The wealthy friends that he made while at Columbia, in particular while fund-raising for the American Assembly, would serve him well when he decided to run for the presidency. These friends included Assembly board member Harry Bullis, chairman of General Mills, from what would become the key state of Minnesota, and Bradshaw Mintener, vice president of Pillsbury Mills, who attended a fundraiser in Minneapolis. In the key state of Texas, the influence of the Assembly was even greater. Oilman Leonard F. McCollum and *Houston Post* owner Oveta Culp Hobby were both on the Assembly Board, as were oilman Jack Porter and Republican Party leader Sid Richardson.[34] As we will see, the argument of historian Travis Beal Jacobs—that "it is conceivable that the nomination would have been impossible without [Eisenhower's] Assembly friends"—has merit.[35]

In 1951, Truman ordered Eisenhower to serve as the first supreme Allied commander in Europe (SACEUR), serving in Paris at the Supreme Headquarters Allied Powers Europe (SHAPE). Eisenhower's assignment was to repair a NATO alliance that had become strained over the issue of the Korean War. This was not an assignment that even remotely appealed to Eisenhower; in the privacy of his diary he called SHAPE "dismaying and unattractive,"[36] and he would later observe, "So far as I know, every senior officer in this hq. [sic] would like to be somewhere else."[37] As if testifying to this fact, Eisenhower did not give up his presidency at Columbia when he returned to uniform; rather, he asked the Board of Trustees for, and was granted, a leave of absence. Nevertheless, Eisenhower was in philosophical agreement with Truman on the need for NATO. As he wrote Kenneth Claiborne Royall, the former secretary of the army, "I am so convinced that the safety of the free world depends on the development of sound, practical, and effective cooperation among us all . . . that I do not see how any man can fail to respond to anything that even has the appearance of a call to duty."[38] The assignment also fit Eisenhower's personality and military experience to a T, a point observed by historian and editor of Eisenhower's papers, Louis Galambos: as SACEUR, Eisenhower was "in effect an American proconsul, spending much of his energy building an ideology of common defense and modifying national ambitions, concerns, and animosities."[39] In this, Eisenhower was diligent. W. Averell Harriman, then serving as the director of the Mutual Security Agency, was Eisenhower's contact in the White House.[40] The assignment also had political overtones. While there is no smoking gun, it is difficult to escape the conclusion that Truman saw Eisenhower—who had yet to even state a party affiliation—as a future political threat and

Harry S. Truman and General Dwight D. Eisenhower, Oval Office,
5 November 1951 (U.S. Army, courtesy of Dwight D. Eisenhower Library)

was banishing him to the hinterland. In terms of Eisenhower's political future, the move to SHAPE had a feeling of finality to it.

Eisenhower looked like a natural-born politician. His grin was infectious; his charisma was best described in the oft-quoted quip by future vice presidential candidate William E. Miller: "With Ike, you always knew he was in the room even before you saw him."[41] Investigative journalist Drew Pearson noted this characteristic when he wrote in his diary of observing Eisenhower's "ability to make people like him and the ability to inspire confidence"—a characteristic that Pearson assessed as being completely "sincere."[42] Journalist Tom Wicker, one of Eisenhower's more recent, and most discerning, biographers, expands upon this point: "His manner suggested always that here was someone to be depended upon, who could handle it—whatever it was—with a confidence that reinforced competence."[43]

His charisma joined with his military success to cause Eisenhower to be rewarded with the greatest title that Americans can bestow—he was immediately christened a hero, usefully defined by philosopher Joseph Campbell as "someone who has given his or her life to something bigger than oneself."[44] A large percentage of Eisenhower biographies has had in its title or subtitle the word "hero." But when compared to his wartime exploits, Eisenhower's postwar positions seemed small. SHAPE was an administrative post out of the limelight, and there is nothing heroic about being a college president. It was only a matter of time—and that time turned out to be remarkably short—until both ordinary Americans and politicos alike, seeing the Truman presidency as tainted goods, would begin to wonder both if the newest American hero wanted the presidency and if there was a way they themselves might step in to make certain that he at least considered the possibility of running.

Their problem was that Eisenhower sincerely wasn't interested.

EISENHOWER COMES TO TERMS WITH THE PRESIDENCY

There can be no doubt but that from 1944 to late 1951—and perhaps beyond—Dwight Eisenhower did not want to be president of the United States. His voluminous correspondence, his candid and detailed diaries, and the memoirs of his confidants are uniformly clear on this point. However, after almost a decade of stating in the most absolute fashion possible that he was not interested in being president, in January 1952 he announced his candidacy for the Republican nomination for president; then, after three months of trying his hand at a long-distance candidacy from Paris, he finally agreed to come home and go toe-to-toe with Robert Taft.

The story of how Eisenhower changed his mind and decided that he would be a candidate for the Republican nomination, when it had been a job that he simply did not want, is one of the great dramas of modern American political history—particularly when it is juxtaposed against presidential elections where it seems that there is no end to the list of candidates who desperately want the job, despite their having what might charitably be called a sparse background of experience. Eisenhower's coming to terms with his own political future is, in many ways, the most important story of the presidential election of 1952.

In 1943, United Press International European correspondent Virgil Pinckney opined that Eisenhower might do well to follow in the "presidential footsteps" of other heroic generals—he noted George Washington,

Andrew Jackson, William Henry Harrison, Zachary Taylor, and Ulysses S. Grant. Eisenhower's response: "Virgil, you have been out in the sun too long."[45] During a lull in the Potsdam Conference in April 1945, Truman turned to a surprised Eisenhower and said, "General, there is nothing you may want that I won't help you get. That definitely and specifically includes the presidency in 1948." Omar Bradley, who witnessed the exchange, "remembered trying to keep a straight face." Eisenhower's response: "Mr. President, I don't know who will be your opponent for the presidency, but it won't be I."[46] Regardless, lapel buttons emblazoned with the slogan "I Like Ike" were around as early as 1946.[47]

In December 1947, John Orr Young, of Young and Rubicam Advertising, placed an advertisement in a Connecticut newspaper, the *Westporter Herald*, advocating for a grassroots effort to foment interest in an Eisenhower candidacy; thirty-five groups appeared, but no more. There is no recorded response to Young's effort from Eisenhower.[48] In 1948, while the general was serving as army chief of staff, Leonard V. Finder, the publisher of the *Manchester Union-Leader*, asked Eisenhower to be allowed to enter his name in the New Hampshire primary. In a 22 January letter to Finder, Eisenhower's response was unequivocal:

> The necessary and wise subordination of the military to civil power will be best sustained . . . when lifelong professional soldiers, in the absence of some obvious and overriding reasons, abstain from seeking high political office. . . . In any event, my decision to remove myself completely from the political scene is definite and positive. I know you will not object to my making this letter public to inform all interested persons that I could not accept [the] nomination even under the remote circumstances that it were tendered me.[49]

Eisenhower followed up this letter with a second letter to Finder, sent only days later, where he reiterated: "So long as I remain active there will never be any diminution of my readiness to work for the good of the country. My decision merely inhibits me from directing these efforts to the strictly political field."[50]

While there were those such as financier and political majordomo Bernard Baruch who empathized with Eisenhower's plight, stating that "anyone seeking to divert Eisenhower's attention to politics" was doing both the nation and the general a disservice (a statement that Eisenhower was quite grateful for),[51] there was no dearth of politicos who tried to convince Eisenhower otherwise. Chief among these was Thomas

Dewey. Resigned to the fact that he could not run a fourth time for the presidency in 1952, Dewey had come to believe that Eisenhower was the only electable moderate Republican—if he could get him to say he was a Republican. Thus, Dewey chained himself to Eisenhower's reluctant star. On 6 July 1949, Dewey met with Eisenhower at the house of the Columbia University president in New York City's Morningside Heights area. Dewey suggested that Eisenhower run for, and be elected to, the governorship of New York and then run for the presidency. In his diary, Eisenhower remembered that he gave Dewey a definite refusal ("So I said, 'I shall never want to enter politics. I shall never willingly seek a vote. I shall always try to do my duty to the United States but I do not believe that anything can ever convince me that I have a duty to seek political office'"). But Eisenhower was sage enough to recognize that Dewey was not hearing what he was saying: "The sad thing is that even as I said this to him I know that to him I meant, 'Why surely, provided I ever become convinced I can win.'"[52]

This seems to have been true because Dewey did not give up. In December 1949, Dewey once again met with Eisenhower; Eisenhower's follow-up letter to that conversation comes close to being a brusque dismissal.[53] Just before he went to SHAPE, Eisenhower granted Dewey one more meeting. Dewey came to Columbia's Faculty Club accompanied by Nassau County executive J. Russell Sprague and Herbert J. Brownell, who had managed Dewey's 1944 and 1948 campaigns and had been chair of the Republican National Committee (RNC). There, Dewey both pledged his organization's support and promised that he would remain deep in the background of any potential campaign. Brownell remembered that Eisenhower "didn't indicate by the flicker of an eyebrow whether he was interested."[54] Once at SHAPE, Eisenhower did his best to stay out of Dewey's sights. This led to a report in Drew Pearson's syndicated column "The Washington Merry-Go-Round" that Eisenhower had "coldly snubbed" Dewey—a charge that Eisenhower, in writing somewhat meekly to Dewey, did not wholly deny.[55]

During his first months at SHAPE, Eisenhower was absolutely clear and absolutely consistent to all who asked; despite his distaste for the assignment, he firmly believed that SHAPE took precedence over any competing call to duty—even a presidential candidacy. He simply did not believe that he *had* to be president; therefore, he could not swap that duty for his duty as SACEUR. He made this clear the day before he left for SHAPE to his friend General Edwin Clark, who had been part of a group that had met with him the day before to gauge his interest in the nomination: "[I told him] it was important that he (and all his associates) understand that I had *not* changed my mind about politics and I still say as I've always said—'I hope always to do my duty to my country; but I cannot conceive of circumstances as of this moment that could convince me I had a *duty* to enter politics.'"[56] In response to the countless letters that Eisenhower received pleading with him to run for president, he sent some form of this reply: "As long as I am assigned to this job I cannot, in justice to America's stupendous effort, become known *as a partisan of any kind*; I must be purely and simply an American public servant."[57] He even refused to answer direct questions regarding his political affiliation, using phrases much like: "I must adhere to my feeling that, as an American soldier in uniform and on active service, I must abstain from claiming membership in a political party."[58]

But if Eisenhower actually believed, as he wrote in his diary, that "my coming to Europe would tend to still the [political] gossip about me,"[59] he was sorely mistaken. Throughout his year at SHAPE, Eisenhower endured a parade of sycophants, elected officials, pseudopolitical experts, and other supplicants, all making the case—either in person at SHAPE headquarters or in what was a seemingly never-ending stream of letters to his office—that he should run for the presidency. Eisenhower tolerated their intrusions, often met with them, patiently heard their appeals, and answered their correspondence. His answer to their entreaties was always no—not, as some historians have gleaned from the correspondence, a Machiavellian "maybe," but a solid no, written and sent so many times that the researcher is left feeling that he is reading a form letter.[60]

Yet Eisenhower's protests that he did not want the job and his refusals to announce as a candidate were simply ignored by those who did not wish to hear them. Charles F. Willis and Stanley M. Rumbough Jr., two former fighter pilots, decided, in the words of Rumbough, that "we would create so much public demand for Ike to run, that he would have to say yes."[61] Thus, in June 1951, "with no contact with or support from Eisenhower or the Republican Party," they launched a grassroots effort named "Citizens for Eisenhower" that would "coalesce public opinion and make the general a candidate."[62] The two men set up an office at the Hotel Marguery on New York's Park Avenue. They solicited the advice of Congressman Hugh Scott (R-PA) and Thomas Stephens, the secretary of the New York State Republican Committee. They developed the *Eisenhower for President Club Handbook* (based on the *General Foods Sales*

Manual and developed in a loose-leaf format for rapid emendation). By November, there were no fewer than 800 "Eisenhower Clubs" in thirty-eight states.[63] Eisenhower ignored their efforts.

While Eisenhower had no trouble dismissing these supplicants like so many gnats buzzing around his head, the entreaties of one friend were different. Lucius Clay's father had been a Georgia senator, and young Lucius received his political initiation as a Senate page. Clay graduated from West Point in 1918 and by 1942 had risen to become the youngest brigadier general then serving in the army. Like Eisenhower, Clay was an outstanding administrator. He had served with Eisenhower in the Philippines, was Eisenhower's deputy as military governor of the American Occupation Zone in Europe, and would serve as the successful strategist of the Berlin Airlift. In 1951, he was named the chairman of the board of the Continental Can Company. The proverbial bull in a china shop, Clay was blustery and clearly saw himself as a kingmaker (Clay to Eisenhower: "I am going to work for you whether you want it or not").[64] But Eisenhower liked Clay's candor and appreciated his understanding of the role that businessmen played in politics.[65] Dewey, who had been rebuffed by Eisenhower at every turn, saw an opening. He welcomed Clay into the inside of his political operation and then used Clay to transmit reports and letters to Eisenhower.

As a result of Clay's entreaties, Eisenhower's stance against running for the nomination began to soften. In May 1951, Clay transmitted to Eisenhower a letter from Dewey that proposed that Dewey and Senator James Duff of Pennsylvania work together to begin to push Eisenhower's name for the nomination, and that Harold E. Talbott, a wealthy industrialist who had been chairman of the Republican Finance Committee in 1948, begin to travel to raise money. Clay clearly hoped that Eisenhower would agree: "I hope that you will let me know that it is satisfactory to proceed. This involves no commitment on your part. All you need to do is to cable me to go ahead. . . . I will take care of the rest."[66] Eisenhower's response, while cryptic, was simply not the outright refusal that he had been giving to that point. While he made it clear that any statement on his part of connection to a party or a campaign committee "would give me the uneasy feeling of being dishonest, if not with others, then with myself," Eisenhower quickly turned to "what others may or should do." Professing to like Dewey, Duff, and Talbott, Eisenhower reminded Clay, "I have always insisted upon the right of every free-born American to do what he pleases." While he would not comment publicly on their efforts,

General Dwight D. Eisenhower and Lieutenant General Lucius B. Clay, Gatow Airport, Berlin, 20 July 1945 (U.S. Army Signal Corps, courtesy of Harry S. Truman Library)

and he warned Clay not to allow the politicos to "put him in a corner," Eisenhower now left the door open: "My present duty is to help develop the defensive power of twelve countries. If I ever have to do any other, I shall have to be *very clear* that I know it to be *duty*."[67]

This was far from a commitment to campaign, but it was enough for Clay, who then spent the summer meeting with various politicians and sending Eisenhower long, melodramatic letters detailing the efforts that were creaking to a start on the general's behalf. Eisenhower was grateful for the reports, although he could not bear the style of the melodramatic Clay, who wrote the letters in a hackneyed code ("A few days ago I lunched with C at his invitation. C is an able financier with wide associations. . . . He is convinced from personal contact that G is expressing an optimism which he does not feel. . . . At the moment, D has all that is needed").[68] But throughout the letters, coded or not, Clay was consistent with his message: "Please remember that no matter how badly you may be needed in Europe you are needed more here, and perhaps if you do not return nothing accomplished there would have any real permanency."[69]

This, Eisenhower would not yet do. He was perfectly happy to let Clay scout the bulrushes, and he was content—albeit more wary—to let Dewey's group begin its exploratory work. This would cost Eisenhower nothing, and he was much too savvy a political warrior not to leave all his options open. But into the fall of 1951, Eisenhower was absolutely consistent both in his refusal to state that he was a candidate and in his unwillingness to allow others to do it for him. He would not allow himself to be pushed. Even when the *New York Herald Tribune* formally endorsed him for the nomination,[70] or when he was informed that a group had formed to formally enter his name in the Oregon primary the following year, Eisenhower refused to budge ("I fail to see why the mistakes of others should induce me to make a serious error of my own").[71]

It would not be the appeals of outsiders that would push Eisenhower into declaring his candidacy. Rather, it would be his belief that he had to save the country, and the collective security of the world, from Robert Taft. Before he went to SHAPE, Eisenhower secretly met with Taft to discuss the Ohioan's impending candidacy against Truman. Eisenhower told Taft point-blank that he would publicly take himself out of the running (with a Shermanesque statement that he had already written and was in his pocket) if only Taft would agree to support NATO and collective security. Taft refused the deal, the meeting ended without an agreement, and Eisenhower tore up his statement.[72] Taft would not waver from his opposition to collective security; in early February, Hoover, Taft, and sixteen other Republicans signed a letter calling for the removal of American troops from NATO.[73] Disillusioned, Eisenhower was a willing audience for those who hammered at the fact that a Taft victory would be disastrous for both the nation and the world. There was a sharp ideological difference between Eisenhower and Taft, one that Eisenhower ultimately could not reconcile. Brownell, at a 1992 conference, remembered that avoiding an isolationist foreign policy was "the one reason that he ran for president, above all else."[74] This was another way of saying what Eisenhower would finally tell reporters on 23 June 1952: "All right, I'll tell you why I'm running for the presidency. I'm running because Taft is an isolationist. His election would be a disaster."[75]

By mid-October, Eisenhower was just about ready to take on Taft. He wrote in his diary on 4 October:

I will never seek any nomination. . . . Of course, because of the remote, very remote possibility that persons may, in spite of my silence, succeed in producing a grass roots draft I have to think more about the subject than is involved merely in a negative attitude. When people like Paul Hoffman, Govs. Dewey & Stassen, Sens. Duff [Frank], Carlson [of Kansas], Lodge, and etc. great friends like Clay, Clark, Roberts etc. . . . all begin to assert that I have a *duty*—it is not easy to just say NO.[76]

All he needed was one final push. It came two weeks later, on 12 October, when Eisenhower met with General Clark, who told him that an exasperated Duff believed that Eisenhower had to put his feelings about the nomination into writing. Should Eisenhower not give those assurances, Clark and Duff both believed that Dewey and Taft would be left to contest for the nomination, and Taft would win. This was enough for Eisenhower. Overnight, Eisenhower wrote a five-page letter to Duff in which, according to Clark's memoir, he clearly identified himself as a Republican and protested that he would not campaign openly for the nomination or resign his commission. However, he also wrote that if he ever was "nominated by the Republicans, I would resign my commission and assume aggressive leadership of the party, working, of course, through the established organization." The letter also gave Duff permission to pursue "whatever course (consistent with what I have said) you may deem proper in organizing like minded people." Clark took the letter to New York, showed it to Duff and several other Eisenhower supporters, and then put it in a safety deposit box for safekeeping.[77]

The actual letter has not survived, although it has been reconstructed by sources close to the event. Assuming that it existed, Eisenhower had now committed to paper that he would accept the nomination. But nothing in the letter said when Eisenhower might announce as a candidate. Moreover, if one accepts Clark's construction of events, only five people knew about the letter. Thus, the entreaties kept coming. But the responses were now different—Eisenhower was now responding like a man who was getting ready to run. To his friend Edward E. "Swede" Hazlett, he wrote, "A man cannot desert a duty, but it would seem that he could lay one down in order to pick up a heavier and more responsible burden."[78] By early December, Eisenhower was writing his brother Edgar, who had argued vociferously against his brother's entering the political fray: "What bothers me is that, if I criticize (and I mean criticize even in my own mind) what is now being done or not being done by our governmental officials, I am forced to ask myself, 'What am *I* doing about it, or what do I *intend* doing about it? . . . *The framers of the Constitution had to assume that citizens would shoulder their responsibilities as such.'*[79]

THE EISENHOWER CAMPAIGN ORGANIZATION

Eisenhower's change of heart converged with the appearance of a political organization that had been created to advance his candidacy, just in case he changed his mind. In September 1951, Dewey called Clay, asking him to come to a meeting at his apartment at New York's Roosevelt Hotel. At that meeting were Dewey, Sprague, Dewey's secretary R. Burdell Bixby, and Clay. Over dinner, Dewey opined that Taft would get the nomination but that he could not be elected. Noting Clay's closeness to Eisenhower, Dewey asked him if he now thought that the general would run. Clay responded that he did not know, but that he was sure that Eisenhower would not run unless there was a demand for him to do so, an actual organization, and a good chance that such a campaign would be well financed.[80]

The next step was taken by Henry Cabot Lodge Jr., the junior senator from Massachusetts and grandson of the Republican senator who had opposed Woodrow Wilson over American membership in the League of Nations. Lodge had met with Eisenhower at SHAPE, coming away with the feeling that Eisenhower "will think that his duty is to prevent the Taft victory from taking place."[81] In September 1951, Lodge suggested that a meeting be held of several senators who were declared Eisenhower supporters. Held in the office of Senator Frank Carlson of Kansas, the meeting included Carlson, Lodge, Duff, and Senator Irving Ives of New York. With Dewey's cooperation, they rented space in Washington for use as an Eisenhower campaign headquarters, an office that was managed by Thomas Stephens, a Dewey supporter and member of the New York State Republican Committee. Everyone understood that this was a temporary measure and that a formal campaign organization, fronted by an official campaign manager with instant name recognition and party credibility, needed to be established.[82] On 11 November, a meeting was held at Dewey's suite at the Roosevelt Hotel for the purpose of formalizing a campaign structure. In attendance were Dewey, Lodge, Clay, Brownell, Sprague, and Duff. A few days after the meeting, both Dewey and Duff called Lodge, asking him to be the campaign manager. Lodge accepted; he was announced as the campaign manager on 17 November.

Throughout November and December, the group that now called itself the Eisenhower Campaign Organization set up offices in New York's Commodore Hotel.

Lodge would later summarize the responsibilities of the committee's leadership: Brownell was "the planner and the thinker. I was the front man, talking to the press, the delegates, the public. But in those early stages, Clay was the key figure."[83] Lodge might well have included Dewey, whose influence was of incalculable value. However, lest Eisenhower be colored as Dewey's man, the governor had to remain in the background. Eisenhower kept his distance from the committee, communicating with it only infrequently, and only through Clay. There were the inevitable problems. Lodge lacked managerial experience; Duff rubbed everyone the wrong way; many resented the control that Dewey had over the operation; money was hard to come by. But the biggest problem was the most obvious—for all its efforts, the committee had no candidate. On 3 December, Lodge wrote to Eisenhower in some exasperation:

> There has been so much talk about your plans that it is becoming vital that you appear and speak in various parts of the United States. People want to know what you think from your own lips and no amount of speaking by Senator Duff or myself or by anyone else can possibly take the place of you. . . . Even people of a patient and conservative turn of mind ask, "When will he get into it?"[84]

Harold Stassen had been asking himself the same thing.

THE "BOY WONDER"

The son of Norwegian and Czech immigrants, Stassen grew up on a small farm in West Saint Paul, Minnesota. He attended the University of Minnesota, where aside from earning his law degree in 1929, he once demonstrated his prowess with a rifle by shooting the tassels off a fellow ROTC student's uniform during practice. During his first campaign for elective office—for Dakota County district attorney in 1929—Stassen discovered that he had tuberculosis in one lung. He spent four months of the campaign, which he won, in a sanitarium recovering from the disease. Elected governor of Minnesota in 1938 at age thirty-one, he was the youngest state governor in American history and had been dubbed the "Boy Wonder" of American politics in the press. It was this notoriety that won him the position of keynote speaker at the 1940 Republican Convention in Philadelphia. He delivered a rousing speech, so much so that Wendell Willkie, the eventual nominee, made Stassen his floor manager.[85] Reelected governor in 1942, Stassen decided to run for the Republican nomination in 1944. In the interim, he enlisted in the navy, where he served in the South Pacific as an aide to Admiral William F. Halsey. A "Draft Stassen" campaign was waged in his absence, but defeats in the early primaries forced him to withdraw from the race. In 1948, Stassen waged a better-planned campaign, and it was more successful. Indefatigable as a campaigner, Stassen crisscrossed the country, touching each state at least once. Nevertheless, both Stassen and Taft fell victim to Dewey at the convention. The year 1950 found Stassen as the president of the University of Pennsylvania, pondering his next move.

Stassen first met with his political advisers on 23–24 June 1951 to discuss a possible 1952 campaign for the presidency. Bernard Shanley, Stassen's campaign manager, who was present at those meetings, confided to his diary that it was decided that Stassen would run, but only if Eisenhower stayed out of the race.[86] Yet Stassen hoped for more. He and his forces believed that if Eisenhower did *not* enter the race, then Stassen would, in Shanley's words, "be in a position to take over the candidacy of the Republican Party as against Mr. Taft, who cannot win against Mr. Truman."[87] In October 1951, Stassen communicated to Eisenhower that while he would remain Eisenhower's "loyal and sincere lieutenant at any time that it becomes clear that you are completely available," if a "vacuum" was created—if Eisenhower did not run—then Stassen would "expect to push ahead on my own."[88] Clay was his usual blunt self: "Please be careful in talking to [Stassen]. He can be very valuable, but no one, I repeat no one, of your group trusts him fully."[89]

By December, Stassen had come to believe that Eisenhower was never going to enter the race, and he could wait no longer. Stassen flew to SHAPE in mid-December and told Eisenhower that he was going to enter the race for himself. He did so on 27 December, proclaiming that he would fight for "humanitarian and liberal" domestic and foreign policies and denying that he was a stalking horse for Eisenhower.[90] No one gave Stassen any chance of winning anything, although Taft quipped to a correspondent: "I suppose his very stupidity will lead him to file in several states."[91]

For Eisenhower, Lodge's warning that the movement could collapse, leaving the hated Taft, the mercurial Stassen, and the too-moderate-for-party-acceptance Earl Warren (to be introduced later in this chapter) as the only candidates for the nomination, was the final straw. While he never once thought that he would be called upon to come home to campaign, Eisenhower was now ready to announce that he was a candidate. On 11 December, Eisenhower wrote in his diary: "[Lodge] says that the project is hopeless without my active *pre*-convention cooperation! That settles the whole matter. . . . But there is no slightest doubt in my mind as to the impropriety—almost the illegality—of any pre-convention activity so long as I'm on this job."[92] The next day, Eisenhower responded to Lodge: "Never have I agreed to any personal pre-convention activity of a political nature. But there is a vast difference between responding to a duty imposed by a National Convention and the seeking of a nomination."[93] Eisenhower had given Lodge half a loaf—he would neither help nor hinder the efforts of the Eisenhower Committee, and he had strongly hinted that he would accept the nomination if offered. Lodge leapt at the straw, writing Eisenhower on 22 December: "It is gratifying to know that you will not oppose our efforts, which have assumed great proportions, to obtain the Republican nomination for you."[94] Eisenhower responded on 29 December that in his view, Lodge "clearly understand[s] the position I shall maintain with respect to the effort you and your friends are making."[95] The committee asked Sherman Adams, the governor of New Hampshire, to take the appropriate steps to place Eisenhower's name on the ballot for the New Hampshire presidential primary, to be held on 11 March 1952.

Given the events of December 1951, Eisenhower's 1 January 1952 letter to Truman stretched the truth to the breaking point. In response to the president's attempt to ferret out Eisenhower's plans ("I wish you would let me know what you intend to do. It will be between us and no one else"), Eisenhower responded:

I do not feel that I have any duty to *seek a political nomination*. Because of this belief I shall not do so. Moreover, to engage in this kind of activity while on my present military assignment would encourage partisan thinking in our country toward a project of the utmost importance. . . . So I shall keep still in all this struggle for personal position in a political party. . . . Because of these beliefs . . . the possibility that I will ever be drawn into political activity is so remote as to be negligible.[96]

Knowing nothing yet of Eisenhower's decision-making process, Truman could have been forgiven if he interpreted this letter to mean that Eisenhower was not going to seek the presidency.

If he believed that, he was wrong. On 5 January 1952, Lodge announced to the press that Eisenhower would be a candidate for the Republican nomination. A perturbed Eisenhower felt that he needed to immediately issue a clarification of his position: that while he saw himself as a candidate, he was not actively running "for" anything.[97] But the ever-impatient Lodge had forced Eisenhower's hand. Two days after Lodge's announcement, on 7 January 1952, General Charles T. Lanham, chief of SHAPE's Public Relations Division, read an announcement to reporters gathered at SHAPE headquarters near Paris. In it, Eisenhower announced that he was a Republican (not a particularly stunning revelation to those who knew him, but a necessity if he was to enter any Republican primaries) and that while he would neither come home to campaign ("I shall not participate in pre-convention activities") nor ask Truman to be relieved as SACEUR, he would indeed "accept a clear-cut call to political duty"—he would accept the Republican presidential nomination if it was offered him.[98] Taft's response the next day was to welcome Eisenhower into the race and remind him of the road he faced, as Taft claimed to have seventy-five delegates already committed to his cause—before the first primary.[99] The response of Taft's manager, David Ingalls, was somewhat less politic: "We don't want to turn the party over to a good looking mortician."[100]

Ten days later, Adams filed a petition of 498 names (only 100 were needed) to put Eisenhower's name on the ballot in the New Hampshire primary, scheduled for 11 March. Eisenhower had ten days to withdraw his name if he wished; he did not.[101]

Dwight D. Eisenhower had not, as many biographers and historians persist in claiming, been drafted against his will. He was now an announced candidate for the Republican presidential nomination. Millions felt as did political operative George Allen, who wrote: "To say that your friends are really jubilant would be the understatement of 1952."[102] But as Eisenhower came to a decision to run on his own terms, so too would he come to a decision to return to the states to actively campaign, in person, against Taft, Stassen, and Warren. When he wrote that "more than this, I shall not do," he meant it.[103] In Eisenhower's mind, a decision to run was not the same as a decision to be a candidate. Indeed, returning to his car after making his announcement, Eisenhower turned to General Alfred Gruenther, then serving as Eisenhower's aide, and asked if Gruenther thought that he would be "bothered" after this statement. Gruenther said yes; a clearly frustrated Eisenhower only grunted.[104]

THE EARLY TAFT CAMPAIGN

The race started with Taft holding a solid lead. His campaign had never really disbanded after his 1948 defeat. The senator's aides had begun to contact potential sources of campaign funds as early as 1949.[105] His top campaign advisers were seasoned party professionals. Closest to the senator was his cousin David Ingalls. A flier in World War I who joined Taft's staff in 1928 and ran for governor of Ohio in 1932 in his own right, Ingalls was, according to Taft's chief biographer, "handsome and genial, [and] had the special advantage of being a millionaire."[106] John D. Hamilton, chairman of the RNC from 1936 to 1940 and architect of the party's successful response to Roosevelt's court-packing plan, was in charge of Taft's campaign in the East.[107] Carrying a special portfolio was Thomas E. Coleman, the chief Republican Party boss in Wisconsin, who was brought into the campaign to help neutralize Joe McCarthy's influence in the Badger State and pave the way for a Taft victory in the primary there; Coleman would also serve as Taft's floor manager at the Republican Convention.[108] The chairman of the RNC, Guy Samuel Gabrielson, was also an avid Taft backer. One voice that was kept in the background was that of Clarence Brown, a former semiprofessional football player, lieutenant governor, and congressman from Ohio who had been Taft's campaign manager in 1948. Many blamed Taft's 1948 defeat on the abrasive Brown, but Taft would bring him out of hiding just in time for Brown to be on the floor of the convention—a decision that was to produce disastrous results.

In January and February 1952, Taft traveled to eleven states, speaking to countless potential delegates. The themes used in his speeches were reminiscent of 1948; in a favorite phrase used over and over on the stump, Taft promised to "return to Washington the principles in which Abraham Lincoln believed—honesty and integrity in government, simplicity and economy, and an unwavering belief in God."[109] Taft was confident of victory, and he exhorted his troops, warning that "there is only one way to win this election, and that is to enthuse those who believe as we do, and then to organize them, [so] that they will do a house-to-house job . . . and bring to the polls the uninterested voter."[110] Taft slashed at Stassen, accusing him of "taking the Truman road to socialism."[111] He also hammered Eisenhower for not coming home to campaign. To this, he added a theme—slapping at the "mugwump" wing of the party—a thinly veiled attack on Eisenhower, whom he portrayed as being deficient in true Republican values.[112] And unlike Eisenhower, who found ways not to speak about McCarthy, Taft, with the help of Coleman, openly courted McCarthy and publicly praised his work in ferreting out communists in the State Department.[113] Yet for all the confidence and support, Taft was still shadowboxing; his main opponent, while now openly a candidate, wasn't yet coming home to fight.

CONVINCING IKE TO CAMPAIGN: THE RALLY AT THE GARDEN

Eisenhower was more than a little disingenuous when he wrote to General Edwin Clark on 9 January: "With the statement that I issued a couple of days ago, I do hope that I don't have to mention the word 'politics' again."[114] But he was now a presidential candidate; he would have to talk and think politics. But he would do so from afar. Leaning on Clay, he prevailed on his friend to take on extra duties in terms of meetings with backers who were aiming for SHAPE, as well as with answering the voluminous correspondence; Clay quickly agreed.[115] He also identified policy areas in which he believed himself to be weak and requested briefing papers on them.[116] Eisenhower also began putting some of his policy thoughts into lengthy letters in which he amplified his ideas— letters that he was clear to note could be shared.[117]

However, those who had wanted Eisenhower to announce his candidacy were not satisfied with him being Cincinnatus. They now begged him to come home to campaign ("Some insist that I come home, possibly, I suppose, as a deserter").[118] In this, they were reacting to the incessant criticism from the Taft campaign, which charged that the Eisenhower campaign was keeping the general away from the action so that the electorate would not learn for what he stood, thereby denying the American people a genuine debate on the issues. The *Chicago Tribune,* consistently a supporter of Taft, put it crudely: "The American people are asked to buy a pig in a poke. [Eisenhower] has the effrontery to tell the American people to take him and like him without . . . lifting a finger to . . . state his position on a single issue."[119] Eisenhower's answer to this charge was public silence; when Clay begged him to respond to Taft's attacks, he simply reiterated, "The statement I issued on January 7th meant exactly what it said."[120]

But events began to conspire to bring Eisenhower home. One such event involved an old-fashioned tug at the heartstrings. Radio personality John R. "Tex" McCrary and his wife, actress Eugenie "Jinx" Falkenburg, came up with the idea for a massive public rally in support of Eisenhower, designed to show the general the depth of his grassroots support and to convince him to come home. McCrary proposed that the rally be held on 8 February at New York's Madison Square Garden. It was not universally accepted as a good idea. Clay was against it; Dewey sniffed, "The Garden? How do you expect to fill it?"[121] But as Clay remembered, once it was decided to hold the rally, "we made damn sure that [it] was filled. We brought in people from all over."[122] Indeed they did. The crowd for the event, which was titled "A Serenade for Ike," was estimated at 20,000 inside the arena and 10,000 more outside, with the show being broadcast on both radio and television.

The show itself was pure star-studded schmaltz. Actors Humphrey Bogart and Lauren Bacall greeted the multitude. McCrary and aviator Jacqueline Cochran, who had been instrumental in bringing women pilots into noncombat roles in the Army Air Corps, emceed the event. Falkenburg hit tennis balls into the crowd. Broadway star Mary Martin sang "I'm in Love with a Wonderful Guy" via the radio, accompanied by Richard Rodgers on piano from the Garden. Clark Gable introduced Irving Berlin, who sang his newest song, "They Like Ike."[123] The crowd loved it, and the radio audience was huge. From any vantage point, the evening was a smashing success.

Cochran immediately flew a film of the event to Paris, where she played it for Ike and Mamie. In his memoirs, Eisenhower recalled that the rally "impressed me more than had all the arguments presented by individuals who had been plaguing me with political questions for many months."[124] In his diary, Eisenhower gushed: "Viewing [the film] finally developed into a real emotional experience for Mamie and me. I've not been so upset in years. Clearly to be seen is the mass longing of America for some kind of reasonable solution for her nagging, persistent, and almost terrifying problems. It's a real experience to realize that one could become a symbol for many thousands of the hope they have!!"[125] He would then write to Swede Hazlett that the film "brought home to me for the first time something of the depth of the longing in America today for change." He added, "I can't tell you what an emotional upset it is for one to realize suddenly that he himself may become the symbol of that longing and hope."[126]

The event at the Garden had moved Eisenhower but not enough to make him change his strategy. Four days after viewing the film, Eisenhower found himself in London, attending the funeral for King George VI. There, he met with Clay, Richardson, and Allen. Eisenhower remembered, "At this meeting I tentatively agreed that I would return home to the United States as soon as I could complete my duties in Europe, and if I was nominated at the convention, would campaign for the presidency."[127] Clay would later remember that this meeting led to Eisenhower's making the "irrevocable decision to run,"[128] but Eisenhower had already made that decision on 7 January. What happened in London was that Eisenhower simply reiterated for Clay what he had said all along: that he would, indeed, come home—he just didn't say when—and as he would later write, "I insisted [to Clay] that I would have to be the one to determine the date of my return."[129] This only increased the pressure brought upon Eisenhower by his admirers to return. They begged that he understand that by virtue of his hard work and organization, Taft was leading the race for delegate support. Eisenhower continued keeping his suitors at arm's length, as he did with one correspondent: "There is also the point of timing. A premature consumption of all the ammunition in a battle is certain to bring defeat."[130]

This is not to say that Eisenhower was not sorely tempted to return to the States to fight Taft. Eisenhower had put a great deal of effort into organizing a meeting of NATO ministers in Lisbon to discuss the situation in Korea. That meeting had ended on 28 February, and on its face the completion of the summit offered the perfect excuse for Eisenhower to proclaim that his job in Europe was done and to come home. For a split second, Eisenhower seems to have considered it. In his diary entry for the day that the conference ended, he mused, "Possibly my work here is not so important as is the work devolving upon the Pres. of the U.S." But he then pulled himself back from the precipice: "But to my mind it is more important than seeking the presidency. But if they will let me alone it is possible that I can soon (several months) turn the job over to another!"[131] It would take more than the Garden, more than a completed summit to cause Eisenhower to come home.

CONVINCING IKE TO CAMPAIGN: THE
NEW HAMPSHIRE PRIMARY

It is important to note that in 1952, the presidential primaries did not serve the function that they do today. Today, the primaries and party caucuses choose the vast majority of the delegates who will go to the party's national convention and vote for a nominee. In 1952, it was just the opposite. There were thirteen primaries, beginning with the New Hampshire primary on 11 March. Only 39 percent of the delegates of both parties would be chosen in the primaries (up from 36 percent in 1948, and compared with 80 percent in 2012); the rest were chosen either by party caucus or by direct wooing of individual delegates by the candidates.[132] Thus, a candidate in 1952 could avoid entering the primaries, work to gain delegate support, and win the nomination behind the closed doors of the convention.

Taft's long service to his party and indefatigable buttonholing had given him a great advantage in the wooing of the delegates. In fact, Taft stood to gain very little by entering any of the primaries. Indeed, those contests did not favor Taft, whose rather wooden style did not endear him to the average voter. On the contrary, Eisenhower's christening as a hero, as well as his consistent personal charm, led observers to conclude—without any immediate evidence—that he would be an instant hit on the campaign trail. However, Eisenhower could not take advantage of his heroic stature or his charisma if he refused to come home to campaign. But if he were to win victories in the early primaries *without* coming home to campaign, those victories would validate Eisenhower's decision to stay in Europe and prove that his organization was good enough to win without him. Those victories could be brandished before the uncommitted delegates by Eisenhower's organization like gleaming trophies, as evidence that their man was a winner and that the delegates better get on board.

The first primary challenge was in New Hampshire, and the Eisenhower campaign invaded the Granite State with a vigor that few expected from an organization with an absent candidate. Visible everywhere was Sherman Adams, who quickly earned the respect and admiration of the

Eisenhower team; Tom Stephens called him the hardest-working man he had ever seen.[133] Adams coordinated a speaking tour of Eisenhower Republicans that included Senators John (CT) and Henry Cabot Lodge, Duff, Carlson, and Leverett Saltonstall (MA). This offensive quickly closed the gap between Eisenhower and Taft. In Keene, Duff accused Taft's managers of "Hitlerian tactics";[134] Lodge charged that "General Eisenhower stands between Taft, [communism], and you."[135] One reporter described the Eisenhower campaign as rather like a "buzz saw."[136]

Taft did not originally plan to meet the buzz saw head-on. Refusing to commit himself to running in the New Hampshire primary, he dispatched John Hamilton to the state to assess the situation. Returning with what he proclaimed to be "surprising and encouraging results," Hamilton told Taft that the primary could be won. Most of Taft's other advisers counseled avoiding the primary. They argued that the spoils of this victory—a mere fourteen delegates—were not worth the effort. Let Eisenhower have the state, they argued. He would gain little, and it would be a hollow victory if the only person he beat was Harold Stassen. However, Taft was spoiling for a fight. Coming to believe that the race was winnable, Taft announced on 30 January.[137]

Choosing instead to court delegates elsewhere in the country, Taft did not campaign in New Hampshire until the first week of March. When he finally came into the state, he campaigned with gusto, undertaking a three-day whirlwind of some thirty speeches. Against the Eisenhower campaign's message that Taft was unelectable in the fall, Taft had a message of his own: "I regret to see that Governor Adams relies on some piffling poll of 400 people to reach his reluctant conclusion that 'Taft can't win.' Why can't I win? I always have won."[138] Taft also denounced his absentee opponent: "I think Governor Adams and Senators Lodge and Duff have done the General a disservice in bringing him into a contest when it is impossible for him to take a position on any controversial issues."[139] Lodge countered by telling voters that he, who had met Eisenhower, knew that the general was not reluctant to run but was just biding his time.[140] Aside from these exchanges, Taft continued to hurt himself by exhibiting a campaign style that was less than welcoming. One journalist noted that Taft was "abrupt and cold in greeting local leaders," and he "brushed off autograph hunters and handshakers, [and] cut short or stopped questioners" during his three-day blitz of the state.[141]

On 11 March, New Hampshire Republicans resoundingly rejected Taft. Eisenhower captured all fourteen delegate contests and won the presidential preference phase of the primary with 50.4 percent of the vote, to Taft's 38.8 percent, Stassen's 7.0 percent, and 3,227 write-in votes for Douglas MacArthur. Eisenhower carried every city except Manchester and carried the state's rural areas by a margin of three to one over Taft. Indeed, Taft did the best in towns that he did not campaign in; he carried only three of the places where he stopped and spoke.[142] Eisenhower's supporters were ebullient. Proclaiming that he was "astonished," Eisenhower gushed that he was "naturally touched."[143]

Eisenhower's New Hampshire victory, along with the defeat of President Truman by Tennessee senator Estes Kefauver in the New Hampshire Democratic primary held the same day (see chapter 2), led some in the press to trumpet that they were witnessing a new era in government.[144] For their part, Taft's associates claimed that the primary meant nothing.[145] The reality was, as is often the case, somewhere in between. While Eisenhower had gained few delegates, he had definitely seized the momentum. But the blow was by no means fatal to Taft, who still held a commanding lead in committed delegate support.

The victory moved Eisenhower, to a point. On 16 March, he announced that he would return to America by 31 May, when he would begin an active campaign.[146] This was about two months before the convention and significantly earlier than Eisenhower had promised on 7 January. But this did little to calm the fears of the Dewey/Lodge Committee. Before Memorial Day, there would be eleven more primaries, not to mention two additional months for Taft to buttonhole delegates while Eisenhower was still at SHAPE. Memorial Day might be too late.

CONVINCING IKE TO CAMPAIGN: THE MINNESOTA PRIMARY

The next primary would be held one week after New Hampshire, in Minnesota on 18 March. It started out, to use a golf euphemism, as a gimme. Grandly announcing that Harold Stassen had a right to his home delegation, Taft refused to allow his name to be included on the ballot. The Dewey/Lodge Committee also tried to keep Eisenhower's name out of the race, less for altruistic motives than out of a fear that their New Hampshire momentum would be stopped after what was expected to be a trouncing in Minnesota by native son Stassen. However, Bradshaw Mintener had already begun a petition drive for Eisenhower, and he refused to halt his efforts, even after the Minnesota Supreme Court ruled that due to the fact that Mintener's petitions had been improperly no-tarized, Eisenhower's name could not appear on the ballot.[147] Buoyed by Eisenhower's New Hampshire triumph, Mintener devised a second strategy. On 13 March—less than a week before the primary—Mintener and his aide, Minneapolis safety manager Forst Lowry, announced that they were spearheading a write-in campaign for Eisenhower, and they asked for an immediate ruling by the Minnesota Supreme Court as to whether write-ins would be counted. The court ruled in their favor, and a blank space to write in another name was included on the primary bal-lot.[148] Despite their furious last-minute efforts, few gave Mintener and Lowry's campaign—which, according to their estimates, had cost them a total of $600—a chance. Even Mintener downplayed expectations: "If we get as many as 10,000 or 15,000 write-ins for Ike, I'll be thrilled."[149]

The expected problems of a write-in contest appeared. On primary day, votes were recorded for Bob Taft, entertainer Arthur Godfrey, evan-gelist Billy Graham, and comic strip character Dick Tracy; many voters just voted for themselves. But Mintener needn't have worried. While Stassen recorded 129,000 votes, 107,000 Minnesotans voted for Eison-hauer, Eausonhower, Ineshower, Eisenhower, or just plain Ike.[150] No matter what the spellings, Eisenhower's second-place showing was little short of a miracle. The Eisenhower campaign was ecstatic. On 20 March, Eisenhower told *New York Times* reporter Cyrus S. Sulzberger II that he was incredibly flattered, and he did not want to disappoint his supporters back in the States.[151] Publicly, Eisenhower termed the outcome "amaz-ing."[152] But he still had no plans to come home.

Delighted with Eisenhower's primary victories but frustrated by his continued absence from the field of political combat, Dewey sent Brownell to Paris to try his hand at convincing Eisenhower to return to America to campaign before 31 May. On 24 March, Brownell visited Eisenhower at SHAPE. He prodded Eisenhower for a statement of his beliefs and told him point-blank that he would have to resign his com-mission and come back and meet delegates, or, despite his early victo-ries, he would probably lose the nomination to Taft. Like so many before him, Brownell was not successful. He walked away from the wide-ranging ten-hour meeting believing that Eisenhower was "politically astute" and "strategic" in his calculations: "[He] had never definitively closed the door on accepting a Republican nomination and at the same time had preserved his image as a non-candidate."[153]

Immediately after the Minnesota primary, however, Brownell proved himself to be a prophet; Eisenhower started losing. On 1 April, having campaigned like a man possessed, Taft defeated both Stassen and Earl Warren in Wisconsin, despite Stassen's pitiful promise that he would give half of the delegates that he won to Eisenhower on the first ballot. That same day, as a write-in candidate, Taft won sixteen Nebraska delegates to one for Eisenhower and one noncommitted (this was, perhaps, a bigger upset than Eisenhower's write-in victory in Minnesota, since in Nebraska, the court ordered that all write-in ballots must have the candidate's name spelled correctly, or the ballot would be invalidated).[154] One week later, in Illinois, Taft won twenty-four delegates to Warren's six and Stassen's none.[155] When he noted, "It's not an easy task to defeat a popular war-time general in successive elections,"[156] that was as close as Taft would get to gloating; the haul from the three primaries increased his committed delegate lead to 191—a two-to-one edge over Eisenhower.[157]

In response to Taft's victories, Eisenhower decided to release more specific information regarding the date of his return. On 2 April 1952, the day after the Wisconsin primary, he wrote Secretary of Defense Robert Lovett, "[I] request that you initiate appropriate action to secure my release from assignment as Supreme Commander, Allied Powers Europe, by approximately June 1, [and] that I be placed on inactive status upon my return to the United States."[158] That same day, Eisenhower wrote to Truman asking the president to relieve him of his command.[159] Truman responded with a handwritten note: "I received your letter about your retirement from military service. It makes me rather sad. . . . I hope you will be happy in your new role."[160] Eisenhower's decision was announced on 8 April—the same day as Taft's win in Illinois. The *New York Times* reported that Eisenhower would return to the United States within six weeks, that he was going on inactive status until the convention, and if he won the nomination, he would quit the army.[161] The timing of this announcement was instrumental in Eisenhower's pulling ahead in what had been a close primary race in New Jersey, where he won thirty-one out of thirty-eight delegates on 15 April,[162] and then defeated Taft by a two-to-one margin in the Massachusetts primary on 30 April.

But in the time that it took Eisenhower to return to actively campaign, the Taft forces showed their tremendous organizational power as they outflanked the Eisenhower forces for a large cache of delegates. Yet by doing so, they sowed the seed for the eventual defeat of Taft at the Republican Convention.

THE "TEXAS STEAL"

In 1950, Henry Zweifel of Fort Worth, an ardent Taft supporter, was elected to the post of Republican national committeeman from Texas. Zweifel's election allowed Taft to gain control of the small Republican machinery in the overwhelmingly Democratic state. However, Zweifel's rise to power did not go unchallenged. He was opposed by H. J. "Jack" Porter, a Houston oilman with excellent fund-raising connections who was decidedly pro-Eisenhower; indeed, in early 1951, Porter had been in contact with both Lodge and Duff, who had helped him to set up an Eisenhower organization in Texas.[163]

The first step toward the choosing of Texas's thirty-eight convention delegates was the precinct conventions that began on 3 May. Held in town halls, churches, schools, and private homes, the precinct conventions were open affairs that resembled a cross between a town meeting and a housewarming party. There was little control placed on who actually voted at these affairs; Zweifel was quick to understand that any independents or even Democrats who managed to attend would probably vote for Eisenhower and could affect the outcome of the vote. Therefore, Zweifel introduced a resolution before the state committee that called for all who participated in precinct conventions to sign an oath: "I am a Republican, and desire to participate in Republican Party activities in the year 1952." The Porter forces were slow to recognize the danger to their cause, and Zweifel's loyalty oath passed.[164] But Porter did not give up; he simply ignored the oath. With the financial and editorial help of William and Oveta Culp Hobby, co-owners of the *Houston Post*, the Eisenhower forces purchased advertisements that publicized the location of the precinct meetings and urged Democrats and independents to attend: "You CAN vote in BOTH Democratic and Republican elections—DO NOT BE INTIMIDATED!"[165] For their willingness to join with conservative Democrats in an effort to defeat Taft, Porter, Hobby, and their supporters earned for themselves the label of "One-Day Republicans."[166]

On 3 May, Republicans, Democrats, and independents alike poured into the precinct meetings. In most cases, the Eisenhower supporters outnumbered the Taft supporters. In his own home, Zweifel was forced to leave his precinct meeting when more than a hundred Eisenhower supporters appeared; he went out onto his front lawn and elected a Taft delegation. All over the state, the results were the same—swamped by Eisenhower supporters, the precinct meetings elected Eisenhower delegates. However, disgusted Taft supporters, furious that the Republican meetings had, in their view, been raided by Democrats, left the meetings and elected their own pro-Taft delegates.[167] Proclaiming that "the majority is not always right," Zweifel vowed that the elected Eisenhower delegates would not be seated at the state party convention.[168] For his part, Porter promised that democracy would prevail.

On 27 May, some 12,000 Texas Republicans descended on Mineral Wells, a town of roughly 7,800, for the state convention. By the time the smoke cleared, the Taft forces had regained the upper hand. Of the 519 delegates who had been challenged after the precinct conventions, the State Executive Committee, controlled by Zweifel, seated only 30 Eisenhower delegates. The rest of the 1,060 convention seats were made up of Taft delegates. When, to no one's surprise, the convention ratified the decision of the state committee, it was now the Eisenhower delegates' turn to walk out. The now solidly Taft-controlled convention chose an "uninstructed" delegation to the national convention, but it was well known that thirty of the thirty-eight delegates chosen were Taft supporters. Meanwhile, across the street, the Eisenhower delegates reconvened. Waving signs that read "Rob with Bob" and "Graft with Taft," they opened their rump convention with a prayer ("We like Ike. God likes Ike. We will nominate and elect him"). Guided by Herbert Brownell, who had flown to Mineral Wells from New York to assess the situation, and with shouts of "Ike" instead of "Aye," the rump convention chose a rival delegation to the national convention, which was instructed to cast thirty-three votes for Eisenhower.[169]

The composition of the Texas delegation would now be decided by the party's Credentials Committee at the national convention in Chicago. But the rhetoric became, if anything, even more heated throughout the month of June. To Taft and his supporters, the issue was simple—he had won the most delegates, period. Lodge termed the Mineral Wells convention "scandalous and shameful";[170] Ingalls sniffed, "We can't have Democrats telling us who to nominate."[171] But it would be the Eisenhower forces who best exploited the issue. The word "Steal" would be on almost all Eisenhower literature from early June until the convention. The Eisenhower campaign now portrayed itself as the aggrieved party, having had its delegates purloined by Taft. Taft missed the point when he attempted to dismiss the Texas issue "not as a moral, but as a mathematical issue."[172] Texas had become a morality play, one that the Eisenhower forces would ride all the way to the convention.

The race was now simply too close to call. Texas had moved Taft ahead in the delegate count. With 604 delegates needed to nominate, Taft was reported to have 399 committed delegates (the Taft forces claimed to have 474) to Eisenhower's 379.[173] And yet by anyone's count, some 380 delegates had yet to make up their minds. Attention now turned to California's 68 delegates, who would make up their minds before Eisenhower returned—and they would initially support neither Eisenhower nor Taft. Rather, California would support a favorite son who had already run a national campaign for the vice presidency.

WARREN

Earl Warren was born in Los Angeles in 1891, but his father moved the family to the tough frontier town of Bakersfield three years later. As a boy, Warren watched as an outlaw shot and killed the sheriff on the town's main street. World War I followed close on the heels of the completion of Warren's work at the University of California Law School, and he enlisted in the army. Although he did not see action, at war's end Warren had worked his way up from private to first lieutenant.

For almost two decades after the war, Warren honed his skills as a prosecuting attorney. He served from 1919 to 1925 in the Alameda County prosecutor's office, and he was elected to three consecutive terms as that county's district attorney from 1925 to 1938. Elected state attorney general in 1938, Warren organized California's wartime defense and, in a move that he later professed to strongly regret, was one of the most vocal supporters of the resettlement of thousands of Japanese Americans from the West Coast to relocation camps in the nation's interior. In 1942, Warren was elected governor of California and was twice reelected—once, in 1946, running on both the Republican and Democratic tickets. When Harry Truman quipped in a 1951 press conference that Warren "was a Democrat and didn't know it," he was not far off the mark. More progressive a governor than even Dewey, Warren embodied what some came to call the infinitesimally small "liberal wing" of the Republican Party. His support of public power, a mandatory FEPC, government-subsidized private housing, and compulsory national health insurance made Warren look a lot like a Fair Dealer.

Warren's electoral successes, his reputation as a moderate, his natural ease as a campaigner, and his ensuing national profile led to his being considered in 1944 as a possible running mate by both Dewey and Taft. However, Warren turned both men down by removing himself from consideration during his convention keynote address. Four years later, however, he accepted the convention's nomination for the vice presidency. The defeat of that ticket did nothing to harm Warren's career trajectory. Several pundits speculated early that he would run for the presidency in 1952. Proving them right, he announced his candidacy on 16 November 1951.

Like Stassen, however, Warren never had a chance to gain the nomination in 1952; unlike Stassen, Warren understood the reality of the situation.[174] He entered the Wisconsin primary, hardly campaigned at all, and, as noted earlier, was trounced by Taft and Stassen. At best, Warren was playing for a deadlocked convention. But the deeper reason for his candidacy lay in the labyrinth of California state politics. Throughout his administration, Warren had been at odds with the California oil lobby. Immediately after Warren's election as governor, William Keck, president of the Superior Oil Company and a large contributor to Warren's campaign, tried to influence the new governor's appointment for the director of the state department of natural resources. Warren refused.[175] In retaliation, Keck let it be known that he would not support Warren for the presidency in 1952, putting his influence behind Congressman Thomas H. Werdel of Bakersfield, who entered the 3 June California primary in opposition to Warren. Both Taft and Eisenhower, conceding that it was Warren's home turf, sat out the primary (Stassen tried to get on the ballot, but his petitions were ruled ineligible).[176] Thus, it would be Warren versus Werdel. If he won, Warren not only would control the sizable California delegation to the convention but also would be in a strong position to influence its outcome, as he would be wooed by both Eisenhower and Taft. If he lost, Warren knew that in California, at least, he would become a "political non-entity."[177]

It was a tough, expensive, and often dirty fight. The most famous incident involved former president Herbert Hoover, who charged that Warren, who had just had surgery for colon cancer before the campaign began, was actually dying—an untrue claim, even though Warren had gone to great lengths to keep the true reason for his surgery away from the public.[178] And for all their statements denying any interest in the campaign, the Taft forces gave direct aid to the Werdel camp. For his part,

Keck met with Ben Tate, Taft's financial director; following the meeting, Keck sent reports to Tate on the progress of Werdel's campaign.[179]

The outcome was not as close as was predicted, even though most observers had conceded the race to Warren by late May. Warren received 1,029,495 votes to Werdel's 521,100 (Werdel carried only one county).[180] In a press conference following his victory, an exuberant Warren proclaimed Werdel's showing to be "rather poor . . . in view of the enormous amount of money that was spent and the enormous amount of deception that was used for the purpose of confusing the voters."

California state law required that all members of a delegation sign a loyalty oath to support the winner of the primary at the convention. All of Warren's delegates did so. However, one who signed was clearly not going to support Warren at the convention. Senator Richard M. Nixon, who had already been courted by both Dewey and Taft as a vice presidential choice, refused; he clearly was going to keep his options open.

As he did so, Ike came home.

ABILENE: 4–5 JUNE 1952

Abilene, Kansas, is a railroad town. The tracks that held so much fascination for young Ike run the entire length of the small midwestern town, whose population in 1952 was about 6,000. Those tracks had carried Eisenhower out of his hometown, to the east, and on to fame. It was only a few yards from these tracks, and a few more yards from his boyhood home, that Dwight Eisenhower would begin his active candidacy for the presidential nomination as he returned home on 4 June to lay the cornerstone for the future Eisenhower Foundation and Museum.

The summer heat in Kansas is often brutal, with a breeze that only makes the stickiness worse. It is this heat that makes the rainstorms there so unexpected and often violent. Such a storm occurred on the morning of 4 June. The park where the dedication was to take place quickly turned into a swamp. Eisenhower arrived in a long, gray raincoat and, coupled with a bald pate that was glistening with raindrops, looked even older than his sixty-one years. After rolling up his trouser legs, Eisenhower walked to the podium, which he shared with three of his brothers. There, within sight of his boyhood home and with a downpour threatening, Eisenhower made his first public speech as a presidential candidate.

It was an unpromising beginning; Brownell was on the mark when he characterized the speech as being as "dismal as the weather."[181] Eisenhower attacked one-party rule, claimed that the loss of China was "one of the great international disasters of our time," and denounced the decisions of Yalta. But none of the Eisenhower charisma came through in Abilene. He read from a script, rarely looked at his audience, plodded through the text, and sounded tired.[182] The press conference the next day took some of the edge off the previous day's disaster. In what would become a significant moment in the history of the modern press, Eisenhower insisted, over the objections of the entire print press contingent and over his own long-standing rule, that television cameras be allowed into the press conference. What those cameras recorded was far more important than what the candidate said. In Abilene's Plaza Theater, Eisenhower demonstrated the skill at thrust and parry with the press that, despite chuckles at his slips of the tongue, would become a trademark of both his campaigns and his presidency. Refusing to say "no comment," Eisenhower often answered, "I don't know"—a novelty for a political candidate, both then and now. When asked about his plan to end the war in Korea, Eisenhower was quick to note, "I do not have any prescription for bringing the thing to an end." He professed that he was "not going . . . to indulge in personalities in anything I have to say." And with terms like "skyhootin'" (what prices do during inflation), Eisenhower sounded for all the world like your next-door neighbor talking politics.[183]

But he was still behind. One week after his return, the *Washington Post* estimated that Taft now had 462 delegates committed to his cause, and Eisenhower had 390.[184] Walter Trohan of the *Chicago Tribune* all but crowned Taft the nominee: "The personal boom of [Eisenhower] has fallen flat on its face before getting off the ground. Only heroic measures can bring Eisenhower into serious consideration as a threat to Senator Taft, and these do not appear to be in the making."[185] But the Eisenhower forces were not disheartened; when a Taft man claimed to have the nomination "on ice," Duff quipped: "They'd better keep it there and not get it out in the sun where it will turn sour."[186]

THE DEMOCRATIC
PRECONVENTION CAMPAIGNS

While he would, throughout the first months of 1952, continue to posture in public, hinting that despite it being against his "personal inclination," he might run for reelection, if only to assure world peace,[1] Harry Truman had long since made up his mind. As noted in chapter 1, he had confided both to his diary and to his staff that he was not going to run, and the last two years had only convinced him that he was right. But for the moment, it served his purposes not to announce his intentions to the public. Keeping the country guessing would allow Truman more time to settle on a suitable heir.

TRUMAN COURTS A SUCCESSOR: VINSON
AND EISENHOWER

Truman honestly believed that the Democratic nomination was his to give and that he could guarantee the nomination to a successor of his choice. His first choice, one that he approached about the position as early as 1950, was Fred M. Vinson, then serving as chief justice of the Supreme Court. The choice astounded Truman's advisers, and with good reason. One can hardly think of a less electable presidential candidate than the sixty-year-old Kentuckian. If his ailing health was not a debit, then the progressive decisions of the Vinson court on civil rights were. There was simply no way that Vinson would be acceptable to southern Democrats.[2]

However, where Truman would have seen these liabilities as fatal in candidates whom he did not like, he ignored them when considering Vinson. The president and the chief justice had been friends for years; Truman appointed him secretary of the Treasury in July 1945, and then appointed him to the court in April 1946. They had long maintained a cheery and informal correspondence; they often played historical trivia games through the mails, quizzing each other on names, dates, and facts. A regular at the poker games attended by the president and held at Truman aide Clark Clifford's home, Vinson even traded murder mysteries with Bess Truman.[3] But Vinson did not want to run. Despite all of Truman's entreaties—and there were many—Vinson always refused, consistently pleading poor health.[4] On 11 October 1951, Truman, Vinson, and Clark Clifford dined together at Blair House. In a last-ditch effort to get his man, Truman promised Vinson his full support. Three days later, Vinson sent Truman his final refusal; Clifford would later confess, "I was greatly relieved."[5]

Truman's second choice may well have been Dwight Eisenhower. He had, as was seen in chapter 1, already offered his support to Eisenhower in 1948, only to be rebuffed. By November 1951, Eisenhower had changed his mind about running and was ready to announce that he would run as a Republican, but Truman did not know that. On 5 November 1951—three weeks after Vinson had turned him down—Truman met with Eisenhower at Blair House. Two days later, Arthur Krock wrote a story for the New York Times in which he claimed that at their meeting, Truman had offered Eisenhower his full support if Eisenhower ran for the Democratic nomination (Krock would later reveal his source to be associate justice of the Supreme Court William O. Douglas, who claimed he had heard the story from Truman). Everyone concerned scrambled to deny the story. On 10 November, Eisenhower wrote C. L. Sulzberger, publisher of the New York Times, protesting that "the story is completely without foundation. In fact, the President said nothing to me that could be so interpreted even by the most tortured and distorted type of reporting." A week later in Key West, Truman himself denied the story.[6] On 15 November, at a birthday party in Paris for Averell Harriman (his sixtieth), Eisenhower repeated his denial personally to Sulzberger; indeed, Sulzberger remembered that Eisenhower denied the story twice. Eisenhower remembered that when he met with Truman at Blair House, "they winked at each other and by mutual agreement said right away there was one subject they weren't going to talk about, and that was the closest they ever came to politics."[7]

Assuming for the moment that the story, which cannot to this day be absolutely verified, is true, Truman was whistling in the wind. Writing in his diary on 25 September 1951, Eisenhower was clear: "I hear that the Democrats still rate me high—but that causes me no concern. I could never imagine feeling any compelling duty in connection with a Democratic movement of any kind."[8]

KEFAUVER

Truman's refusal to announce his intentions, as well as his inability to corral an heir, led to a logjam in the Democratic race. Despite his problems, Truman was a formidable electoral opponent; his complete control of the machinery of the Democratic Party would make any potential challenger for the nomination reconsider his priorities. Not so Estes Kefauver. The senator from Tennessee had spent his entire career leading highly publicized crusades against the machinery of his own party, crusades that advanced his career but brought him into a blood feud with the president of the United States.

Young Estes signed a classmate's friendship book: "Nickname: Big Bill. Character: Mean and Lazy. Ambition: To Be President."[9] After his 1927 graduation from Yale Law School, Kefauver tried his hand at an independent law practice but quickly became bored. In 1938, he ran for the state senate from Chattanooga and was soundly defeated. However, his service to the party in a losing cause did not go unnoticed. He was appointed state finance and taxation commissioner, a position he resigned within a year. In 1939, Kefauver was elected to the U.S. House of Representatives on a platform supporting public power for the Tennessee Valley.

Kefauver quickly gained a reputation for himself as a maverick by speaking out strongly against the poll tax and the filibuster, issues that the Roosevelt administration had consigned to the back burner, and speaking ever so delicately in favor of civil rights.[10] In 1948, taking advantage of a split between the forces of Memphis boss Ed Crump, who was bitterly opposed to Kefauver, and the rest of the party, Kefauver entered a three-way battle for the Democratic nomination for the U.S. Senate. He often trailed his opponents by as much as twenty-five points in the polls, but Kefauver's optimism on the campaign trail was contagious. His simple, down-to-earth style appealed to Tennessee voters in much the same way that the Missourian at the top of the Democratic ballot would appeal to the entire nation that fall. An example of his folksiness became Kefauver's trademark. When responding to a Crump editorial that likened the congressman to a "pet coon" rummaging about in a drawer when he thought no one was looking, Kefauver donned a coon-skin cap and, to the delight of his audience shouted, "I may be a coon, but I ain't Mr. Crump's pet coon."[11] For the rest of his career, Kefauver was expected to don the cap whenever he made a speech; he usually obliged. In winning this primary election and the general election that followed, Kefauver went to the Senate with a national reputation as a crusader against the vested interests.

Kefauver's Senate seat was barely warm before he latched onto the idea of chairing a high-profile investigatory committee that would look into interstate crime. What would become known as the Kefauver Crime Committee visited fourteen cities, issuing subpoenas and questioning various members of the criminal underworld, with many of its sessions broadcast on live television. As such, it became television's first great political extravaganza. The public response to the parade of criminal lu-minaries through their living rooms via television was staggering. The most famous example of the committee's success was the New York City hearings, for which an estimated 30 million people tuned in, vastly out-numbering any televised program to date.[12] What these viewers saw was a soap opera of chillingly real magnitude. The most memorable scene was that of underworld leader Frank Costello, who was so afraid of the camera that his lawyer demanded that only his hands be shown on tele-vision. The contrast of Costello's sweaty, wringing hands and Kefauver's calm demeanor and penetrating questions was impossible to miss.

The crime hearings made Kefauver a household name. But they also made him persona non grata in his own party. In his zeal for the headlines, Kefauver showed little regard for local party politics, and he proceeded to implicate and embarrass many Democratic Party leaders. In Miami, for example, the committee discovered that a Capone fam-ily associate had contributed $100,000 to the 1948 campaign of then governor Fuller Warren. Incensed by the committee's exposure of the contribution, Warren unleashed a barrage of vitriol against Kefauver in the press. The hatred that Warren expressed would find its way into the Florida primary a year later.[13] In the committee's investigation of Chi-cago, enough questions were raised about the relationship between or-ganized crime and the Democratic Party that in that fall's election, both houses of the Illinois legislature fell to the Republicans. Democrats lost all over the state; even Senate majority leader Scott Lucas was defeated by former congressman Everett Dirksen.[14]

Kefauver elicited true extremes of attitude—he was either loved by his contemporaries or detested. Paul Douglas (D-IL) represented one pole of opinion when he described Kefauver as "a true soldier of the people. . . . He deserves to be rated as one of the best Senators of the last half-century."[15] Clinton Anderson (D-NM) represented the other pole: "From his first days in the Senate, Kefauver had his eye on the presidency and was determined to let nothing stand in the way of his winning it."[16] Truman was definitely in the latter camp. In his memoirs, Truman wrote that he "approved of what [Kefauver] undertook to do with his investigating committee, but I did not approve of the methods he used and the way he went about it."[17] This was an understatement; Truman was seething. For Truman, Kefauver's disregard for Lucas's position and his recklessness when placing the Democratic Party on trial in city after city showed that the senator had no party loyalty—a sin that Truman could forgive in no man. Privately he referred to Kefauver as "Senator Cow-Fever" or as the "demagogic dumb bell."[18]

Well aware of Truman's antipathy toward him, Kefauver, who had decided to try for the presidency in 1952, nevertheless felt that he had to move quickly. He had to prove on the primary trail that he had the vote-getting ability that the Democrats could not afford to ignore. This meant that he would have to enter as many primaries as he could, regardless of what Truman did or did not do. In December 1951, Kefauver told the *New York Times*, "If I decide to seek it, I will go on notwithstanding. I don't think the president will announce his decision until shortly before the convention."[19] Privately, Kefauver reportedly chortled, "I hope Truman decides to run. I'll beat the socks off him."[20] On 15 January, Kefauver met with Truman at the White House; eight days later, on 23 January, Kefauver made it official, announcing his candidacy and proclaiming that he was "in it to the finish."[21] Kefauver's entry into the race before Truman had publicly announced his plans only confirmed for Truman that the Tennessean was a Democrat who did not respect, or care about, the Democratic Party. Furious, Truman would nurse a slow-burning loathing for Kefauver that he would not hold for any other candidate in 1952—Democrat or Republican.

Sharing their boss's dislike of Kefauver, Truman's staff tried to get the president to change his mind and run for another term. But Truman

Estes Kefauver leaving the White House, 15 January 1952 (National Park Service, Abbie Rowe, courtesy of Harry S. Truman Library)

would hear none of it.[22] He was not running, but he would not leave the choice of his successor to chance. Truman wanted to have an heir apparent in place before he announced to the nation that he was not running. Although Vinson and Eisenhower had disappointed him, Truman had already settled on a third choice. On 8 May 1951, he had scribbled himself a short note: "I've said that no third term appeals to me. On 16 April 1950 I expressed my opinion on that. Now if I can find a man who will take over and continue the Fair Deal. . . . It seems to me now that the

Governor of Illinois has the background and has what it takes. Think I'll talk to him."[23]

STEVENSON

Adlai Ewing Stevenson II had strong ties to the history of the Democratic Party—his grandfather had been Grover Cleveland's vice president during Cleveland's second term. The younger Stevenson was born in Los Angeles, but when he was six years old, Adlai's father, a newspaper executive, moved his family to Bloomington, Illinois. Stevenson received his basic educational training in the East, graduating from Choate in 1918 and from Princeton University, with a major in literature and history, in 1922. He began law school at Harvard, but poor grades and financial difficulty forced him to withdraw. After a stint as the managing editor of the family paper, the *Bloomington Pantagraph*, Stevenson enrolled at the Northwestern University School of Law, where he took his degree in 1926.

Stevenson worked as a lawyer in Chicago until 1933, when he signed on as a foot soldier in the New Deal. From 1933 to 1935, he was special counsel to George Peek, the administrator of the Agricultural Adjustment Administration (AAA). After a six-year hiatus spent building up his law practice, Stevenson returned to Washington as special assistant to Secretary of the Navy Frank Knox. During World War II, Stevenson headed a civilian commission that studied plans for the occupation of Italy, served as assistant secretary of state under both Edward Stettinius and James Byrnes, and was chosen as a delegate to the first General Assembly of the United Nations. When Stevenson returned home to Illinois in 1947, he was a well-known figure in the Democratic Party.

Stevenson had considered a run for the U.S. Senate from Illinois as early as 1942, but he ultimately dismissed the idea as being premature.[24] In 1948, a group of supporters moved to convince Colonel Jacob M. "Jake" Arvey, the boss of Illinois Democratic politics, that Stevenson would make a good candidate for the Senate. Arvey needed little convincing—he had been made aware of Stevenson by Jimmy Byrnes ("you have a gold nugget in your own backyard").[25] However, Arvey had already thrown the machine's support in the Senate race to Paul Douglas, a college professor, war hero, and alderman from Chicago. But Arvey as yet had no candidate for governor. Despite his doubts as to how the Illinois electorate would react to the cultured, sophisticated Stevenson, Arvey took a calculated risk and backed Stevenson for governor. The gamble paid off. Stevenson proved to be an adept campaigner, and his persistent attacks against the scandal-ridden Republican administration in Springfield resonated with the public. Stevenson defeated his opponent by 572,067 votes; it was the largest plurality in the state's history, and some 539,000 more than Truman won in the state.

Stevenson's forty-two months as governor earned him a reputation for honesty and fairness, as well as the label of progressive reformer. He intervened, when local governments would not, to break the back of downstate gambling interests. He established a merit system in the police force and introduced a law calling for a permanent Fair Employment Practices Commission (FEPC) in Illinois (Stevenson in a radio report: "I think this legislation is not only simple justice, but will actually strengthen our economy and our society by reducing prejudice and discrimination and their ugly offspring—racial tension").[26] On 30 July 1949, Stevenson ordered: "There shall be no racial segregation nor shall there be any discrimination in accepting enlistment . . . [in] the National Guard or Naval Militia because of race, creed, or color."[27] Taking a high-profile stand against McCarthyism, on 26 June 1951 Stevenson vetoed a bill requiring all public officials to take a loyalty oath. In his veto message, Stevenson was at his most articulate: "We here in Illinois need not now do something *bad* just for the sake of doing *something*. . . . We must not burn down the house to kill the rats."[28] Stevenson's veto was strong rhetoric that appealed to the liberals; it also brought him national attention (the progressive journal the *Nation* called the veto "a sharp reversal for the witch hunters"),[29] but it made him even more of a target for the Republicans.

But his tenure was not without its controversies. On 2 June 1949, two days after Alger Hiss's first trial for treason had begun in New York (see introduction), Stevenson, who had refused to testify in person, submitted a written deposition to a U.S. commissioner in Springfield. The deposition stated that, in Stevenson's opinion, the reputation of Hiss, the governor's colleague at the AAA, the United Nations, and the State Department, for loyalty, integrity, and veracity was "good."[30] Criticism was sharp against Stevenson's depiction of the disgraced Hiss (the *Chicago Tribune* claimed that Stevenson had lied when he gave Hiss a favorable recommendation; Stevenson shot back, "I can hardly believe the *Tribune* is recommending that politicians protect themselves in unpopular situations by lying").[31] Potentially more damaging was Stevenson's

12 December 1949 announcement that he and his wife, Ellen, had divorced. In addition, a horrific accident, an explosion at Orient No. 2 Coal Mine in West Frankfort, Illinois, killed 119 men on 22 December 1951 and led to much public debate about the competence of the administration when it came to mine safety. Pundits were beginning to predict that he would lose a bid for reelection in 1952.

The speculation in 1951, then, was not whether Stevenson would run for president; it was whether he would choose to stand for reelection as governor. On that score, Stevenson bared his soul in a letter to close friend Alicia Patterson, the founder and editor of *Newsday*:

> I literally don't know whether I could physically survive another campaign and four more years. Yet if I slow up as everyone advises, I dread the possibility of the administration slipping back, losing the momentum and the public confidence I've gained. . . . Moreover if Ike runs and it turns into a landslide as well I'm not sure I could win [reelection as governor] against the deluge.[32]

Thus, he played his cards close to the vest. To future biographer Porter McKeever, Stevenson wrote: "I can see little prospect of articulating a future course until I can first feel the wind."[33] He did not feel that wind until the new year; on 5 January 1952, Stevenson announced that he would run for reelection.

As the nation turned into the 1950s, American liberals were in a state of crisis. Roosevelt had been their hero, but now his successor was widely seen to be a failure. The war in Korea slogged on, McCarthy's boorish attacks were cheapening politics, and with Eisenhower on the horizon, it seemed possible that the country was going to entrust its leadership to the Republican Party. Liberals longed for a leader who could both excite and educate the public: a candidate who read more widely than dime store westerns, one who could write, think, and argue not just with conviction but with style. They were looking for the idealized FDR; until he was supplanted by John F. Kennedy, Adlai Stevenson was treated by liberals as the epitome of the American liberal.

Stevenson seemed to be exactly what American liberals, particularly eastern liberals, had longed for. They saw in Stevenson not an average politician but in many ways the complete antithesis of the stereotypical politician. He was elegant, polished, erudite, self-deprecating, a well-read intellectual. His speeches were crafted with grace and wit—as a whole, they were revered by liberals as political manna. New York publishers fell over each other to win a contract to print his speeches (in early 1952, before the nation at large had been introduced to Stevenson as a possible presidential candidate, John Bartlow Martin, a writer for the *Saturday Evening Post*, was editing Stevenson's speeches as governor for publication, and in 1952 *Adlai's Almanac* offered the reader a Stevenson saying for each month).[34] He was seen as the most gifted public speaker of a generation (reporter David Halberstam claimed Stevenson "seemed incapable of uttering a sentence that did not seem polished").[35] He constantly complained about his job, a trait that many took to mean that he was somehow above it all.[36] Stevenson was viewed by the faithful as a political neophyte; a miscast college professor or preacher; someone who was somehow above politics—in short, as an anti-Truman.

This reputation has largely survived the test of historical time. Indeed, few politicians have been better served by scholars in general, and by biographers in particular, than has Adlai Stevenson. He has yet to find a truly balanced, critical biographer, and Stevenson scholars have, even more so than Eisenhower scholars, all too often slipped into hyperbole. One observer compared Stevenson to Woodrow Wilson and Thomas Jefferson in terms of "scholarly excellence."[37] Another, conveniently ignoring his electoral victories in Illinois, opined that Stevenson was "not really designed by nature to be a politician."[38] One biographer, whose book was subtitled *Patrician among the Politicians*, described Stevenson as "The Upper Class Man as Moral Crusader";[39] to another, whose book was subtitled *The Politics of Honor*, Stevenson grew, "slowly, steadily, with a seeming inevitability—into greatness."[40]

All such hyperbole aside, it is clear that liberals wanted so desperately for Stevenson to be the second coming of Roosevelt, and his sycophantic biographers were all so certain that he had filled that role, that they were all willing to overlook, or were not aware of, certain flaws in the narrative. Those who would paint him as an intellectual need to confront the claim of two of his closest advisers that he actually read few books.[41] Those who would portray him as a liberal can with certainty point to his record on civil rights as governor. But they tend to ignore his own words, published in the *New York Herald Tribune* under the title "What Kind of Democrat I Am," that make him sound decidedly right of center: "I do not identify big government with good government. . . . I think government should be small in scope and as local in character as possible."[42] They also ignore the assessment of Martin, who would serve as a Stevenson speechwriter as well as the author of a two-volume biography of the governor, that he "favored balanced budgets, feared executive power, looked with favor on business, [and] deplored what he considered labor's excesses."[43] Stevenson disagreed with Truman on federal aid for education, on the repeal of Taft-Hartley, on the Brannan Plan for agriculture, and on national health insurance—hardly what one would expect of a card-carrying New/Fair Dealer.

His most often cited legacy—that of being a great orator—also needs qualification. There is no question but that his speeches read on paper as eloquently today as they did when written. Of American politicians of the postwar period, only Stevenson, John F. Kennedy, and Ronald Reagan have had volumes of their edited speeches go on to be best sellers. But his eloquence can also be seen as inaccessible, high-flown verbiage that only served to distance himself from an audience of everyday Americans. And, more interested in educating than in convincing, those speeches were all too often delivered in a detached, nasal, almost condescending manner that led his listeners to feel as if Stevenson were talking down to them. When he spoke, Stevenson did not turn off the liberal intellectuals like himself, but he all too often turned off everyone else.

John Kenneth Galbraith, an economist who would serve as a speech-writer for Stevenson in 1952, is perhaps the most critical of the Stevenson image, remembering a Stevenson who presented himself as more intellectual, more doubting, and more detached than he really was: "He felt compelled to picture himself and to believe that he was something he was not. . . . More perhaps than any political figure of our time, Adlai Stevenson was committed to personality modification for public purposes."[44] Perhaps. But even had they been presented with incontrovertible evidence that Stevenson was just another politician, American liberals in 1952 would not have believed it (in much the same fashion they chose to ignore evidence of Kennedy's philandering lest it tarnish their view of him). What mattered to them was that Adlai Stevenson looked and acted the part of the liberal intellectual's answer to the malaise of American politics. He looked, acted, and sounded like an intellectual, like a liberal, like a candidate who could bring reasonable discourse back to American politics. Indeed, he was their hero. The Eisenhower-loving *Time* magazine dubbed Stevenson "Sir Galahad," noting in late January 1952 that he was "politically hot, and Harry Truman feels the need for a little warmth."[45]

Harry S. Truman and Adlai E. Stevenson II, Oval Office, 4 December 1952 (National Park Service, Abbie Rowe, courtesy of Harry S. Truman Library)

TRUMAN COURTS A SUCCESSOR: STEVENSON

Truman first approached Stevenson through James Loeb Jr. and David Lloyd, both of the White House Special Counsel's Office. They went to see George Ball, then one of Stevenson's law partners (Ball would serve as undersecretary of state in the Kennedy and Johnson administrations and also serve as the U.S. representative to the United Nations); they told Ball that Truman wanted to talk to Stevenson and asked Ball to arrange the visit. When Ball approached Stevenson, he found the governor "stonily resistant" to such a meeting, but Ball convinced him that it was impossible for a governor to ignore a direct request from the president. On 22 January 1952, Stevenson flew to Washington. He first dined with Ball, who had correctly surmised the reason behind Truman's request. Ball begged Stevenson not to refuse Truman if he did indeed ask Stevenson to run for the presidency and offer his help. Stevenson ignored Ball's advice. After dining with Ball, Stevenson met with Truman at Blair House. But no amount of Truman flattery or cajoling would work ("Adlai, if a knucklehead like me can be President and not do too badly, think what a really educated smart guy like you could do in the job."). At the end of the meeting, Stevenson bluntly told Truman that he was not interested in running for the presidency.[46] Truman tried again, but the result was the same. In a second meeting with Truman, held in Key West on 4 March, Stevenson was, if anything, even clearer about his refusal to run than he had been in the initial meeting, as he turned down the president in language that could not be misinterpreted.[47]

Of course, the subject of the meetings between Truman and Stevenson leaked almost immediately. Eisenhower had broken down and agreed to run; now the press had another reluctant politician to bore in on. And bore in they did; Stevenson was now hounded by the press on a daily basis. But he was absolutely consistent in his answers to the oft-repeated question of whether or not he would be a candidate—he was too busy (to Archibald MacLeish: "How can I neglect this brutal job and find the time for the other . . . ?").[48] And he was already running for something. He wrote to Alicia Patterson: "Stevenson wants nothing except to be Gov. of Ill. again—and his heart won't break if the people deny him that.[49]

Truman was genuinely perplexed. Why was someone *else* turning down his offer of the presidential nomination on a platter? He simply could not bring himself to believe that Stevenson did not want to run. To Truman, Stevenson must have been confused; the fact that he had spurned the president must have meant that he had difficulty making up his mind. Several years later, Truman would tell an interviewer: "If a man doesn't enjoy running for office and doesn't think he can do some good for people by doing it, I don't know what the hell he is doing in politics in the first place."[50] Despite Stevenson's refusals, Truman did not consider the matter closed.

As was the case with Eisenhower, Stevenson's denials also meant nothing to his supporters—they simply went on without him. Immediately after the 22 January meeting with Truman, Ball set up a "Stevenson Information Center" in his Washington office (reminiscent of Clay's coded letters to Eisenhower, Ball melodramatically code-named it "Project Wintergreen"), from which he began to raise money and publicize Stevenson's record as governor. An upset Stevenson wrote to Ball specifically asking him to "restrain" one of the project's staffers, telling his old friend that "the unwilling candidate becomes more unwilling daily!" But Ball reasoned that since Stevenson "interposed no veto," he could continue his work.[51]

At the same time, Leo A. Lerner, publisher of the Chicago Northside

Newspapers and the director of the Independent Voters of Illinois, began to look for someone to head a Stevenson for President Committee.
He contacted Walter Johnson, then the chairman of the Department of
History at the University of Chicago. Johnson had run, albeit unsuccess-
fully, for the Chicago City Council in 1943; he had also done some fund-
raising for Stevenson's 1948 gubernatorial campaign. Together, Lerner
and Johnson assembled the "National Committee, Stevenson for President," better known as the Draft Stevenson Committee. They printed
and distributed fact sheets on Stevenson, bought an advertisement in the
Chicago Sun-Times, and sent a brochure to all Democratic governors, senators, and committeemen. Operating on a shoestring, they were fiscally
cautious—the buttons they made up only said "Stevenson" on them, just
in case he did as he promised he would and remained a candidate for
governor.[52] But Stevenson did not authorize either the Ball Committee or
the Draft Committee. Indeed, he specifically and consistently instructed
members of his reelection campaign not to cooperate with either movement.[53] To Johnson, who would send Stevenson unsolicited quotes, draft
speeches, requests for appointments for friends, and the like, Stevenson would reply with gentle thanks but with unmistakable rebuffs.[54]

Thus was the myth of Stevenson as "Hamlet" born.[55] No part of
the Stevenson character is so embedded in political lore as the belief
that when the chips were down, he could not make up his mind about
whether or not to run for the presidency. Journalist Carl Rowan put it
crudely: "Stevenson was one of the most indecisive men I have ever met
in high office. He lacked balls."[56] To put it charitably, such claims are
nonsense. Stevenson had made up his mind—he was running for governor and nothing else. He had said just that, and he said it plainly. However, Truman and other Democrats chose to ignore Stevenson's decision,
and when he snubbed them, they could only explain that rejection by
believing Stevenson was indecisive—if only he was approached differ-
ently; if only promises were made; if only he had time to think about it,
Stevenson would change his mind. He didn't. He had decided not to run
for the nomination, and, unlike Eisenhower, he would remain true to his
word, right through to the convention.

RUSSELL

In the middle of his courtship of Stevenson, Truman learned that another Democratic notable was about to enter the race for the nomination.

The family of Richard Brevard Russell Jr. had lived in Georgia since the founding of the colony. His father, Richard Brevard Russell Sr., was a judge who served on the Georgia Supreme Court, as well as being an unsuccessful candidate for governor, senator, and Congress. Born in 1897, young Richard grew up in a sternly religious home with twelve brothers and sisters. He graduated from the University of Georgia in 1918 with a law degree. He then joined his father's law firm, and in 1921 he won a seat in the Georgia state legislature, where in 1923 he was elected speaker. In 1930, at age thirty-three, Russell was elected the youngest governor in the history of Georgia—making him a gubernatorial contemporary of New York's Franklin Roosevelt. Within eighteen months, he had reduced the state's Depression-induced debt by a third (one step that was highly popular was Russell's cutting of his own salary by $40,000), launched a highway construction program, and begun a program of agricultural research. In 1932, following the death of U.S. senator William J. Harris of a heart attack, Russell ran in the special election and won, making him, at age thirty-five, the youngest serving U.S. senator. He was given a seat on the powerful Appropriations Committee, and from that perch he became the force behind the creation of the school lunch program, which not only would help needy schoolchildren but also would help farm prices through purchases of agricultural surpluses. Following the war, Russell became an unabashed cold warrior, generally using his membership on the Armed Services Committee to support Truman's foreign policy of containment.

A chain-smoking bachelor with a fear of airplanes, Russell was formal, almost regal in his manners. Solitary, he spent his evenings home, memorizing Senate rules and procedures and reading, for relaxation, the *Congressional Record*. Although he rarely socialized, Russell was well liked—and trusted—on both sides of the aisle.[57] This tended to obscure the depth of his opposition to any advancement in the civil rights of blacks in the South. In terms of civil rights, Russell was less bombastic than the majority of his southern colleagues but no less racist. He couched his racism in terms of a constitutional opposition, arguing that the South was making great strides in terms of the race question, and even if it wasn't, the federal government had no right to meddle in any affairs of any state. He saved particular bile for the FEPC, which had been created by executive order, thus bypassing the advice and consent of the Senate. Russell consistently voted to cut its funding, but he couldn't do away with it. He called the report of Truman's executive committee on civil rights "the most outrageous affront to the people of our section that we have had to face since Reconstruction days." While he did not follow the Dixiecrats in their walkout, in 1948 Russell had allowed his name to be put in nomination for the presidency as a symbolic gesture in opposition to Truman's civil rights policies.[58]

By the summer of 1951, several southern senators—including the powerful Harry Byrd of Virginia, who had also vociferously supported the Dixiecrat movement—began to search for a southern candidate who could be a power broker at the convention, and perhaps even swing the nomination away from a liberal successor to Truman. Russell's reputation, plus his evenhanded work as chair of the Senate committee investigating the dismissal of General Douglas MacArthur, made him the perfect choice. While on 20 October Russell declared that he would not be a "front man" for those opposing Truman, the pressure continued on him from all directions; on 30 January, the Georgia House of Representatives unanimously passed a resolution advising him to run for the nomination.[59]

On 28 February, calling himself a "Jeffersonian Democrat," Russell announced his candidacy for the Democratic nomination. Claiming that he was running regardless of what Truman might decide to do, Russell said nothing about civil rights in his prepared text. But in the question-and-answer period that followed, he sneered at Truman's "civil wrongs legislation."[60] He was immediately endorsed by Byrd, former secretary of state Jimmy Byrnes, and other leading southerners—both Dixiecrats and Loyalists. Northern Democrats feared that Russell's real intent was to position himself to lead another walkout of the Democratic Convention and be nominated by the States' Rights ticket. Russell did nothing to squelch such talk. Indeed, in a 2 March interview with a reporter for the *St. Louis Post Dispatch*, Russell responded to a question on whether he would automatically support the platform and candidate of the Democratic Party: "Without knowing what the platform of the Chicago convention will be, I would not commit myself unalterably to the support of the candidate and the platform. . . . I put my country above my party."[61]

NEW HAMPSHIRE

Russell was not foolish enough to enter a New Hampshire primary he was certain to lose. That left Kefauver running, for the moment, unopposed. Initially Truman acted as if he, too, was willing to cede the primary to Kefauver. On 31 January, Truman ordered that his name be taken off the New Hampshire primary ballot (it had been entered without his consent by several of his supporters).[62] This was a wise strategy. A victory in New Hampshire against no opposition would be a hollow victory for Kefauver, and he would have no claim of electoral superiority. However, Truman could not leave well enough alone. In the same statement, he observed that "all these primaries are just eyewash," and "when it comes to the national convention meeting, it doesn't mean a thing."[63]

As Truman was to prove at the convention in July, he was right. But he had played right into Kefauver's hands. Kefauver was quick with the comeback: "I feel that the primaries are a very necessary way for the people to express themselves for their party candidates. . . . The selection of party candidates . . . ought to be as democratic as possible."[64] Truman's gaffe had allowed Kefauver to hammer home his campaign theme: he was leading "the people" against the uncaring, corrupt political bosses. Truman was furious, and it didn't take him long to momentarily forget his promise to his staff that he wasn't running and jump back into the fight against the detested Kefauver. On 5 February, without formally announcing that he was running for reelection, Truman sent a letter to the New Hampshire secretary of state, declaring that he would be a candidate in the New Hampshire primary.[65]

It was now Kefauver versus the president, and the senator left nothing to chance. Kefauver spent three weeks campaigning in the Granite State, more than any other candidate in either party. Although he rarely mentioned the president by name, there was no mistaking his message. In a 10 February speech in Nashua, Kefauver said, "And *since I don't consider it eyewash at all,* but rather take it as a democratic method for you to express your choice for the nominee for the highest office in your power to give, I shall be back frequently."[66] Truman did not travel to the state to campaign, nor did any member of his cabinet. In an ironic Dewey-like fashion, Truman acted as if his victory in the primary was assured.

The results, however, were as shocking on the Democratic side as they were on the Republican. Kefauver handily defeated Truman in the presidential preference phase of the primary: 20,147 to 16,298, gaining 54 percent of the vote. Even more striking was the fact that the senator won all twelve delegates in the delegate selection phase of the primary. The workers in Kefauver headquarters, located in Manchester's Eagle Hotel, were ecstatic. With his customary scotch highball in his hand, Kefauver walked slowly around the room, putting his arm around the shoulder of every person, saying, "I certainly appreciate your help." As he claimed his victory, Kefauver proclaimed that "people are interested in a new vigor" in politics.[67]

Truman's defeat was complete. He lost nine of twelve cities, including the largest five, as well as eight of New Hampshire's ten counties.[68] More important was the fact that Kefauver carried the labor vote—a key Truman constituency in his 1948 upset. One onlooker from Tennessee summed up the feeling of the moment: "Handshaking seems to work as well in New Hampshire as it does in Tennessee."[69] Kefauver was on a roll; one week after the New Hampshire primary, he won some 20,000 votes in the Minnesota primary—a primary in which he did not campaign and had conceded to the state's favorite son, Senator Hubert H. Humphrey. Humphrey quickly announced that he supported Kefauver.[70]

THE JEFFERSON-JACKSON DAY DINNER: 29 MARCH 1952

As Kefauver's candidacy led Truman to abandon his promise not to run, so, too, did Kefauver's New Hampshire victory lead Stevenson to rethink his own refusals to enter the race. On 13 March, two days after the New Hampshire primary, he wrote to Alicia Patterson that he would continue his campaign for and service as governor "unless the Democratic convention should nominate me." Stevenson quickly dismissed the idea as being "very unlikely,"[71] but he dangled the possibility before Charles Murphy, one of Truman's closest aides, who met with Stevenson on 14 March in Key West and attempted to sell Stevenson on the merits of being president; Stevenson wrote him three days later: "I do not want to be a candidate for the nomination. I do not want to run for president, and I do not want to be president at this time," but if "in these strange circumstances I should still be nominated I would work as if I really wanted to be elected—and I probably would *want* to win *very much indeed* after I recovered from the shock!"[72] Stevenson's implicit agreement to accept the nomination was never made public. Stevenson was sticking to his original plan, convinced that he could never be nominated without his assent. In private, he refused to welcome Truman's offer of support; in public, he continued to protest that he would never seek the nomination.

But Truman could no longer wait for Stevenson to come around to his way of thinking. Truman had joined a rather elite club—that of sitting incumbents who had run in a primary and been defeated.[73] Even had he changed his mind about running, with Russell in the race Truman stood virtually no chance of winning the votes of the South at the convention and stood a very real chance of having to watch the Dixiecrats walk out on the Democrats a second election in a row. To make matters worse, Truman now found himself facing a steel strike, as well as failed negotiations to end the Korean War (see introduction). Truman was finished; all that was left were the formalities.

The Jefferson-Jackson Day Dinner, held annually in Washington, had very little to do with honoring the two great Democratic leaders. Rather, it was one of the most important fund-raisers of the year, particularly a presidential election year (it was to raise $450,000 for the party's coffers).[74] On 29 March, more than 5,300 Democrats gathered at the National Guard Armory and ponied up close to half a million dollars ($100 per plate) to eat filet mignon and ice cream molded in the shape of a donkey.

Truman was the final speaker. He initially sounded like he was ready to go out on the campaign trail and give the Republicans hell one last time. He attacked Taft's "dinosaur school of Republican strategy," which would "try to make people believe that everything the government has done for the country is Socialism," and Taft's desire to "pull out of Korea, abandon Europe, and let the United Nations go to smash." But Truman would not be leading that charge in 1952. Without pausing for a breath, he set aside his typed script and glanced at a longhand addendum, written out moments before he entered the hall and not released to the press. The Armory fell silent as Truman announced, "I shall not be a candidate for reelection. I have served my country long and, I think, efficiently and honestly. I shall not accept a renomination." When reporters, caught totally off guard, shouted, "Is that decision subject to any change?" Truman quickly replied, "None whatsoever." A woman's voice shouted, "Oh my God!" Truman shut his leather binder and turned to kiss his wife. Once outside the Armory and inside their limousine, both Trumans wept.[75] One person who attended the banquet would later write that after Truman made his announcement, "the effect upon the gathering was electric. The bottom fell out of the whole dinner."[76] In the excitement of the moment, the press abandoned the now lame-duck president and rushed to get the impressions of one of the distinguished guests, one who had just soared in national importance—the governor of Illinois.[77]

The Jefferson-Jackson Day Announcement, 29 March 1952 (National Park Service, Abbie Rowe, courtesy of Harry S. Truman Library)

KERR AND NEBRASKA

The next primary, however, would not feature Stevenson. The Nebraska primary, held just three days after Truman announced his withdrawal, would feature another Truman favorite who had thrown himself against what was now becoming a Kefauver juggernaut.

Robert S. Kerr was descended from Irish immigrants who fought for the Confederacy in Missouri during the Civil War. He was born in a tent house on 11 September 1896 in Oklahoma Indian Territory, near the village of Ada. When the territory became a state in 1907, Kerr's father was elected first county clerk of Pontotoc County. Kerr earned his teaching certificate at East Central Normal School in 1913. He enrolled for a short time at the University of Oklahoma but had to withdraw because of a lack of money. He served as a second lieutenant in World War I, studied law with an Ada attorney, and passed the bar in 1920. In 1924, both his wife and his baby boy died in childbirth; he would remarry in 1925. In 1926, Kerr threw his lot in with the Oklahoma oil boom as he joined the Dixon Brothers Oil Company in Anadarko, Oklahoma. In 1929, he bought the company and changed the name to Anderson and Kerr Drilling Company; later it would become the Kerr-McGee Corporation. At the time of his 1948 election, Kerr was the richest man in the U.S. Senate.[78]

Following an unsuccessful run for the office, Kerr was elected governor of Oklahoma in 1942 by the slimmest margin of victory for any Oklahoma Democrat since 1914.[79] Kerr proved to be an excellent governor, freeing Oklahoma—a state virtually destroyed by the Great Depression—from its state debt. He also dealt effectively with the widespread flooding throughout the state in 1943; as a result, he became a lifelong apostle for planned water development. His successes led Roosevelt to choose him to keynote the 1944 Democratic Convention, a speech that was universally seen as a success.[80] At the convention, Kerr was one of the first to throw his support to Harry Truman for the vice presidency. Truman did not forget. When Kerr ran for the Senate in 1948, while in the midst of his own close race for the presidency and with Oklahoma guaranteed to go for the Democrats, Truman spent a full day in the state campaigning for Kerr. This support was most likely crucial—although Kerr won, he ran far behind Truman.[81]

Clark Clifford, a Truman aide and a friend of Kerr's, described him perfectly when he called him a political "pirate."[82] In the Senate, Kerr was primarily interested in securing as much pork as he could gather up for Oklahoma. The most noted example of this was his attempt in 1950 to pass a law that would exempt natural gas producers from being controlled by the Federal Power Commission (FPC). Although Truman vetoed the bill, Kerr eventually got what he wanted, convincing the FPC to refuse jurisdiction over independent gas producers.[83] On most other matters, however, Kerr was a loyal Fair Dealer. While he was far from the "uncrowned King of the Senate" that he would become in the Eisenhower and Kennedy years, Kerr's reputation was nonetheless large, and he was being mentioned as a presidential possibility as early as January 1951.[84] Kerr began to beat the bulrushes, but it was a quiet effort—he had made it clear to Truman that if Truman ran, he would support the president.[85]

Kerr was an imposing figure, both on and off the Senate floor. After watching the big man (six foot three), one awed observer commented that Kerr resembled "a Sherman Tank looking for its target."[86] Competitive, driven, and one of the most powerful debaters in Congress, Kerr seemed the perfect candidate. Senator Clinton Anderson (D-NM) spoke for many: "He's the smartest man I know."[87] But Kerr was not without his liabilities. His less than convincing stand on civil rights would hurt him in the East. Liberals were unnerved as well by his comment, which compared himself to William Jenner, the reactionary senator from Indiana ("The difference between us is that I have never learned to hate").[88] Kerr's millions, as well as his localism and his support for the natural gas bill, seemed to define him as the type of politician that many Democrats felt they were fighting *against*. Many echoed the opinion of Truman, who, despite the senator's loyalty, felt that Kerr's "background of representing the oil and gas interests made him ineligible" for the nomination.[89]

Kerr had entered the Nebraska primary, to be held on 1 April, to keep Kefauver from winning the state's delegates by default. He publicly stated that if he won, and if Truman decided later to enter the race, then Kerr would immediately deliver his delegates to Truman.[90] This gave Kefauver the perfect line of attack, as he charged Kerr with being Truman's "stand-in." Because it was true, Kerr could not respond. It was a dirty campaign. Kerr hammered on Kefauver as being "soft on communism"; Kefauver charged that Kerr had campaigned for Hoover in 1928 rather than support the Catholic Al Smith. Kefauver also hit Kerr hard in the wet city of Omaha for his teetotaling.[91] When Truman withdrew on 29 March, Kerr announced that he was now running on his own and would keep whatever delegates he won. The results were a mixed bag. While Kefauver easily won the presidential preference phase (64,531 to 42,467), the results of the delegate selection phase were much closer, with Kefauver winning five to Kerr's four, Stevenson's two, and one for Russell.[92] Kefauver had been slightly wounded, but the damage was momentary. Kerr would continue to campaign with no hope of gaining the nomination, and pundits began to wonder if *any* Democrat could stop Kefauver.

HARRIMAN AND THE DISTRICT OF COLUMBIA

Immediately before they left for the Washington Armory to attend the Jefferson-Jackson Day Dinner, Stevenson had met with W. Averell Harriman, then the director of the Mutual Security Agency (MSA), and Harvard historian Arthur M. Schlesinger Jr. at the Metropolitan Club, right around the corner from the White House. None of those present were privy to what Truman would announce only a few hours later. But the president's defeat in New Hampshire had exposed his political vulnerabilities, and the three men discussed the very real possibility of a presidential race without Truman in it. None of the three were Kefauver supporters. Harriman believed that Stevenson would make a good candidate and told him so. Stevenson made it clear once again that he wasn't running, but he thought he had found the solution to both his crisis and that of his party. He had mentioned this two weeks earlier in a letter to a friend: "My only escape—aside from the flat refusal—would now be to deflect the attention to Harriman."[93] Stevenson told Harriman that he should run; if he did, Stevenson promised him that he would deliver the Illinois delegation to him at the convention. Harriman, who had been yearning to run for the presidency since he had learned, along with Truman's other advisers, that the president was planning to withdraw, took heart.

A few days after this meeting, and after Truman had announced that he would not be a candidate, Harriman flew to Chicago to meet with Stevenson again. At that meeting, Stevenson told him plainly and clearly that he was about to announce that all he was interested in doing was running for reelection as governor. According to Harriman's most thoughtful biographer, he was "secretly pleased" that Stevenson had tapped him as his candidate. He told his New York friends to begin putting together a campaign.[94]

The public career of William Averell Harriman up until 1952 was extraordinarily vast. Raised on the 20,000-acre family estate at Arden, New York, Harriman graduated from Yale University in 1913 and jumped directly into a vice presidency of the railroad that his grandfather had built: E. H. Harriman's Union Pacific. In 1932, he went to Washington, a convert to the New Deal because of his irritation with Hoover's tariff policy. With the aid of close friend and Roosevelt confidant Harry Hopkins, Harriman soon landed several plum foreign policy assignments. He served as Roosevelt's special emissary to London to expedite the Lend-Lease program and as ambassador to the Soviet Union from 1943 to 1946. Indeed, for his "exceptionally distinguished conduct in a role of great importance" in Moscow, Harriman was awarded the National Medal of Merit in 1946. In the Truman administration, he served as secretary of commerce (he had been a member of the cabinet committee that had drafted the Marshall Plan) and served briefly as a foreign policy adviser. As the director of the MSA, he had closely advised Truman on the recall of Douglas MacArthur.

Harriman was undoubtedly the most liberal candidate in the Democratic field, particularly in the area of civil rights. He was uncompromising in his support for a permanent FEPC and equally uncompromising in his promise to get Taft-Hartley, a bill that he called "punitive," repealed.[95] He drew to a possible candidacy the support of such liberal luminaries as Eleanor Roosevelt, Franklin D. Roosevelt Jr., and Henry Wallace.[96]

Harriman's strategy was simple enough: he avoided talking about Eisenhower and declared that Taft "had been wrong for years on every issue."[97] This put him on the right side of the issues for Truman, who was still reeling from being spurned by Vinson, Eisenhower, and Stevenson. But Truman believed Harriman to be unelectable. The first problem was his patrician background. In a private memorandum to himself, while conceding that Harriman was the "ablest of all" the potential candidates, Truman sighed, "He has been a Wall Street Banker, [and] is son of one of the old time pirates of the first score of this century. Can we elect a Wall Street Banker and railroad tycoon President of the United States on the Democratic ticket? Ask someone else. I can't answer!"[98]

An equal problem turned out to be Harriman's lack of polish as a campaigner. For Harriman to mount a viable campaign, he had to morph from being a career statesman and diplomat to being a politician on the national level—all in four months. This would be a daunting task for any person but particularly so for Harriman. When on 22 April it came time to announce his candidacy, Harriman was on the phone, dealing with a foreign-aid question. Despite the plethora of reporters who had assembled to cover the announcement, Harriman never did make an appearance—the gaggle had to make do with a press release.[99] And, to put it bluntly, as a speaker, Harriman was terrible. While attending one of Harriman's speeches, Stevenson jotted down on the back of an envelope, "He can't even read a script."[100]

And yet Harriman's command of the black vote made him a force to be reckoned with. On 17 April, before he had even formally announced as a candidate, Harriman faced Kefauver in the District of Columbia primary. In a district that in the 1950 census was 39 percent black, this would be a test of Kefauver's claims to being a southern liberal; it would also be a test of his vote-getting power in the black community.[101] In both areas, Kefauver failed miserably. Harriman was aided by a large number of black volunteers, all of whom wore buttons proclaiming "I Crave Ave." In a record turnout, Harriman received 14,075 votes to Kefauver's paltry 3,337, carried forty of the forty-five polling places, and won all six delegates.[102] Five days later, on 22 April, Harriman announced his candidacy; the next day, New York leaders pledged their delegation to Harriman.[103]

Harriman then took his campaign out West, where, despite having to have minor surgery while in Montana, he made some small inroads in formally uncommitted Colorado.[104]

To Truman, despite Harriman's liabilities as a campaigner, he was a more palatable choice than was Kefauver. Harriman had been loyal to Truman and, as the DC primary showed, could be counted on to keep the blacks in the Roosevelt/Truman coalition. But Truman was not about to endorse Harriman—not as long as Truman continued to believe that Stevenson could be made to see reason. Truman laid down the facts of life to Harriman, even before Harriman had announced his candidacy: "I assured Harriman that, if it came to a showdown between him and Stevenson, I was committed to Stevenson, because I felt that he would be the strongest candidate the Democratic Party could offer at this time."[105] Never mind the fact that Stevenson was not committed to Truman.

Writing his brother Vivian, a member of the Missouri delegation to the convention, in late May, Truman said that Harriman was "perfectly alright with me." But then he quickly warned his brother: "Don't get the Missouri delegation committed to the point where we can't place it in the Convention where it will do the most good."[106] Continuing to hope that he could crown an heir apparent before the balloting began at the convention, Truman planned to order Harriman to withdraw if and when Stevenson changed his mind.

"WHO WINS THIS FALL IS LESS IMPORTANT THAN WHAT WINS"

But Stevenson was not behaving in a manner that satisfied the president. On 31 March, returning to Chicago from the Jefferson-Jackson Day Dinner and Truman's bombshell announcement, Stevenson simply confused the reporters at Midway Airport who were clamoring for a statement as to his status by saying, "My status is quo—or my quo is status."[107] Later that day, professing to be "stunned by your announcement," Stevenson wrote Truman, telling him again, "I had hoped long and prayerfully that it might be otherwise." Stevenson then reiterated his stance: "I hope you don't feel that I am insensitive to either that confidence or the honor you have done me. Perhaps the reasoning underlying my hesitance is unsound, but my heart is not."[108] But Truman hung in there, responding to Stevenson, "I sincerely hope you will not take yourself completely out of the picture."[109]

Stevenson, however, had decided to do exactly that. On 16 April, he released a statement that he believed would take him out of consideration for good. He began by making his dilemma clear: "I cannot run for two offices at the same time." For good measure, he declared, "I could not accept the nomination for any other office this summer."[110] This was, in Stevenson's mind, final; it was also a reversal of what he had been saying to selected friends and to the president through Charles Murphy—that if cornered, and presented with the nomination on a platter, he would accept it. Stevenson sent a copy of the statement to Truman, meekly writing in the enclosed note, "I know you will be disappointed in me."[111] This was an understatement of colossal proportions—Truman was furious. On 22 April, he penned an angry reply to Stevenson's statement, "I am sorry that you felt it necessary to make this statement, although you are your own best judge of what you should do. I am very certain that if you had left the door open there would be no difficulty about your nomination and I think you could be elected."[112]

Stevenson's announcement should have closed the door on any talk of a candidacy. But the very next day, his own glibness erased that possibility. The day should have been Harriman's; he had just won the DC primary, and he was the guest of honor at a fund-raiser in New York City. All the candidates showed up—Kefauver, Kerr, and Russell were there, as well as Vice President Alben Barkley, who was soon to become a candidate. Harriman spoke and, as usual, froze the room with his wooden stage presence. Stevenson, who followed Harriman, stole the show with one of his patented eloquent speeches. Rather than celebrate Harriman, Stevenson began by talking about himself: "I am told that I am here at the head table by misrepresentation and fraud; that you invited a candidate for President but got a candidate for Governor instead." Then he transfixed the audience with political language of a kind they had not heard in years: "Perhaps it isn't exactly the thing to say at a partisan meeting, but who wins this fall is less important than what wins—what ideas, what concept of the world of tomorrow, what quality of perception, leadership and courage." This line literally made people in the hall sit up and take notice. No speech line did more to cement in the minds of adoring Democrats the belief that Stevenson was somehow above the political fray.[113] Even poet Carl Sandburg wrote Stevenson that he was so enthralled with the speech that he had been carrying around a copy of it.[114]

Rather than cementing his previous day's decision in the minds of his audience, Stevenson's erudite speaking style had made him all the more desirable. Stevenson wrote Alicia Patterson: "I think I did allright [sic] in N. Y. . . . too well for my peace and security from renewed pressure which broke out after the meeting."[115] Stevenson was now constantly surrounded by reporters demanding to know when he was going to enter the race. Thanks to the speech, as well as the presence of the Draft Stevenson movement, which Stevenson had consistently disavowed, the reporters' questions turned from whether or not he would run to whether or not he would accept a draft. To Stevenson, this was ludicrous. He thought his 16 April statement had explained his position; moreover, he had not the slightest doubt that a draft was impossible. It was difficult not to let his frustration get the better of him. A week after the speech in New York, while traveling in Portland, Oregon, Stevenson snapped at a reporter who had asked him once again if he was really a candidate: "Why don't you put that question in German? It has been put in every other language, it seems."[116]

FLORIDA

Harriman had badly bloodied Kefauver in the District of Columbia. This made the 6 May primary in Florida a crucial test. Kefauver had to show that he could recover from a licking; Russell and Kefauver, both southerners, had to prove that they could win in the South. Many believed this to be the last chance to stop Kefauver from sweeping the convention. For Russell, it was even simpler. He had tried retail politics, flying all over the country to speak to individual delegates. But while impressed with his bearing, northern Democrats could not ignore or forgive his stand on civil rights. If Russell could not win in his native South, if he could not win in Florida, his campaign was over.

However, Russell could afford to be optimistic. Kefauver was more vulnerable than he had been in the northern primaries. Because of his stance in favor of a permanent FEPC, in favor of federal rather than local control of the Tidelands oil, and in favor of civil rights legislation, Kefauver was distrusted in the South. Moreover, in Florida, Kefauver faced not only Russell and a debate on the issues but also political payback. Governor Fuller Warren, whom the Kefauver Crime Committee had charged with having ties to Capone family money, was now ready and willing to take Kefauver down. He challenged Kefauver to a televised debate on the senator's fitness to be president. Kefauver accepted, but when he arrived at the agreed site in Tallahassee, he was informed that the governor was "out of town."[117] After leading Kefauver on a wild goose chase around the state, Warren's forces disseminated virulent anti-Kefauver literature (one handbill read: "If elected president, this power-crazed man, with his cynical contempt for the U.S. Constitution, would make a shambles of states' rights. . . . This ambition-crazed, power-hungry opportunist will be for anything that will help him get into the White House. It would be no surprise if he should come out for a concordat vote with the Kremlin").[118]

Nevertheless, Kefauver stumped the state for the better part of late March and early April. Russell, on the other hand, did not campaign in the state until late April. Rather, he utilized several well-known Florida surrogates—Governor Fuller Warren, Senators Spessard L. Holland and George A. Smathers, and all six Democrats in the House of Representatives—to campaign for him until he arrived in the state, spending a total of ten days there immediately before the primary.[119] The two men sparred on the FEPC and the issue of a potential Dixiecrat walkout. In Tampa, Russell told his audience, "If FEPC legislation were enacted," he would not be "bound" by the law.[120] Kefauver was equally clear: he would support the party platform, even if there were a plank calling for a compulsory FEPC.[121] Russell also hit Kefauver for his support of a proposed Atlantic Union—a plan that was before Congress to join the United States, Canada, and the Western European nations in a union that would present a common foreign and defense policy. Russell cagily tied the union proposal to the issue of states' rights; showing that he was not above hyperbole, in Gainesville, he charged that the proposal would "write a new constitution to supersede our own," and that it would "submerge the sovereignty of the U.S. with other nations."[122]

On 5 May, the night before the primary, Kefauver and Russell met in a dramatic and bitter televised debate. The debate swirled around the FEPC. Russell attacked Kefauver for his support of the FEPC; Kefauver accused Russell of planning to "pick up [his] marbles and run out" if he disapproved of the platform. Despite the fact that he had kept the door open all along to a refusal to accept the platform, an angry Russell shouted at his opponent: "If you mean that I'm going to leave the party, oh, no! I'm not going to leave the party!"[123]

The next day, Russell received 367,980 votes (54 percent) to Kefauver's 285,358 (42 percent). Two weeks later, in the delegate selection phase, Russell picked up 17 delegates to Kefauver's 7.[124] Russell had won, and he was far from finished as a force at the convention—and one estimate gave Russell 262 of the 616 necessary to nominate.[125] But he had not knocked Kefauver out. Russell's Florida victory was treated in the press as a regional victory—one that Russell had been expected to win. Moreover, his refusal to embrace the FEPC cost him any chance he may have had at building a wider national constituency. The *Atlanta Constitution*'s postmortem was accurate: "Candor compels us to say that . . . Russell's victory . . . was a disappointment. It was not a landslide and it did not destroy the Kefauver legend."[126] The primary season was over; Kefauver would enter the convention scarred but with his campaign intact.

MISSISSIPPI AND TEXAS

As the Democratic candidates jockeyed for position that spring, the delegate selection process in the South was creating delegations that promised no more support for a pro-Truman/"liberal"/civil rights platform or candidate than they had been willing to give in 1948. The infighting was particularly bitter in Mississippi and Texas; if they were any indication, the chances of another Dixiecrat walkout in 1952 was very real indeed.

An active states' rights group in Mississippi had long been vocal in its support of Russell. The group was led by Hugh White, who had participated in the 1948 Dixiecrat walkout and had been elected governor in 1951. The state committee, controlled by White and the States' Rightists, recommended that Mississippi's twenty-two delegates be bound by a "good faith pledge," which would require the delegate, among other things, to "endorse the action of the delegation in its refusal to participate in the national convention if an anti-Southern platform were adopted."[127] On 28 June, the States' Rights Democratic Party convention met in Jackson, chose its delegation, and endorsed Russell. But the States' Rights faction had issued a warning, in language that was blunter than many southerners were willing to use. If the platform read like that of 1948, particularly in the civil rights plank, Mississippi was, once again, leaving.

However, a "Loyalist" faction, led by national committeewoman Mrs. John A. Clark, formed its own delegation to the convention. They, too, met in Jackson on 5 July and formed an uninstructed delegation that was bound to support the decision of the convention.[128] Kefauver, desperate for delegates but not willing to tie himself to a States' Rights delegation, refused to support either Mississippi delegation. Truman, who was single-mindedly determined to prevent another walkout like the one that had almost cost him the White House in 1948, immediately supported White's delegation.[129] In Mississippi, it would be a question of loyalty to state party or loyalty to national party—just as it was in Texas.

In Texas, the leader of the States' Rights faction was also the state's governor, as well as an outspoken critic of the president. Allan Shivers demanded, in his words, no less than the "recapturing and redeeming [of] the National Democratic Party from left-wing domination and machine control." He demanded that Texas send an uninstructed delegation to the convention, and that the party's platform call for state, not federal, ownership of the Tidelands oil (see introduction).[130] He was swimming against strong tides. Senator Lyndon B. Johnson was openly working for Russell, and Speaker of the House Sam Rayburn was willing to send an uninstructed delegation, but only if that delegation took a pledge to support the nominee of the convention.[131] Shivers would have none of it. Early in 1951, he made it clear that he would not support any kind of a pledge that would bind the sixty-two Texas delegates to the decisions of the convention.[132] It was clear that the governor and his forces, dubbed "Shivercrats" in the press, controlled the state's party machinery, but the "Loyalists" soon had a champion in Maury Maverick, the former congressman and ex-mayor of San Antonio. While in the House, Maverick had been a Roosevelt soldier. He was also a vocal Fair Dealer and a frequent correspondent with Truman. Impulsive, boisterous, and completely dedicated to the national party, Maverick was the ideal leader for the Texas Loyalist faction.

The Shivercrats first showed their control of the party organization with victories in the local precinct meetings. On 3 May, helped by a record voter turnout, the Shivercrats won 1,009 out of 1,152 precinct contests. In the county conventions, held three days later, the Loyalists were once again swamped, losing the majority of the 241 conventions.[133] Shivers boasted that his supporters now controlled all but 91 of the 1,227 delegates to the state convention, to be held on 27 May in San Antonio.[134]

At the convention, Maverick immediately moved the adoption of a minority report, which would require that the Texas delegation take an oath of loyalty to the national party. Defeated on a point of order, Maverick called for his delegates to leave the auditorium ("Let us go. It's time for us to walk out into the rain"). The remaining Shivercrats easily ratified a sixty-two-member, fifty-two-vote delegation that was uninstructed regarding a candidate, but was nevertheless instructed by the convention to "vote for and fight for" a candidate and a platform that Texas could accept. Meanwhile, the Maverick forces met at La Villita, a Works Progress Administration (WPA) reconstruction of the original San Antonio villa. They wore donkey lapel buttons emblazoned with the promise "No Phony." They voted for their own uninstructed delegation to the Chicago convention.[135] Maverick would later write Truman that his supporters had merely reacted against a "vicious attack on the Democratic party, its principles, and our President," to which Truman replied, "You certainly did a good job."[136]

STEVENSON OPENS THE DOOR

As the calendar turned to June, the chaos in the Democratic Party showed no signs of abating. Thus, more and more people looked to Stevenson to save the party from itself. Stevenson still did not want the job. But he had come to regret his 16 April statement—that he would not accept the nomination even if offered. He was now leaning toward a revised statement that made public what he had told Truman through Charles Murphy on 13 March—that if nominated, he would reluctantly accept. On 15 May, he wrote Alicia Patterson: "I thought I had it all settled and for keeps but it seems hotter than ever now." He wondered if he would have to issue a Shermanesque statement—if nominated, he would neither accept nor serve. But he couldn't bring himself to do it. As he wrote Patterson, "It's a cocky, contemptible, distasteful thing to do and I hate to have a place in the history books by saying I *won't* do something honorable that has come to few people."[137]

Stevenson decided that he would articulate what he had come to feel was his duty. On 30 June, when he arrived in Houston at the Conference of State Governors, Stevenson got right to the point:

I think we can anticipate some of the questions which will be asked, and I think we can save both your time and mine. I will now say what I have to say and all I have to say on the Presidential situation, and then we can go on to other subjects. . . . Some time ago I said that for many reasons, including my prior candidacy for re-election as Governor, I could not be a candidate for any other office. I have not been nor am I now. . . . I am not being coy or trying to select my opponent.

I have not participated, nor will I participate, overtly or covertly, in any movement to draft me.

Then came a shocker: "Without such participation on my part, I do not believe that any such draft can or will develop. In the unlikely event that it does, I will decide what to do at that time in the light of the conditions then existing."[138]

Truman no longer cared. Stevenson had had his chances, and now he was off Truman's list. But Truman refused to allow an open convention. Instead, he inexplicably gave his support to a Democrat who dearly wanted to be president but who was also seventy-five years old and nearly blind.

TRUMAN BACKS BARKLEY

Alben W. Barkley was born in Lowes, Kentucky, in 1877. His father moved the family to the town of Clinton so that young Alben might more easily attend nearby Marvin College. Barkley worked his way through Marvin as a janitor, and then through Georgia's Emory College by peddling earthenware on horseback. His legal training consisted of a few courses taken at the University of Virginia and a subsequent clerkship. In 1905, he was elected county attorney for McCracken County, and the following year he was elected a county judge. In 1912, in his first political race, he was elected to the House of Representatives, where he would serve seven consecutive terms. From 1927 to 1949, he represented Kentucky in the U.S. Senate, and for ten of those years—1937 to 1947—he was the Senate majority leader, serving longer in that position than had any other Democrat.

Barkley was described quite accurately by *Time* magazine as the most loved man in the Democratic Party—"the glue that holds the party together."[139] Much of this affection came as a result of Barkley's ability to exact his demands without seeming to be demanding. Much of it also came about as a result of his celebrated feud with Franklin Roosevelt. In 1944, Barkley publicly disagreed with a Roosevelt veto of a tax bill that the majority leader had stewarded through the Senate. Barkley rose at his desk and in a low voice slapped at the president for "his effort to belittle and discredit Congress." A cheering Senate quickly overrode the veto. After the vote, Barkley immediately resigned as majority leader, only to be unanimously reelected to the position only minutes later.[140] It was this challenge that led Roosevelt to bypass Barkley for the vice presidency in 1944 and to choose Harry Truman as his running mate. But the Kentuckian would be the unanimous choice for Truman's running mate in 1948, aided by his delivery of an outstanding keynote address to the convention.

Dubbed the "Veep" by his grandchildren, Barkley was a man of unimpeachable integrity and gritty common sense. His homespun demeanor made him an unquestionable public favorite, and he had proved himself to be a completely loyal vice president to Truman. But Barkley would be seventy-five years old by Inauguration Day 1953, and he had had major cataract surgery in early February 1952. As it had always been, and as it continues to be, a candidate's age and health were major hurdles to overcome in 1952. Barkley also had the onus of a tainted Truman administration on him. To many Democrats, the popular Barkley was too risky a gamble.

Throughout the primary season, Barkley made it clear that he supported Truman for reelection. He also claimed in his memoirs that he told Truman that he would accept the vice presidential nomination again.[141] But when Truman withdrew, Barkley came to see himself as a potential dark horse if there was a logjam at the convention. Even before Truman had announced his plans, Barkley had brought up the subject of a potential candidacy for himself with Stevenson, who was Barkley's distant cousin. Barkley emphasized, "I've got a lot of friends who over the years have been urging me as a possible nominee and I don't know what is going to happen." When Stevenson carefully suggested, "Theoretically your age is against you," Barkley quickly parried with a defense that he would use almost verbatim during the coming months: he named leaders—Winston Churchill, Oliver Wendell Holmes, and Johann von Goethe—who did their best work after they had reached the age of seventy. Barkley closed the subject by telling Stevenson, "I'm not a candidate but my name is being mentioned and I will be compelled to give it consideration."[142] Barkley remembered that immediately after the Armory speech, "many party stalwarts were quoted as declaring themselves, then and there, for me."[143] If that was the case, there is no record of it. Regardless, on 29 May, the vice president issued a statement: "While I am not a candidate in the sense that I am actively seeking the nomination, I have never dodged a responsibility, shirked a duty, or ignored an opportunity to serve the American people. Therefore, if the forthcoming Chicago convention should choose me to lead the fight in the approaching campaign, I would accept."[144]

On 11 July, only ten days before the convention was to open in Chicago, while vacationing at his Paducah, Kentucky, farm, Barkley received a call from Leslie Biffle, secretary of the Senate and a Truman confidant. Truman wanted to see Barkley in Washington the next day. Truman's and Barkley's recollections of that conversation fundamentally agree. With Truman were Biffle, Democratic National Committee chair Frank McKinney, Democratic public relations expert Clayton Fritchey, and several other Truman staffers. Barkley relates what happened next: "Chairman McKinney opened the parley by telling me right off that President Truman had decided to back me for the nomination. This statement was made in the presence of Mr. Truman, with his implicit approval. President Truman would not make a public announcement that he was backing me, Chairman McKinney went on, but he would urge his own Missouri delegation, of which he was a member, to support me." When the meeting was done, the men had agreed on Barkley for president and Secretary of the Interior Oscar Chapman for vice president.[145]

In the privacy of his diary, Truman had expressed misgivings about a Barkley candidacy: "[Barkley] wants to be president more than anything else in the world. He can't see, he shows his age. . . . It takes him five minutes to sign his name . . . my good friend Alben would be dead in three months if he should inherit my job!"[146] But Truman was not concerned enough with Barkley's health to counsel him to return to Kentucky. Instead, Truman's desire to name an heir won out. On 16 July, he did, indeed, send a note to his proxy for the convention, Thomas Gavin: "Dear Tom: I hope you can see your way clear to vote for Alben Barkley when nominations for President are in—and try to get the Missouri delegation to go along."[147]

3
THE CONVENTIONS

No one had been too surprised when both the Republicans and the Democrats chose to move their national nominating conventions back to Chicago in 1952, each party having held its 1948 convention in Philadelphia. The quintessential metropolis, Chicago was made to order for a huge gathering, offering all the necessities right in the downtown area. For the Republicans particularly, the Windy City had long been their favorite convention town. Since 1860, the party had held twenty conventions there; their Democratic associates had held seven. But there was a political consideration in moving back to Chicago as well—the need of both parties to capture the swing state of Illinois in the fall, a state that held twenty-eight crucial electoral votes that Harry Truman had won with a bare 50.07 percent of the popular vote.

In 1952, both parties turned away from the spacious Chicago Stadium, the home of many of their past conventions, and moved their enclaves into the Chicago Convention Building and Amphitheatre. Built in 1934, the Amphitheatre was situated about three and a half miles south of the Loop, on the easternmost edge of the stockyards. Although it sat five thousand fewer people than the Stadium, it had several features to recommend it. It had a larger center arena, with more space on the aisle and fringe areas for independence of movement. It had a newly installed air-conditioning system— something that the Stadium could not boast—and it had a larger total platform and stage area than had the Stadium. It was, in short, made to order for television coverage.[1]

TELEVISION COVERAGE

Television had first played a role in presidential politics in 1948, with both parties choosing Philadelphia as their site largely because the city sat squarely in the middle of a recently laid New York to Washington, DC, television line. Both parties broadcast a portion of their conventions to an Eastern Seaboard audience of about 1 million people.[2] However, by early 1952 the television craze had exploded. There were over 18 million television sets in 39 percent of the living rooms in the country, and the numbers were rapidly increasing.[3] The Kefauver Crime Committee hearings (discussed in chapter 2) had proved that there was a large market for political programming, and the four major networks—NBC, CBS, ABC, and Mutual—decided to broadcast the 1952 conventions in their entirety.

There were no precedents to follow in 1952 regarding such important considerations as equal access to the convention hall for all networks, whether or not advertising time should be sold for a public service program, and, if ads were sold, where they should be placed in the programming. To address these questions, a committee was formed, composed of representatives of all the networks and both major political parties. This committee, chaired by Thomas Velotta, the vice president of ABC, met regularly throughout the first months of 1952. The first roadblock for the Velotta Committee was the question of whether the networks or the parties would pay for the construction of the needed camera platforms and studios in the Amphitheatre. After weeks of wrangling, the networks gave in and agreed to pick up the entire tab for the construction costs.[4] It was also agreed that small, portable cameras (nicknamed "peepie-creepies") would be allowed on the convention floor and that no network would have exclusive rights to convention coverage.[5]

However, the most vexing problems that the committee faced related to advertising. While the networks wanted to have a free hand to offer any client any kind of suitable commercial to air, both parties argued that coverage should be on a noncommercial, public service basis. After two months of discussion, the committee announced that both sides had agreed in principle to the selling of commercial time for the conventions, but that they had also agreed to a commercial code that would regulate the type, length, and style of commercials that would be aired. Among other things, the code called for a disclaimer at the beginning and end of each commercial, stating that the political party involved did not necessarily endorse that product and that commercials "must meet the highest standards of dignity, good taste, and length."[6]

Whether or not the commercials were dignified was a matter of opinion. What could not be denied, however, is the ubiquitous reach of convention programming in 1952. The networks broadcast a total of 57.5 hours of the Republican Convention and 61.1 hours of the Democratic Convention. The average household viewed a total of 10.5 hours of the Republican Convention and 13.1 hours of the Democratic Convention.[7] By way of comparison, the networks broadcast a total of 3 hours of live coverage of each party's convention in both 2008 and 2012.[8]

THE REPUBLICAN NATIONAL CONVENTION: 7–11 JULY 1952

As the delegates arrived for the Republican Convention, set to convene for committee work on 1 July and for public deliberation a week later, they found that all of the candidates had established their headquarters and reception areas in the enormous Conrad Hilton Hotel. Taft commandeered the ballroom, turning it into "Taft Town," where a wandering delegate could stop (if he wasn't collared by a Taft volunteer first), relax, and catch up on the latest in Taft literature. If the delegate was of a sightseeing bent, he could walk to the nearby Congress Hotel and view one of the biggest tourist attractions of the week—the new, eight-room, $40,000 Presidential Suite, complete with solid gold faucets. However, our roving delegate could only peer into the room, as it was roped off with museum ropes until its occupant for the week, Bob Taft, arrived in Chicago.[9]

Or our delegate could go souvenir hunting. It was not hard to find an Eisenhower button—the catchiest slogan in American political history adorned lapels in twenty-seven different languages ("Yo Prefiero a Ike," "I Mi Place Ike," "Fur Mich Ike").[10] If simplicity was not our delegate's cup of tea, he could always grab one of the thousand buttons made by the Earl Warren organization—six inches in diameter, they outdid the largest Ike and Taft buttons by a good two inches (when asked to whom he would give such a gaudy item, Warren's campaign manager sighed, "To anyone who'll wear 'em").[11] But our delegate was wise to be careful; tempers were flaring, and all sides genuinely hated each other. One altercation, comic on its face, showed the depths of the antipathies between the two sides: actor John Wayne, an outspoken Taft supporter, jumped out of his taxicab and threatened Marty Snyder, a World War II veteran who was driving an Eisenhower sound truck. Red-faced and furious, the Duke shouted at Snyder, "Why don't you get a red flag?"[12]

Courtesy of Dwight D. Eisenhower
Presidential Library and Museum

Credentials Challenges

In the week before the convention was gaveled to order, the Republican Party Platform Committee haggled over a document that had no bearing on the events of the convention and would have little bearing on the fall campaign.[13] The real issue that week, as it would be throughout the convention, was the issue of the delegate "steal." Aside from the 38 delegates of Texas, delegate contests had been filed from seven other states: Florida (18 contested delegates), Louisiana (6), Mississippi (4), Georgia (4), Puerto Rico (3), Kansas (1), and Missouri (1). The stakes could not be higher. Even if Taft won all the contested delegates, he would still, by his own count, be 65 votes short of the 604 votes necessary to win a first-ballot nomination, but the momentum would clearly be his, and most observers agreed that if Taft won the delegate fight, there would be a flood of uncommitted delegates to his banner at the end of the first ballot—if, indeed, the convention went *that* long.

The Republican National Committee (RNC), sitting as a committee of the whole, would be the first body to hear the delegate contests and to rule on the fate of the seventy-five contested delegates. The Eisenhower forces had their work cut out for them. The Republican national chairman, Guy Gabrielson, was an ardent Taft supporter, and it would be he who controlled the hearings. The chairman of the Contest Committee, George T. Hansen, also supported Taft. Beginning its deliberations on 1 July, Gabrielson's first move was to close the Contest Committee's deliberations to television (the Velotta Committee had only struck agreements on broadcasting the public events of the convention); his decision was supported by a 60–40 full committee vote.[14] This turned out to be the first of many blunders by the Taft forces during the convention. Fruitlessly arguing that their First Amendment rights had been violated, reporters did the best they could; NBC took up a position immediately outside the committee room and used "peepie-creepie" cameras and interviews to flesh out the proceedings.[15] Thomas Dewey telegraphed the RNC, demanding open, televised hearings, but to no avail.[16] But the visual of shut-out reporters played right into the hands of the Eisenhower forces. The *Atlanta Constitution* echoed the feelings of many when it labeled the Taft forces "ruthless and arrogant."[17] The Taft forces had made their candidate—who was on record as favoring the broadcast of the hearings[18]—look petty and secretive; it played right into the Eisenhower forces' narrative that there was thievery afoot.[19] Nevertheless, the television vote was a fair predictor of the decision of the RNC. First, the Florida delegation was divided sixteen for Taft, one for Eisenhower, and one uncommitted. Next, Taft's forces graciously conceded the one vote of Kansas to Eisenhower. In the Louisiana, Mississippi, and Puerto Rico delegations, Eisenhower was granted only three seats.[20]

Then the Taft forces once again overplayed their hand. No one had given the Georgia delegation a second thought. Under Georgia law, the state Republican Committee had selected a delegation, divided thirteen for Eisenhower, two for Taft, one for Warren, and one uninstructed. This delegation was led by Taft supporter Harry Sommers, an RNC member. A competing Georgia delegation, boasting a solid seventeen votes for Taft and led by Roy Foster (who had led the contending delegations that had been ejected from both the 1944 and the 1948 conventions), was given no chance, as no prior charges of improprieties with regard to the Sommers delegation had been filed with the RNC.[21] Then came a jolt. Monte Appel, Taft's attorney and his chief representative at the hearings, publicly announced that if the Foster group was seated, Sommers could count on being reelected as a national committeeman. An Eisenhower supporter leapt to his feet to ask Sommers if he was going to denounce what was an obvious offer of a deal. Sommers meekly replied, "In view of all the controversy, I will not make any comment." Everyone in the room knew what that meant—Sommers had abandoned his delegation to keep his RNC seat. The full committee voted 62–39 to seat Foster's delegation.[22]

Georgia had, for the moment, gone to Taft. However, the Taft forces had once again fumbled the morality ball over to Eisenhower, who was then on his way to the convention from Denver by train. Grabbing the high road by the throat, the general proclaimed that he was going to "roar out across the country for a clean, decent operation. The American people deserve it."[23] Taft now found himself in a quandary. Thanks to the decisions of the committee, he was well ahead of Eisenhower in committed delegates, and the big prize, the thirty-eight delegates of Texas, was about to come before the committee. But Taft had to find a way to gain Texas delegates while at the same time squelching talk of a "steal." If he could not do so, he might either lose all uncommitted delegates on the second ballot, and eventually lose the nomination, or win the nomination and be unable to gain the support of the aggrieved Eisenhower supporters in the fall. Either way, he stood to lose.

Taft tried to resolve his problem by offering Eisenhower a compromise. On Friday, 4 July, with the hearings already under way, Taft sent a note to Gabrielson and authorized the chairman to offer a deal to the Eisenhower forces. Taft, who had only two weeks before proclaimed that "the law was on the side of Henry Zweifel,"[24] now proposed that Texas be split pretty much right down the middle—twenty-two votes for Taft, sixteen for Eisenhower. In the note, Taft complained, "While I will suffer a delegate loss in making this proposal, I am doing so because I think it is so generous that its equity cannot be questioned."[25]

Someone in the Eisenhower camp saw through Taft's proposed deal. Lodge would later say it was he;[26] Brownell would later say it was he.[27] Regardless, someone in the Eisenhower camp refused to let their opponent defuse the morality issue. Speaking for the Eisenhower committee, Lodge rejected Taft's offer outright, as well as an offer from former president Herbert Hoover, who would soon suggest that he act as an "honest broker" in the Texas matter.[28] Yet even without a deal in place, the RNC voted to divide the Texas delegation exactly as Taft had requested.[29]

Taft had won all his battles before the RNC. Each challenge had been decided in a manner that favored the stand taken by the senator. A temporary roll of the delegates was constructed; it would now go to the Credentials Committee for appeals, emendation, and approval. The temporary roll showed that Taft had 527 committed delegates to 427 for Eisenhower. While he was still short of an assured first-ballot victory, Taft held the upper hand. From the Eisenhower perspective, the only thing that could be done was to somehow decrease the number of committed votes that Taft would receive on the first ballot. There was only one way that that could be done—the Eisenhower forces would have to get the convention to change its own rules.

The "Fair Play Amendment"

At the 1912 Republican Convention, also held in Chicago, temporary chairman Elihu Root ruled that delegates on the temporary roll, whether they were contested or uncontested, could vote on any issue that came before the convention, save their own contest. In no small bit of irony, the "Root Rule" helped Taft's father, then president William Howard Taft, secure his renomination against the Progressive insurgency of Theodore Roosevelt. For four decades, the "Root Rule" sat as an arcane bit of political history, not well known to anyone—that is, until the spring of 1952, when someone in the Eisenhower campaign, doing some research in order to find an edge for their candidate, came across the existence of the rule. Brownell later claimed that it was Stephen Benedict, the research director for the Citizens for Eisenhower, who found a reference to the rule while combing the stacks of the New York Public Library; Lodge would later say that it was he who came up with it.[30] Regardless, it was Brownell who immediately saw in the "Root Rule" both potential danger and a sliver of an opportunity. The "Root Rule" would demand that all seventy-five contested delegates—a group that strongly supported Taft—be allowed to vote on the floor. But if somehow that rule were to be challenged and overturned, those seventy-five votes would be taken out of the equation, and anything could happen.

On 30 June, at the annual Governors' Conference in Houston, Governors Sherman Adams of New Hampshire, Walter Kohler of Wisconsin, and Dan Thornton of Colorado drafted a telegram that demanded that none of the seventy-five contested delegates be allowed either to be seated at or to vote at the convention until the entire convention had a chance to vote on whether or not these delegates should become credentialed. The telegram, which was soon dubbed the "Houston Manifesto," was, thanks to the influence of Dewey, signed by almost every Republican governor.[31] It was also, not surprisingly, dead on arrival in Chicago; Gabrielson immediately shelved it.

But in light of the defeat of the Eisenhower forces before the RNC, Brownell decided to go for broke. With the help of Boston lawyer Ralph Boyd, Brownell refashioned the telegram as an amendment to the rules of the convention. Hugh Scott of Pennsylvania, an Eisenhower supporter, dubbed the proposal the "Fair Play Amendment." If the Eisenhower forces could somehow convince the uncommitted delegates that they were being railroaded by Taft, and if those uncommitted delegates cast their lot with Eisenhower and the rules changed, the tide on the first ballot might shift to Eisenhower.

Once again, the Taft forces did not see the threat to their campaign. With an air of haughty invincibility, Gabrielson, who would open the convention as its temporary chairman, assured Lodge that nothing would be done from the podium to block the introduction of the Fair Play Amendment.[32]

Suddenly, Chicago sounded like it was hosting a holy war. A typical Eisenhower broadside, designed and written by Sig Larmon of Young and Rubicam advertising, hit the themes of political morality, the delegate steal, and, just for good measure, Taft's inability to win in the fall:

DON'T LET THE NOISE OF THE STEAMROLLER DROWN OUT THE VOICE OF THE NATION!
Vote for the Fair Play Amendment!

To All Republican Delegates:
The Eyes of the Nation Are On You. The nation may *differ* as to WHO should be nominated. But the Nation *agrees* that there must be no shadow of doubt that the winner of the Republican nomination— no matter who he may be—was *honestly* nominated in a *free* and *unrigged* convention by delegates *whose right to vote was established beyond question.*

No Republican Candidate whose nomination rests on corrupt methods can attack effectively the corruption of the Democratic administration.... Remember November! Vote the Fair Play Amendment!
You can't fight corruption with corruption![33]

To counter the Eisenhower onslaught, Taft backers took out full-page ads in several Chicago newspapers that read, with the first line in three-inch-high block letters:

DON'T BE FOOLED!!
. . . Every representative assembly in the free world follows this method of organizing for business. . . . The Eisenhower managers now realize that their cause is lost. In a desperate, last minute effort they want to change the rules under which the nomination is to be made. They want a "strike out" in the ninth inning to count as a home run. . . .

LODGE PROPOSAL UN-AMERICAN . . . it is a repudiation of everything for which the Republican Party stands.[34]

The shift to Eisenhower began behind closed doors. In caucus, the two largest uncommitted delegations—New York and Pennsylvania—voted to support the Fair Play Amendment. Recognizing that the situation was starting to get away from him, Taft tried to broker a last-minute deal with the Eisenhower forces. On Monday evening, 7 July, ten minutes before the convention was to open, Gabrielson telephoned Lodge and asked him to come immediately to his office, which was directly behind the speaker's platform. When Lodge arrived, he found himself out-numbered—in the office were Gabrielson, Ingalls, and Taft supporters Senator William Knowland, Tom Coleman, and former Taft campaign manager Clarence Brown. Brown offered Taft's proposal: the senator's backers would be willing to have the contested delegates *voluntarily* agree not to vote on any contests until their own credentials had been estab-lished. Astounded, Lodge asked for fifteen minutes to consult with other members of the Eisenhower Committee. Once again, Lodge had spotted a Taft trap—if the Eisenhower forces were denied their moment to argue the Fair Play Amendment on the floor of the convention, even though they might win the point on the voting rights of the contested delegates, they would not have the momentum to sway uncommitted delegates to support Eisenhower over Taft on the first ballot. Lodge huddled with Brownell, and it did not take them long to reject Brown's offer. When Lodge emerged from Gabrielson's office, he headed straight for mem-bers of the press and proclaimed, "We are taking the fight to the floor."[35]

After Lodge left, Coleman and Brown met outside Gabrielson's office and came up with a plan that strained parliamentary procedure to its breaking point. They decided that immediately following the formal in-troduction of the Fair Play Amendment, Brown would go to the podium, be recognized by Gabrielson, and raise a point of order regarding the Louisiana delegation. Brown would argue that because the seven Loui-siana delegates had had their fate settled by their state committee, they technically were not "in contest"; thus, the delegation should remain as it had been before the RNC reallocated it—committed to Taft. Once Gabri-elson rammed this motion through on a voice vote, Brown, who would still hold the floor, would quickly move to pass the Fair Play Amendment without any debate from the floor.[36] Thus, the Taft forces would, without having to endure an embarrassing vote, regain the high ground.

Never mind that this thinly veiled sleight of hand completely violated parliamentary procedure. The real problem was that the Taft forces had momentarily stopped talking to each other. Everything hinged on Gabrielson recognizing Brown and calling for a voice vote on his motion—but Coleman and Brown did not bother to tell Gabrielson about their plan. Apparently, no one told Taft either. He had arranged for John Bricker, Taft's Ohio colleague in the Senate, to make a motion that the 1948 convention rules, which included the Root Rule, be adopted. Bricker made his motion, and before Brown could react, Governor Arthur Langlie of Washington sprang to his feet, was recognized by Gabrielson, and offered the Fair Play Amendment as a substitute for Bricker's motion.[37]

Once more, Taft's lieutenants had stumbled. The correct strategy, seen in hindsight, was what Taft had wanted Bricker to do—simply *accept* the Fair Play Amendment. The delegate loss would have been minimal, and a floor fight would have been averted. But it hadn't happened that way. Taft now found himself in a floor fight against the forces of fair play. Attempting to recover from their error, the Taft forces drove the stake in deeper. Immediately after Langlie had recorded his motion, Brown rushed to the podium; once recognized, he offered an amendment to Langlie's amendment—that Louisiana's seven delegates would be *excluded* from the Fair Play Amendment.[38] When Taft, who was watching the action on television in his Hilton headquarters, saw Brown moving to the stage to take over, he audibly gasped, and with good reason.[39]

Brown's action defies logical explanation—only if one sees his fixation on Louisiana as gaining for Taft some kind of moral victory does fighting so hard for seven delegates make any sense at all. Besides, Brown's actions had once again made Taft look as if he was making an exception for one delegation on an issue of ethics. Before the convention was even three hours old, Brown had bumbled his way into a critical roll call that, if Taft *won*, would make him emerge more tainted with steamroller tactics than he had been before.

The vote bore out Taft's fears as he sat stunned in his headquarters. After two hours of debate, in which Louisiana was predictably lost in the shuffle and fair play tactics became the center of attention, the convention voted 648 to 548 to reject Brown's amendment and then unanimously approved Langlie's Fair Play Amendment.[40] A beaming Eisenhower, who had bet Frank Carlson that his vote would be nearer to 650 than to 600, collected a dollar from the senator.[41] As he left the convention, Lodge summed up the Fair Play fight: "We have defeated the Taft forces on the ground of their own choosing."[42]

The next day the Credentials Committee gave its approval to all the Taft delegates who had been seated by the RNC, save the seven unlucky pawns of Louisiana who were sacrificed by Taft in a measure of conciliation. But it mattered little. The full convention would now vote on the decision of the Credentials Committee, but thanks to the Fair Play Amendment, the contested delegates could not vote. The fate of those delegates was sealed; Taft still controlled his other committed delegates, although the count was now considerably closer.

Now Lodge moved in for the kill. He announced that on Wednesday night, when the motion was made to approve the entirety of the Credentials Committee's report, the Eisenhower forces would challenge the Credentials Committee's ruling on Georgia and Texas from the floor, decisions Lodge claimed were "stains on the integrity of our party that we must erase if we are to go to the people with clean hands."[43] It would be Taft's last chance. The Fair Play Amendment already showed that uncommitted delegates were starting to drift to Eisenhower; if Taft lost the fifty-five total votes of Texas and Georgia, his chances for a first-ballot victory would disappear.

Speeches: MacArthur and McCarthy

Sandwiched in between rounds of the Fair Play fight, the television audience endured countless speeches of varying length and interest. Here, the Taft forces ruled unchecked. Historian Jeff Broadwater makes an important point when he observes that while the party's conservatives were losing their chance at the nomination with Taft, they controlled the podium throughout most of the convention.[44] Taft had chosen most of the speakers without serious input from the Eisenhower forces. Thus the views of the conservative wing of the Republican Party were not lost on Chicago; rather, they were heard by a rather sizable television audience.

In terms of advance publicity, Taft could not have made a better choice for the convention's keynote speaker than Douglas MacArthur. Aside from MacArthur's military prominence, and the fact that he was the obvious choice to deliver a speech designed to be a frontal assault on Truman, it had long been speculated that Taft had offered MacArthur the chance to be his running mate.[45] Keynote addresses had often propelled the speaker into the political stratosphere—as recently as 1948, Alben Barkley's rafter-raiser had won him the second spot on Truman's ticket.

It is likely that MacArthur thought that he, too, could benefit from a deadlocked convention but in a more exalted fashion—perhaps the convention would turn to him with its presidential nomination.

However, in front of the largest television audience to view any speech at either convention, MacArthur flopped dismally.[46] For nearly an hour, to a convention that had been entertained that afternoon by the Fair Play fiasco, the general flailed wildly at the shortcomings of the Truman administration.[47] The speech was universally condemned. William Manchester, MacArthur's most perceptive biographer, called the keynote "probably the worst speech of [MacArthur's] career";[48] C. L. Sulzberger of the *New York Times* recorded in his diary that during the speech, "one could feel the electricity gradually running out of the room." He added, "I think he cooked his own goose and didn't do much to help Taft."[49] MacArthur, who quit the army days after the convention adjourned to take a position as chairman of the board of Remington-Rand,[50] would eventually be drafted without his consent by Gerald L. K. Smith's far-right Christian Nationalist Party (formerly the America First Party). Both that party and its candidate were unimportant in the fall campaign.[51]

Joseph McCarthy's speech, however, was different. He had endorsed neither Taft nor Eisenhower (his only real statement of position had been his refusal to support Stassen in the Wisconsin primary).[52] Nevertheless, his growing stature had won him a prime slot in the convention program, and he made the most of it. He used it to deliver one of his best-remembered speeches, a rousing declamation against the past two Democratic administrations and how their ennui had allowed the communists to infiltrate American government. It was McCarthy at his most effective, goading the delegates into a frenzy: "My good friends, I say one Communist in a defense plant is one Communist too many (applause). One Communist on the faculty of one university is one Communist too many (applause). One Communist among the American advisors at Yalta *was* one Communist too many . . . (applause)."[53]

It was the first time that most Americans had seen McCarthy speak; it would not be the last, even during this election.

Georgia, Texas, and the Balloting for President

Everyone knew that Wednesday night's session would decide the nominee. The convention was going to vote on the Credentials Committee report, and Lodge had promised to challenge the Georgia and Texas decisions. Taft's men circled the wagons for Eisenhower's final charge.

As soon as Oklahoma's Ross Rizley, the chairman of the Credentials Committee, moved that the convention accept his committee's report on Georgia, Senator Donald Eastvold, the young attorney general of Washington State, rose to present the Eisenhower minority report, which argued against Rizley's motion. The debate went on for close to an hour. It was raucous, and it was personal. Eastvold spoke for the Eisenhower forces, and Senator Everett Dirksen of Illinois spoke for the Taft forces. Of all Taft's supporters, including Taft himself, Dirksen was the best speaker. His gravelly voice and anecdotal speeches were fast becoming Senate legends. Yet on this night, Dirksen's equally famous temper would put the final nail in Taft's coffin. After a smooth beginning, which painted a picture for the delegates of a Republican Party that was a vast sea waiting to cascade on the Democrats in the fall, Dirksen slowly picked up steam. After charging that it was Eisenhower's supporters, not Taft's, who had truly been corrupted, he looked straight at Thomas Dewey, who was sitting with the New York delegation. As Dewey sat with a tight, fixed smile, Dirksen roared: "We followed you before and you took us down the road to defeat." Amid a mix of boos and applause, Dirksen raised his finger, pointed right at Dewey, and growled in a low, threatening voice, "And don't do this to us again." Permanent chairman Joseph Martin, himself a Taft supporter, tried to quiet the crowd by reminding them that "this is no place for Republicans to be booing other Republicans," and a flushed, chastened Dirksen continued: "I assure you that I didn't mean to precipitate a controversy."[54] But the damage had been done. Now Taft forces not only were seen by many to be attempting to steal the convention but also seemed to have cornered the market on bad taste.

The thirty-two-year-old Eastvold, who was running for Washington's attorney general that fall, made the best of Dirksen's lapse of judgment. He opened his defense of his minority report by stating in a soothing voice, "I did not come here tonight to deal in personalities." And then, after reminding his audience of the old adage "Beware the young attorney with a book," he hoisted above his head a sizable law book and cited a Supreme Court decision that said that the party convention should make the final decision in delegate contests.[55]

When the vote finally came, the shift to Eisenhower was complete. The final vote was 607 votes in favor of the motion to 531 against. The uncommitted delegates had broken to Eisenhower. Warren's California, Stassen's Minnesota, and Duff's Pennsylvania all voted for the minority report. There was no longer any doubt as to how Warren and Stassen would react in case the convention deadlocked while balloting for president—they would turn their delegations over to Eisenhower.

There was little point in debating Texas—an ironic turn of events, since it was the "Texas Steal" that had given the Eisenhower Committee the issue that it had, to this point, used so effectively. Taft yielded on the Texas credentials fight, thus giving up twenty-two delegates.[56] Most agreed with Eisenhower's assessment of the evening's events: "I'm going to win."[57]

On Friday morning, 11 July, the voting began for the presidential nomination. Eisenhower was going to get 68 new votes, the spoils of his victories on the Georgia, Texas, and Louisiana contests. But these would be balanced, for the moment at least, by the 68 votes controlled by Warren and the 26 controlled by Stassen—votes that had been for Eisenhower on the Brown and Georgia votes but would now return to the control of their favorite sons. As RNC secretary Katherine Howard called the roll, shifts and changes were minimal. Then came a shock. Despite Stassen's tearful pleading, the Minnesota delegation broke ranks—it cast 19 votes for Stassen and 9 for Eisenhower. At the end of the first ballot, Eisenhower had 595 votes, 9 short of the nomination. Taft had 500, Warren 81, Stassen 20, and MacArthur 10. Watching the televised spectacle at his headquarters, Taft sadly mumbled, "There will be some shifts."[58] The big shift came from Minnesota. With an Eisenhower nomination a near certainty, Stassen released his delegation.[59] Minnesota quickly changed its vote; the entire delegation went for Eisenhower. While it was never made unanimous, as is often the custom after convention balloting, Dwight D. Eisenhower was now the Republican nominee for president.

Immediately following his victory, Eisenhower, who had spent the better part of the convention in his suit, suffering from an ileitis attack, ignored the counsel of all his advisers, and decided to pay a call on his vanquished foe. Leaving his suite at the Blackstone Hotel, Eisenhower walked over to Taft headquarters for a personal talk with the senator. Eisenhower would later profess to be surprised by the surly, booing crowd that met him at the Hilton. Eisenhower and Taft smiled for the cameras, Taft saying that he would "do everything possible in the campaign to secure [Eisenhower's] election" and Eisenhower calling Taft "a very great American."[60] But the booing and catcalling persisted as Eisenhower tried to make his way out of the Hilton. It only stopped when a Taft aide stood on a chair and asked the crowd to be "good sports and cheer both the Senator and General Eisenhower."[61] No such cheer broke out; no breach had been healed. Taft was gracious in defeat, but neither he nor his staff was promising anything specific for the fall. The meeting was all too brief for that—Eisenhower had to leave immediately for the Amphitheatre, where he would announce his choice for his running mate.

The Choice of Nixon

Born in 1913 and reared in southern California, young Richard M. Nixon was known for his scholarly nature, his thoughtfulness, and his love of reading. No one was surprised when this stoic young man signed up for prelaw in high school. A strong student who excelled at rhetoric and debate, Nixon would nonetheless be kept from attending an elite college, thanks to his family's marginal financial status and the need to care for an elder brother with tuberculosis. Forced to settle for little Whittier College, Nixon commuted every day to classes, then returned to work in the family grocery store. Nevertheless, he stayed on the honor list all four years and continued his passion for debate. Seeing his mind as first-rate, several of his teachers helped him to procure a full-tuition scholarship (of $250) to Duke University Law School in 1934. Despite the trials of the Great Depression (at one point Nixon lived in a toolshed with no wood stove), Nixon once again proved himself a superior student, making the law review and graduating third in his class in 1937.

After a brief and fruitless job search in New York, Nixon returned to Whittier and joined the law firm of Wingert and Brewley. The work was tedious, and Nixon had time on his hands: time that he filled by entering local politics. He had two short-lived candidacies for city attorney and the State Assembly and campaigned widely for Wendell Willkie in 1940. His career trajectory, like those of so many others of his age, was cut short by the attack on Pearl Harbor. In 1942, he moved to Washington and took a job at the Office of Price Administration, the agency in charge of wartime price controls and rationing. It was here that Nixon developed a distaste for government bureaucracy in general and the Democratic New Deal in particular. In short, he hated it. In 1942, Nixon volunteered for service in the U.S. Navy. He saw active service in the Pacific, where as a lieutenant (J.G.)—the same rank held during the war by John Kennedy, Lyndon Johnson, Gerald Ford, and George H. W. Bush—Nixon supervised the loading and unloading of cargo planes in a combat zone.

Following the war, he wasted no time in parlaying his veteran status into political capital. In 1946, he ran for a congressional seat, representing California's Twelfth Congressional District. He blitzed his opponent, Democratic incumbent Jerry Voorhis, with a veritable smorgasbord of lies—he falsified Voorhis's voting record, understated the number of bills that Voorhis had introduced, and linked him to a labor political action committee that had disavowed Voorhis not two years earlier. But it was his tying of Voorhis to domestic communism that would become Nixon's signature political approach. Nixon ran ads that declared, "[Voorhis's] voting record in Congress is more Socialistic and Communistic than Democratic," later defending the smears as just hard-knuckle politics. Nixon was practicing what Garry Wills, his most thoughtful biographer, would later term the "denigrative method" of politics—attack your opponent before he gets a chance to attack you, and keep him on the defensive, no matter the truth of the charges.[62]

As a congressman, Nixon identified with the moderate, internationalist wing of the party that would ultimately support both Dewey and Eisenhower; for example, he strongly supported the Marshall Plan. Thanks to his superlative constituent service, he was popular and influential in his district, and he was returned to office in 1948 by a wide margin. Yet it was the Hiss case (see introduction) by which Nixon's congressional career is ultimately judged. As a member of the House Un-American Activities Committee, Nixon made sure that there were plenty of reporters and cameras around when he left no stone—or pumpkin, the well-publicized hiding place for Whittaker Chamber's cache of documents—unturned. For all the questions that still remain regarding the Hiss trial, one thing is absolutely certain—it served to identify Nixon in the public mind as, for the moment at least, one of the nation's leading communist hunters. The 1950 Senate campaign in California found Nixon keeping Congresswoman Helen Gahagan Douglas constantly off guard with exaggerated charges of her communist leanings. With the help of public relations specialist Murray Chotiner, Nixon turned red-baiting into an art form, berating Douglas's voting record and labeling her the "Pink Lady." In a direct-mail piece that would make political history, Nixon compared Douglas's voting record in the Senate to that of radical Democrat Vito Marcantonio of New York. Nixon defeated Douglas by some 680,000 votes.

Richard Nixon was now a certified Republican superstar. He was a proven winner, and he was young and vigorous—only thirty-nine years old in 1952. Not surprisingly, both the Taft and the Eisenhower forces wanted his support. But Nixon had made up his mind. In November

1951, Nixon traveled to Europe to attend a meeting of the World Health Organization. While there, he met with Eisenhower at SHAPE headquarters, where, according to Nixon, the conversation "steered away from American politics" and concentrated mostly on European postwar recovery. Nixon wrote, "I felt that I was in the presence of a genuine statesman, and I came away convinced that if he ran for the nomination, I would do everything I could to help him get it."[63]

But Nixon first had to abide by California state law, which mandated that all members of a delegate slate sign a loyalty oath to support the winner of the California primary at the convention. That meant that Nixon was bound, by oath, to Earl Warren—at least through the first ballot (see chapter 2). But to Nixon, this was but a minor roadblock. When Taft went to Nixon's office to ask for his support, Nixon told the senator that although he had signed an oath to support Warren, he was actually an Eisenhower man.[64] Nixon took several steps to assure the Eisenhower camp that, despite the oath, he really was one of them. On 15 November, accompanied by his personal lawyer Dana Smith, he met with Lodge for several hours. Lodge later wrote for his file, "It is now pretty much an open secret that the support pledged by him . . . and others to support Warren was only to the extent of cooperating in the selection of a representative delegation which will have considerable freedom of action at the convention."[65] Nixon also lent a hand to a boomlet designed to get him chosen as the keynote speaker at the convention, where, ostensibly, he could sing Eisenhower's praises.[66] But that plum went to MacArthur with, as we have seen, disastrous results.

On 11 June, Nixon sent a letter on Senate letterhead to some 23,000 California Republicans. In it, Nixon explained that he wished to find out, just in case Warren released the delegation, whom the delegation should support next. Below the letter was a ballot that read: "From my conversations with other voters and my analysis of all the factors involved, I believe that _____ is the strongest candidate the Republicans could nominate for President."[67] The result, as Nixon no doubt knew it would be, was overwhelmingly for Eisenhower. While on the train bringing the California delegation to Chicago, Nixon leaked the results of this ballot to the press, infuriating Warren in the process.[68] As things worked out, Nixon did not have to break his oath to Warren. Eisenhower won the nomination without California's votes, which were cast for Warren on the first ballot and which Warren did not release.

There is some evidence that suggests that even before Nixon left for the convention, Dewey had offered him the vice presidential slot on an Eisenhower-led ticket. If he did, and the evidence is contradictory,[69] the position was ultimately not Dewey's to give. It was Eisenhower's, and there are two contending stories explaining how Eisenhower came to choose Nixon as his running mate. One is told in essentially the same manner in both Eisenhower's and Nixon's memoirs. According to Eisenhower, sometime before the convention he had written an "eligible list" for the vice presidency, which he carried in his wallet. Nixon headed this list, followed by Congressman Charles Halleck, Senator Walter Judd, and Governors Dan Thornton and Arthur Langlie. Immediately after Eisenhower's nomination, he gave the list to Brownell, who held a meeting of party leaders at Brownell's suite. There, they unanimously approved Eisenhower's first choice.[70]

There is, however, a competing story, sourced by Brownell. This one begins on Thursday, 10 July, at a dinner meeting in Eisenhower's suite at the Blackstone. At that dinner were Eisenhower, Clay, Brownell, and Dewey. When the conversation came around to the vice presidency, Eisenhower professed not to know that the candidate could actually choose the second man on the ticket—he thought it was totally up to the convention. When pressed, Eisenhower did, indeed, produce a list, but on it were the names of two businessmen—Charles Wilson, the president of General Motors (who would be chosen as Eisenhower's first secretary of defense) and Cyrus R. Smith, the president of American Airlines. It was left to Eisenhower's friends to steer the conversation back to political reality. Let Brownell tell what happened next: "I said that General Clay and Governor Dewey and I had talked it over and that, unless he expressed a preference otherwise, we would recommend Senator Nixon of California to him. He thought for a moment, said he had met Senator Nixon, and that he would be guided by our advice. Then he told us to clear Nixon's name with the other leaders of the party. And that was it." The next day's meeting in Brownell's suite was remembered by Brownell in essentially the same way that Eisenhower and Nixon related it.[71] In his memoirs, Brownell tells this story, only remembering that list had five or six names on it, including Nixon's.

Regardless of how he eventually got there, Eisenhower called Nixon with the news. Nixon would later remember that when he got the call, he was "speechless." Without even bothering to shave or to phone his wife (he was taking a nap at the time of Eisenhower's call, and Pat Nixon heard the news on the radio while in a restaurant), he sprinted up to

Convention victory: Richard M. Nixon, Dwight D. Eisenhower, and
Arthur Summerfield (Republican National Committee, courtesy of
Dwight D. Eisenhower Library)

Eisenhower's suite at the Blackstone to confer for the first time with the
head of the ticket.[72] He would be nominated later that evening.

Epilogue

Later that evening, the Amphitheatre rocked to the screams of the delegates: "We Want Ike!" A disappointed Joseph Martin, whose job it was
to introduce "the next president of the United States," did so with grace
and style, as he asked the convention to "unite behind this great leader,
soldier, and statesman."[73] Dressed in a blue suit, blue shirt, and blue tie,
Eisenhower looked out on a cheering crowd that only hours before had
been locked in mortal combat over his candidacy. His wife, Mamie, who
like her husband had been ill for much of the convention, smiled behind
him. Eisenhower then accepted the nomination in a speech that did less
to define his policies than it did to label the upcoming campaign: "You
have summoned me on behalf of millions of your fellow Americans to
lead a great crusade—for freedom in America and freedom in the world.

CAN NATIONAL CONVENTION

The nominee addresses the delegates, 11 July 1952 (Republican National Committee, courtesy of Dwight D. Eisenhower Library)

I know something of leading a crusade. I have led one. . . . I will lead this crusade."[74]

Such was the euphoria. But during the convention, Eisenhower also faced the torment felt by thousands of parents in wartime. His son, John, was heading for active duty in Korea. He came to see his father in Chicago, just before he was to deploy. John remembered, "In the course of conversation Dad gave me one admonition: never get captured." Worried about the possibility of blackmail for his son's life, Eisenhower was clear: "If you're captured, I suppose I would just have to drop out of the presidential race."[75]

How did Dwight Eisenhower win the nomination? Despite the plethora of explanations that point to how a moderate Republican won over a conservative one; how an internationalist won over an isolationist; how an optimist won over a pessimist; how a potential winner won out over a three-time presidential loser, the answer is quite simple. It was the issue of the "Steal" and the resulting fight over "Fair Play" that gave Eisenhower the victory. Depending on one's point of view, it happened either because Taft's advisers fumbled away a win (this was put acerbically by Harry Truman in a letter to his cousin: "It looks very much like my candidate for the Republican nomination [Taft] has beaten himself. Of all the dumb bunnies, he is the worst")[76] or because Eisenhower's advisers, particularly Lodge and Brownell, were astute enough to sniff out every trap laid for them by Taft and successfully negated each one. Either way, one thing is clear—Eisenhower had not been a major player in any strategy at the convention that had won him the nomination. He was indebted to the political skill—or inanity—of others for his nomination. What remained to be seen was whether or not Eisenhower would run his own campaign in the fall.

THE DEMOCRATIC NATIONAL CONVENTION: 21–26 JULY 1952

In the one week between the Republican and Democratic Conventions, several changes were made to the setup in the Amphitheatre—the one most obvious to the public was the installation of a center-aisle camera platform, which would provide the television viewer with a cleaner, less obstructed picture.[77] There had been no change, however, in the status of the Democratic nomination. Truman had yet to produce an heir, but he had given Barkley his promise of support. Kefauver was continuing to hope that his showing in the primaries would sway uninstructed delegates to his side (Kefauver circulars, given to the delegates as they entered the Amphitheatre, stressed his lead in the popular vote through to the end of the primaries—"Senator Estes Kefauver has won nearly six times the popular support of his nearest competitor . . . an overwhelming endorsement, unprecedented in American political history").[78]

And Stevenson still hoped to escape Chicago without being nominated.

Adlai E. Stevenson II arriving at the Democratic National Convention, Chicago, Illinois (courtesy of Library of Congress)

On 12 July, he released a statement saying that he was "a candidate for re-election as Governor of Illinois, and as he has often said, wants no other office." Stevenson further asked the Illinois delegation to "continue to respect his wishes, and he hopes all of the delegates will do likewise."[79] On 18 July, the night he arrived in Chicago, he said to the press, "I'll not ask anybody to vote for me here. On the contrary. I'll do everything possible to discourage any delegate from putting me in nomination or nominating me."[80] This he did. On Sunday, 20 July, he met with the Illinois delegation and asked the delegates not to vote for him.[81] Stevenson continued to try to stop all campaigning on his behalf. For example, Senator Brien McMahon of Connecticut was calling delegates and pushing Stevenson's name; Stevenson called pollster Elmo Roper, a friend of McMahon's, and asked him to call the senator and implore him to stop.[82] On the night before the convention was to open, Stevenson begged Jake Arvey: "You got me into this—you've got to get me out."[83]

The Platform and Civil Rights

The Republican platform was of little consequence to the whole of the election of 1952. Not so the Democratic platform. Four years earlier, the Dixiecrats had walked out of the party over the civil rights plank in its platform. In 1952, the party held its collective breath to see if its platform would lead to the same result.

No one was more concerned about another Dixiecrat split in 1952 than was Harry Truman. Indeed, he was so concerned about the chance of a second southern walkout that he left nothing to chance—he drafted the platform himself. As early as May 1952, Truman had entrusted the job of drafting the platform to his chief assistant, Charles Murphy, and to Richard Neustadt, one of his special assistants. It took five attempts for the two men to develop a thirty-six-page draft that satisfied Truman.[84] Truman sent this draft to Chicago with Neustadt, and on 8 July, Neustadt hand-delivered the draft to John McCormack (D-MA), the chairman of the Platform Committee.

In this draft, Truman deliberately avoided a volatile issue. Despite the actions of his administration, the draft did not call for a compulsory Fair Employment Practices Commission (FEPC). This, of course, ran counter to the stand that Kefauver had taken throughout the primaries. Truman did, however, hit another issue head-on. The draft called for changes in congressional procedures so that issues could be brought to a vote more quickly. This was a direct slap at Rule 22 of the Senate, which permitted filibusters by requiring a two-thirds vote of the Senate to close debate—a cloture vote. With a two-thirds vote on any measure notoriously hard to come by, Rule 22 effectively guaranteed unlimited filibusters, which had been used by southern Democrats to kill any bill that smacked of civil rights. Truman seemed to hope that his dodging FEPC would please the South while his attack on Rule 22 would please the North.

When the inevitable debate over the platform began, it centered around two of the most influential members of the committee. Representing the interests of the North was Senator Herbert Lehman of New York. Wealthy, dapper, and handsome, Lehman was a former governor of his state and head of the United Nations Relief and Rehabilitation Administration, and he had served in the Senate since his defeat of John Foster Dulles in 1950. Second only to Hubert Humphrey in his outspoken advocacy of civil rights, Lehman had naturally gravitated to the candidacy of fellow New Yorker Averell Harriman. When speaking of the expected fight before the Platform Committee, Lehman told the press that he was totally committed to the cause of civil rights, and while he hoped that the South would not bolt, he would "press for it [a strong civil rights plank] anyway."[85]

Representing the interests of the South was John J. Sparkman, the junior senator from Alabama. Sparkman was an interesting blend of moderate and conservative southern beliefs. Son of a poor sharecropper, Sparkman worked his way through the University of Alabama Law School by shoveling coal. Ten years of practicing law and teaching at Huntsville College led to an interest in politics, and he was elected to the House in 1936 and to the Senate ten years later (by a fluke, in 1946 he became the only person in American history to be simultaneously elected to the House and to the Senate in the same election). Like most southerners, Sparkman disliked Truman, but as a strong party man he disliked the Dixiecrats even more. Following the 1948 election, Sparkman worked tirelessly to expunge the Dixiecrats from his state's party machinery. In 1952, he supported Russell's candidacy, largely because he believed that Russell would not lead a second Dixiecrat walkout. As Sparkman would write to a constituent, "The potential of a Southern Revolt is much greater this year than it was in 1948. I do not believe that potential can be converted into actuality without Dick Russell's help. I am convinced that those who would lead the South in revolt will not have that help from [him]."[86] To those Alabamans who argued to their senator that Russell was a Dixiecrat in sheep's clothing, Sparkman countered with statements like the following: "It was largely due to the fact that he could be counted upon to continue to be a loyal Democrat that [Russell] was endorsed [by me]."[87] While Sparkman made it clear to a friend, "I have not liked the attitude expressed by President Truman, Averell Harriman, Hubert Humphrey, and others threatening our platform,"[88] Truman trusted Sparkman more than he did Lehman to fight for a noninflammatory platform, one that would not lead to a Dixiecrat walkout.

The result of the committee's hours of debate brought a victory for Truman. After bitter wrangling on Wednesday, 23 July, the committee recommended a very bland civil rights plank that called not for a compulsory FEPC but rather for "the cooperative efforts of individual citizens and action by state and local governments . . . [and] . . . federal action." The plank made no reference to Rule 22 but instead asked Congress to "improve congressional procedures so that majority rule prevails and decisions can be made after reasonable debate without being blocked by a minority in either house."[89] The *New York Times* observed that that plank lacked the "fighting words" of the 1948 plank, and it was right.[90] Neither the Dixiecrats, nor those whom Neustadt had called the "simon-pure civil rightsters,"[91] had carried the day. Indeed, it was Truman who had gotten the civil rights plank he had wanted—a compromise plank that would halt a Dixiecrat walkout, at least for the time being.

Many southerners were stunned to find that the author of the compromise plank on civil rights was John Sparkman. But avoiding an impasse over civil rights had been Sparkman's goal all along.[92] It was his work on the platform that led to Sparkman's portrayal in the press—only partly accurate—as a southern moderate. It was an effort that would eventually lead to his consideration as his party's vice presidential nominee.

Credentials Challenges, the Loyalty Pledge, and the "Northern Coalition"

The debate over the platform was not, however, the only fight that threatened to take the South out of the convention. The credentials fight over Texas and Mississippi loomed large. Frank McKinney, the chair of the Democratic National Committee (DNC), had learned a lesson from one of the many mistakes of the Taft forces a few weeks earlier; he announced on 16 July that there would be gavel-to-gavel coverage on radio and television, and the print press would have unfettered access to the deliberations of the DNC Subcommittee on Credentials, chaired by Senator Calvin Rawlings of Utah.[93] Those hearings certainly made for entertaining watching. Hugh White, Mrs. John A. Clark, Allan Shivers, and Maury Maverick had all stormed into Chicago at the head of their respective delegations, girded for war. Over three hours on Saturday morning, 19 July, the debate was furious.

The Texas case took the dramatic lead, primarily due to the oratorical flourishes of both Shivers and Maverick. Maverick charged the Shivercrats with conspiring to return the party to its 1840 platform, which backed "white supremacy" and slavery. Words like "prostitute" and charges like exchanging "white women" for "black wenches" were thrown out at a television audience as yet unaccustomed to such fare.[94] When offered a compromise—a delegation made up of half Loyalists and half Shivercrats—Maverick growled, "We don't want any so-so split. Kick us out like dogs, or seat us as the only legal delegation from Texas."[95] Maverick said that he would stop his challenge only if the Shivercrats signed a loyalty pledge stating that each member of the delegation would support the nominees of the convention. Shivers refused.[96]

The subcommittee was as unimpressed with Maverick's histrionics as Truman was unimpressed with a telegram from Kefauver that predicted that the Shivers delegation would "do what they pleased at the end of this convention. Under these circumstances they have no right to be here" (Truman scrawled in the margin: "Not answered").[97] But the party leadership *was* impressed by a promise that Shivers gave to Sam Rayburn, who would soon serve as the convention's chairman (if his delegation was seated, Shivers promised to support the eventual nominee of the party), as well as by the arguments of Lyndon Johnson that Shivers could be trusted.[98] The subcommittee voted unanimously to seat the Shivercrat delegation in its entirety; it would later vote unanimously to seat Hugh White's Mississippi delegation in its entirety. Later that morning, the subcommittee's decision was ratified by the full DNC. The Maverick and Clark delegations were assigned balcony seats, far from the convention floor.[99] Thus, the DNC had seated two delegations that had expressly stated that they would sign nothing and would not promise anything that would bind them to the decision of the convention.

However, the DNC was leaving nothing to chance. As a precondition of accepting the credentials of the Shivers and White delegations, the committee adopted a resolution proposed by Jonathan Daniels of North Carolina, and clearly aimed at keeping the Shivercrats, the Mississippi States' Rightists, and any other recalcitrant Dixiecrats inside the party: "Be it resolved: That it is the consensus of this convention that the honorable course of every delegate who participates in its proceedings is to support the majority decisions of the convention here and hereafter."[100] In other words, if you were seated as a delegate, you were bound to support the nominees of the convention. Such a strategy certainly fit in with Truman's desire to keep the Dixiecrats from bolting. The Daniels resolution also had the virtue of being a moderate one—delegates didn't have to do anything; they just took their seats, and by virtue of their attendance it was assumed that they would support the nominees.

However, a vocal group of northern liberals immediately protested that the Daniels resolution did not keep the South on a short enough leash. Later that Saturday, the formation of a "Northern Coalition" between the Kefauver and the Harriman forces (conveniently forgetting, for the moment, that Kefauver was a southerner) was announced. The coalition, which had been unable to force the seating from the Loyalist delegations from Mississippi and Texas, now demanded that each and every delegate be required to recite a loyalty pledge, promising to support the nominees and decisions of the convention and work to have the nominees put on their state's ballot in November.[101]

Harriman, who came to the convention with the commitment of 17½ delegates outside of the New York delegation, never articulated a reason for joining the coalition. His most thorough biographer suggests that he may have been driven to the coalition out of spite, feeling betrayed by Truman's support of Barkley.[102] Kefauver's motivation, however, is much clearer. Indeed, there were two ways that the coalition's stance could work to Kefauver's advantage. The most obvious was a scenario that led to a decision by the convention to overturn the decision of the DNC to seat the White and Shivers delegations. Both White and Shivers were virulently anti-Kefauver; Maverick, on the other hand, had spoken favorably of Kefauver on several occasions. Should the Maverick and Clark delegations be seated, Kefauver stood to gain the lion's share of the seventy combined votes from the two states on the first ballot. But even if the decision stood, and the Shivers and White delegations were seated, Kefauver could still gain from the situation. A southern walkout played right into Kefauver's hands. When the votes of the South were subtracted from the equation, Russell was effectively eliminated from the contest (he had 130½ committed delegates, all but 9 from the South), and Kefauver, while still being some 66 votes short of what he would need to win, would nevertheless hold a solid first-ballot lead.

For those who wanted to stop Kefauver, there seemed to be only one way out. If an anti-Kefauver candidate, one who stood a chance of actually getting the nomination, was to step forward, preferably with Truman's blessing, then Kefauver and the coalition might be stopped. Stevenson continued to deny adamantly that he was that man. And on Sunday night, in an event that changed the entire complexion of the convention, a major candidate was forced to withdraw from the race.

Barkley's Withdrawal

Alben Barkley came to Chicago with a promise of support from Harry Truman. As far as political promises went, it seemed ironclad; as we have seen, it had been given to Barkley in the presence of both the president and his political advisers in the Oval Office, and Truman had informed his convention surrogate to vote for Barkley. But no one knew this, as all who were at the meeting, including Barkley, had agreed to a high level of secrecy. Now, as the loyalty pledge issue threatened to tear the convention apart, one can assume that Barkley, who coveted the presidency, was waiting for Truman to announce his support for the "Veep," thus offering to the convention a less threatening southern candidate, which might well lead the southerners to stand down on the loyalty pledge.

It never happened, largely because Barkley took an ill-advised meeting on Sunday, 20 July, with several leaders of organized labor, including Walter Reuther (president, United Auto Workers), Jack Kroll (president, Congress of Industrial Organizations Political Action Committee), and Joseph Keenan (former director, Labor League for Political Action). The assembled leadership stunned Barkley by telling him that they could not support him. The reason that Truman remembered they gave was his age; Barkley remembered that they were concerned that if he was not nominated, the Dixiecrats would choose him as their nominee.[103] Regardless, Barkley saw the handwriting on the wall. There was no way that Truman would continue his support for Barkley, promise or no promise, if labor was not on board. Monday afternoon, Barkley was visited by Leslie Biffle, Senator Earle Clements, Governor Lawrence Wetherby, and Lieutenant Governor Emerson Beauchamp of Kentucky, all telling him what he already knew—that he would have to withdraw. He met with the press on Monday, 21 July—just before the convention was gaveled to order—and withdrew, blasting "certain self-appointed labor leaders" who had precipitated his fall, as well as, in a thinly veiled slap at Truman, the "leaders . . . who have been encouraging my candidacy, [who] now find it expedient to withdraw their proffered support of me."[104]

What happened? It is clear that labor had chosen a candidate, but it was not Barkley—it was Stevenson. Documents show that Walter Reuther had been for Stevenson from the start; indeed, after the convention was over, he wrote to Stevenson, extending his best wishes "as one of your many friends who plotted to get you into this."[105] The question of whether or not these leaders were acting on their own, or on the orders of the president, has never been answered with complete certainty. Truman would later write that none of this would have happened if Barkley had acted on the advice of Truman and his staff and simply refused to take the meeting.[106] But Barkley did not believe for a second that labor had acted independently of the wishes of the president. He believed that Truman had lost faith in his vice president's ability to both gain and maintain the support of labor, as well as to hold the party together in the face of another Dixiecrat walkout; thus, the president had, according to Barkley's reading of the situation, given labor its marching orders. As Barkley remembered the meeting, the leaders told him that they had been informed by a good source that Truman was shifting his allegiance to Harriman; thus, labor was compelled to support Harriman as well. In Barkley's mind, Truman had given him the "kiss of death," and he could not go on.[107]

With no transcript having been kept of the meeting between Barkley and labor, it is Barkley's word against Truman's. But it is simply not reasonable to assume that labor would act independently of the wishes of the president. Whether or not they wanted Stevenson, it is difficult to believe that they would have jettisoned Barkley—Truman's choice—for Stevenson without direct orders from Truman. For his part, there is nothing in the correspondence to suggest that Truman believed that Stevenson was going to change his mind and run: quite the opposite in fact. But Truman did, indeed, dump Barkley; even if he did not give the order, he did not step in and defend Barkley from labor's decision. Barkley would never forgive Truman. The tone of his memoirs is decidedly bitter on the event, and a careful reading of the evidence suggests that Barkley was justified in his anger. His campaign logo—his name with a streak of lightning through it—was eerily prophetic of his brief candidacy, which had been speared by his "supporters."

The Welcoming Address

The oppressive heat that met the delegates on Monday morning, 21 July, was but a portent of things to come. Tempers and temperatures would get a great deal hotter before the Thirty-First Democratic National Convention left Chicago. However, this morning had been reserved for platitudes. The delegates would salute, pledge, pray, and endure the seemingly endless stream of opening procedural and welcoming speeches.

Few delegates would have guessed that they were about to hear one of the most extraordinary speeches in American political history.[108] In one of his ceremonial functions as governor of Illinois, Adlai Stevenson was about to welcome the delegates to the convention. Paying only slight attention to the wild demonstration that followed his introduction by temporary chair Frank McKinney, Stevenson began slowly in a voice that cracked slightly as he adjusted to his audience. He welcomed the delegates to Chicago, where they were "about to choose . . . candidates for the greatest temporal office on earth," and to the state of Illinois, where the "modern Democratic story began," reminding the delegates that the Land of Lincoln had elected a Jew, an Irish immigrant, and a Catholic as Democratic governors in the past century.

However, any resemblance to a mere speech of welcome ended after Stevenson had spoken but a few moments. His voice got stronger as he denounced the "pompous phrases" of the Republicans. He accused them of "first slaughtering each other" before they went after the Democrats, a carnage he wryly attributed to the "proximity of the Stockyards" to the Amphitheatre. The hall roared with approval, but what struck all who heard the speech was not Stevenson's humor but his warning to his party not to repeat its past mistakes: "This is not the time for superficial solutions and endless elocutions, for words are not deeds. . . . Where we have erred, let there be no denial; where we have wronged the public trust, let there be no excuses. Self-criticism is the secret weapon of democracy, and candor and confession are good for the political soul." His final call was an eloquent and moving demand that his party return to the values of Wilsonian idealism during the upcoming campaign: "What counts now is not just what we are *against,* but what we are *for. Who* leads us is less important than *what* leads us—what convictions, what courage, what faith—win or lose. A man doesn't save a century, or a civilization, but a militant party wedded to a principle can. . . . I hope our preoccupation here is not just with personalities but with objectives."

Although Stevenson left the stage immediately upon the completion of his speech, the applause that he left behind was long and deafening. John Bartlow Martin, a future Stevenson speechwriter and biographer, gushed that the speech was "incandescent."[109] The *Chicago Daily News* underestimated the case when it observed that the place had gone "slightly daft."[110] Stevenson had spoken nearly the same words before on 9 April 1952, at the New York fund-raiser honoring Harriman (see chapter 2). Nevertheless, many observers remember the welcoming speech as the moment that Stevenson became a bona fide alternative to the declared candidates: a man of eloquence and honesty who could bring the party's warring factions together. Other observers, with absolutely no evidence to support their conclusion, walked away believing that Stevenson had somehow done it on purpose—that the speech was deliberately designed to jump-start a draft. But for a moment, at least, Stevenson held the convention in the palm of his hand. It remained to be seen if he chose to let it go.

The Floor Fight over the Loyalty Pledge: Round One

The first part of Tuesday's session was dominated by a rather dull keynote, delivered by Massachusetts governor and temporary chairman

Paul Dever.[111] The second part of the session gave the delegates all they could handle. McKinney delayed the start of the business session, which would take up the issue of the loyalty pledge, until 12:20 a.m., hoping that he could broker a compromise. When no one moved, McKinney reluctantly reconvened the convention. Senator Blair Moody of Michigan rose to offer the coalition's alternative to the Daniels resolution—that no delegate would be seated "unless he shall give assurance to the Credentials Committee that he will exert every honorable means available to him . . . to provide that the nominees of the convention for President and Vice President . . . appear on the election ballot under the heading . . . of the Democratic Party." Moody was asked from the floor whether a delegate who refused to take the pledge could be seated at the convention; Moody growled, "The answer is no." The hall exploded into a mixture of boos and cheers; the coalition had drawn its line in the sand.[112] The South immediately took up the challenge. Governor Herman Talmadge of Georgia argued that the laws of his state did not permit any member of his delegation to take a pledge of any kind.[113] Senator Spessard Holland of Florida, who introduced the Daniels resolution as an alternative to the Moody resolution, directly charged the coalition with "fixing to do the very thing [that will] tear down this convention."[114] A roll call vote was called for on Holland's motion; it was 1:30 a.m.

Dever then stole the show. The convention rules stated that one-fifth of the delegates present had to rise from their seats to indicate that they wished a roll call vote to be taken. Dever asked for those wishing a roll call vote to rise, and in the pandemonium that followed, he quickly declared that not enough had risen. He then quickly called for a voice vote, and after screaming and yelling, Dever declared that the Holland motion had been defeated. The hall was in chaos; Dever then called for a voice vote on the Moody resolution; in the pandemonium, that motion was passed. With southerners still in the aisle screaming for recognition, the convention was adjourned by Dever at 2:05 a.m.[115]

The next day, the Credentials Committee upheld the Moody resolution. It further declared that all delegates must sign their names to written loyalty pledges within twenty-four hours. Sparkman tried to broker a compromise, getting the committee to agree that the loyalty pledges were for "this convention only," but it was not enough to convince all southern delegates to sign. On Wednesday morning, it was announced that forty-five states had signed and returned their pledge sheets. However,

Virginia, South Carolina, and Louisiana had refused to sign.[116] The possibility of a walkout was now acute, and Stevenson's name was now openly floated as the only candidate whose nomination could forestall such a walkout.

Stevenson Changes His Mind

Despite the governor's desire to make himself unavailable, the Draft Stevenson Committee was now ready to deliver his name to the convention. After several days of heated negotiation, Walter Johnson convinced Henry Schweicker, the governor of Indiana, to nominate Stevenson—whether or not Stevenson approved. But suddenly, and quite unexpectedly, Stevenson stepped in. By Johnson's own reporting, Jake Arvey communicated to Johnson that he had already arranged to have Governor Elbert Carvel of Delaware place Stevenson's name in nomination; Schweicker's services were not needed.[117] Rather than completely embarrass Johnson, Arvey arranged for Schweicker to give the first half of the nominating speech, Carvel would give the second half, and there would be no seconding speeches.[118] But it was clear that Arvey did not make this move without Stevenson's approval. Adlai Stevenson was not drafted, not by Johnson's committee, not by anyone. He had decided—albeit at the last possible second—that he would put his own name into nomination.

As we have seen, literally until that moment, Stevenson had continued to say that he was only a candidate for reelection to governor of Illinois. But, as Eisenhower had done that January, Stevenson had changed his mind. This moment is, from the Democratic point of view, the most important moment of the prenomination period. It is also one of the most poorly documented moments of the entire election. Virtually every observer has fallen lockstep behind Walter Johnson's assessment of his own effort in *How We Drafted Stevenson*—that at this point the draft committee placed so much pressure on Stevenson, even to the point of having a fellow governor ready in the wings to place his name in nomination, that Stevenson capitulated and reluctantly gave in. The problem with this conclusion is that there is no evidence to support it, and much to refute it. Stevenson had, right down to this moment, written and said that he wanted no part of the draft movement. That simply did not change at the convention (Stevenson had no contact with Johnson's committee), and there is nothing in the correspondence, oral histories, or contemporary assessments—other than Johnson's book—that suggests that Stevenson acted because of the draft movement. Stevenson had, right down to this moment, written and said that he wanted no part of the draft movement.

There are no documents to help the researcher learn why Stevenson made this all-important move. All conclusions are conjectural, but two have credibility. One presents an opportunistic Stevenson—Stevenson had assessed the situation and had come to believe that the convention was about to deadlock and he *could,* on a later ballot, be the nominee. A second presents a more altruistic Stevenson—he had assessed the situation, seen that the situation was rife for another destructive southern walkout, and allowed his name to be put into nomination so as to stop such a walkout.[119] Both are plausible; neither is ultimately provable. Only two things can be said with certainty: throughout the entire primary campaign, Stevenson did not want to run and did nothing to advance any kind of a candidacy—that is, until the second day of the Democratic Convention, when, like Eisenhower, he changed his mind.

Now that Stevenson had decided to run for the nomination, he had to bite his lip and tell Truman. On Thursday afternoon, he called the president, then still at the White House. Stevenson asked, by Truman's recollection, "If the situation developed to the point where he could be put into nomination would it embarrass me?" Truman's response was a mixture of fury and relief; he had wanted Stevenson all along, but Stevenson had spurned him—until the last minute. Using the colorful language that dotted many a Truman conversation, the president made it clear, in no uncertain terms, that it was about time. Truman immediately called his alternate, Thomas Gavin, and gave him a change in instructions—the vote of the president's alternate would no longer be for Barkley but for Stevenson.[120] Stevenson had not run in the primaries, and he had no campaign machinery ready. But he did have the president, who was about to make his presence known.

The Floor Fight over the Loyalty Pledge: Round Two

As Stevenson began his two-day candidacy for the nomination, the coalition's strategy was evaporating. On Wednesday, without serious incident, the convention seated the Shivers and White delegations, adopted the loyalty pledge, and adopted the platform. However, the coalition's trump card had yet to be played. If Virginia, Louisiana, and South Carolina persisted in their refusal to sign the Loyalty Oath before the voting for the presidential nominee took place, they might yet lead a southern walkout to protest the pledge—or they might yet be thrown out of the convention for refusing to sign.

When the convention reconvened at noon on Thursday, 24 July, the main order of business was the placing of names into nomination for president. Six nominating speeches were the curtain riser for a tumultuous session. As the speakers droned on, bored delegates began to leave the hall for dinner. By the time all nominating and seconding speeches had been completed, it was about 7:00 p.m. Then, completely unexpectedly, the Louisiana delegation was recognized. Louisiana yielded to Virginia, and Governor John Battle rose to a point of order. Reiterating that Virginia, as well as Louisiana and South Carolina, would "not give the assurances demanded" by the pledge, Battle demanded to know of Sam Rayburn, now serving as the convention's permanent chair, "whether we are, or are not, members of the convention . . . entitled to full partnership in the deliberations and votes of this convention."[121]

Rayburn had one goal in mind—to prevent a second southern walkout. Related to this goal was the fact that "Mr. Sam" despised Kefauver and his renegade tactics. Through a debate that lasted for seven hours, and featured at least two delegates fainting from the heat and a small fire breaking out in the delegate seating area, Rayburn played a major role in the final ruin of Kefauver's chances for the nomination. After hearing several impassioned speeches, Rayburn ruled from the chair that "South Carolina, Virginia, and Louisiana have not complied with the rules adopted in this convention."[122] Amid screams of protest, Rayburn recognized Maryland congressman Lansdale Sasscer. Sasscer, whose motion had been prearranged with Rayburn, moved that Virginia and South Carolina be immediately seated, despite the fact that they had yet to sign the pledge. The motion required a roll call vote.

As frantic chairmen tried to get their delegations back from dinner, most of the states passed on the first reading of the roll, which dealt with the fate of the Virginia delegation. At the end of the ballot, Rayburn personally spoke to delegates, attempting to ascertain which side of the issue they supported. Suddenly, at 8:50 p.m., Cook County clerk Richard Daley demanded to be recognized. Declaring that "Illinois had confidence in the Governor of Virginia," Daley announced that Illinois was reversing its first-ballot vote, which had gone against Virginia, and that Illinois was now voting 52–8 in favor of Virginia.[123] Everyone in the hall knew what had happened—through Daley, one of Stevenson's political appointees, Stevenson had spoken and had ordered the shift. Stevenson was siding himself against the coalition and against the walkout; if you wanted him as your nominee, you had to vote to keep the three states in the convention. Delegations shouted to have their vote changed. Within an hour, Virginia had been seated—615 votes for, 529 against, and 89 not voting.[124]

The coalition tried to get an immediate adjournment so that it might try to prevent South Carolina and Louisiana from being seated. Paul Douglas, senator from Illinois and a Kefauver supporter, stood not ten feet away from Rayburn, screaming for recognition until he was red-faced. Hubert Humphrey, also a coalition member, shouted, "Follow the rules!" at the speaker.[125] Rayburn, however, would have none of it. He stared straight ahead and completely ignored Douglas until he knew that he had enough delegates in the seats to defeat Douglas's motion for adjournment (which could hardly be heard by the delegates because Douglas was so hoarse). By 1:50 a.m., the convention had voted to seat both South Carolina and Louisiana despite the fact that they, like Virginia, had not signed the loyalty pledge. The coalition had been defeated. Most important, there would be no southern walkout.

The Balloting for President

Kefauver was now in the same position as all the other contenders for the nomination. The balloting would begin on Friday, 25 July, and he now had to hope that there would be a deadlocked convention and that he could deal his way to the nomination on a later ballot. However, Kefauver had few friends in those smoke-filled rooms. The first ballot went as expected. A surprisingly quick roll call had Kefauver in the lead with 340 votes; Stevenson followed with 272, then Russell with 268, Harriman with 123, Kerr with 65, Barkley with 48½, and the eight favorite sons with a total of 111.

As soon as the first ballot ended, Harry Truman boarded his plane in Washington (2:41 p.m. Chicago time) and started the two-and-a-half-hour flight to the convention. For the entire trip, he would watch the proceedings of the convention on television—the first president to do so.[126]

The second ballot saw the release of many uncommitted delegates, but the deadlock only tightened. Kefauver still led with 362½, followed by Stevenson with 324½, Russell with 294, Harriman with 121, Barkley with 78½, and favorite sons still controlling 48 delegates. As the convention recessed for dinner, all bandwagons had stopped.

As noted earlier, Truman had made it clear to Harriman that he expected him to withdraw from the race in favor of Stevenson at the request of the president. When Truman landed in Chicago, he went by motorcade to the Stockyard Inn, where he dined with Stevenson, Jake Arvey, Sam Rayburn, and Frank McKinney. During dinner, Truman pulled the plug. He sent word to the governors of Massachusetts and Arkansas—then controlling their delegations as favorite sons—to release those delegates. He then dispatched his aide Charles Murphy to contact Harriman and tell the New Yorker that his candidacy was over. Ever loyal, Harriman sent fellow New Yorker Paul Fitzpatrick to the Amphitheatre just before the start of the third ballot. Fitzpatrick withdrew Harriman's name from contention and asked Harriman's delegates to vote for Stevenson.[127] Truman would later tell an interviewer, "If I had not flown to Chicago, Stevenson could not have been nominated."[128] As was the case with many "Trumanisms," while exaggerated, this one had a grain of truth. When Stevenson's candidacy stalled on the second ballot, Harry Truman broke the logjam.

The convention was in the midst of the third ballot—the first time that committed delegates could legally switch their vote (committed as they were, by party rules, through two ballots). Suddenly, down the center aisle of the Amphitheatre, walked Kefauver and Douglas. The two men were arm in arm, patiently working their way through the throng of supporters that spilled out into the aisles to give solace to their champion. Kefauver was hoping to secure the recognition of the chair so that he might concede and turn his delegates over to Douglas; Douglas would then turn those delegates over to Stevenson.

Kefauver would later claim that his actions were meant to "help bring unity to the party and heal many political wounds, and [to get] a well-deserved ovation for Senator Douglas."[129] If so, Rayburn, who saw Kefauver's motive as little more than a cheap stunt, wasn't buying. Rayburn ordered his chief parliamentarian to tell Kefauver and Douglas to sit down. The two men were then forced to wait on the stage for two hours until the third ballot was over, a ballot that now left Stevenson only 2½ votes short of victory. When Rayburn finally recognized the humiliated Kefauver, all the senator could say was, "I know all of my friends will join in doing everything to bring the Democratic Party to victory and to elect Governor Adlai Stevenson as President of the United States."[130] Utah demanded to be recognized and switched its vote to Stevenson. The final tally: Stevenson 615½; Kefauver 255½; Russell—who never released his delegates—262; and Barkley—who, in a last gasp for an enhanced legacy, allowed his name to be placed into nomination even after he had formally withdrawn from the race—67½.[131]

"Let's Talk Sense to the American People"

A brief recess was ordered before the nominee was presented to the convention. Truman appeared to a polite ovation, and his introduction of Stevenson was short, tense, and disappointing.

Stevenson's acceptance speech on 26 July was another matter entirely. As he had done five days earlier, Stevenson once again astounded the delegates with his oratorical skill. He began hesitatingly, constantly clearing his throat and moving his eyes from the television camera at the back of the hall to the eyes of the delegates. In his usual self-deprecating manner, Stevenson spoke truth when he said that he had "not sought the honor you have done me," and then paused and waited for the applause to swell. There were audible gasps from the audience when he metaphorically threw his hands in the air and accepted his fate with a biblical injunction: "If this cup may not pass from me, except I drink it, Thy will be done." He got short, polite applause when he mentioned Barkley's service to the party, but when he mentioned Truman near the end of the speech, there was wild applause for several minutes. He also won both hearty applause and laughter when he referred to "*both* Republican parties"—the party of Taft and the party of Eisenhower—and he received wild applause when he dryly noted that Eisenhower had been called upon to "minister to a hopeless case of political schizophrenia."

Thoroughly warmed up, Stevenson boomed his way through the peroration, as he set the stage for the coming campaign. Slowly, emphatically, and with precise diction, Stevenson repeated his call from his welcoming address, reminding both the delegates and his television audience, "More important than winning the election is governing the nation. . . . Better we lose the election than mislead the people, and better we lose than misgovern the people." The lofty theme for the Stevenson campaign was set: "Let's talk sense to the American people."[132]

The Choice of Sparkman

Immediately following Stevenson's acceptance speech, the party leadership adjourned to a room behind the stage and under the speaker's platform to discuss a vice presidential candidate. Given the history of the 1948 Dixiecrat walkout, as well as the nature of the close call at the convention over the loyalty pledge, there was only one nonnegotiable requirement for this position—he had to be a southerner. Truman knew this, and he knew that despite the fact that his party had a new nominee, his input would have great weight. However, as had been the case in the process of choosing the top of the ticket, Truman did not get his first choice for veep.

Truman's first choice, and the first one who was offered the second spot on the ticket, was Richard Russell. When being interviewed in 1969 for a WSB (Atlanta) special on his life ("Richard Russell: Georgia Giant"), Russell disclosed that in 1952 he had been contacted directly by DNC chairman Frank McKinney, as well as other men whom he refused to name, and had been offered the vice presidential spot.[133] This story was corroborated by Margaret Rutledge Shannon, an *Atlanta Journal* reporter. When preparing a biography of Russell for her files, she asked the senator about the 1952 offer. Russell wrote her a letter marked "Personal/Confidential," in which he wrote that it was, indeed, McKinney, as well as "a number of Stevenson's leaders, including those who were responsible for putting his name in nomination," who had contacted him and offered him the spot.[134] While Russell would not directly say that Truman was behind the offer, he indirectly corroborated this claim when he told a member of his staff, "I resent Harry Truman bringing these people in here and bringing all this pressure on me."[135] Although the nomination was his for the taking, Russell turned McKinney down.[136] When Russell told a reporter for the *New York Times* on 1 July that the rumor that he had made a deal to run as vice president on a Stevenson-led ticket was "as despicable a falsehood as ever uttered by any man," he wasn't kidding.[137] Truman had once again been unable to corral his man.

As the leadership met underneath the stage to discuss the vice presidency, any attempt to even bring up Kefauver's name was squashed by the vindictive president. He had another southerner in mind. Truman would later remember that he "left the meeting before a decision was reached, but before leaving I suggested that Senator John Sparkman of Alabama would be the best asset to the ticket."[138]

When explaining in 1966 why he believed he had been chosen for the vice presidential nomination, Sparkman listed three factors:

1) I was a member of the drafting subcommittee of the Resolutions Committee. We had a most difficult time in drafting a civil rights plank. We had both extremes. . . . I worked very hard trying to find a

solution to this problem. . . . 2) From the time of the establishment of the Senate Small Business Committee in 1950, I had been its chairman. . . . Adlai was interested in a program for small business and took note of my activity in that field. 3) Selection of me, a Southerner, as his running mate, would help unify the party geographically.[139]

It is safe to say that no one in Chicago cared about Sparkman's concern for small business. But Sparkman was as acceptable a southerner as Truman hoped to find. His moderate voting record on all aspects of the Fair Deal, short of civil rights, made him palatable to all sections of the party. For Rayburn, for whom loyalty was as important as it was for Truman, Sparkman had been Rayburn's whip while he was in the House, and Sparkman had, pro forma, spoken out in favor of Rayburn for the presidential nomination in 1952.[140] Moreover, his crafting of a moderate civil rights plank in the 1952 Platform Hearings endeared him not only to Truman but to all Democrats who had prayed that there would not be another Dixiecrat walkout.[141]

Epilogue

Immediately following Stevenson's speech, Truman wrote the new nominee a note, gushing that the last night of the convention was "one of the most remarkable I've spent in all my sixty-eight years" and assuring him, "You have my whole-hearted support and cooperation."[142] Stevenson immediately replied to Truman, "I am grateful beyond expression for your charity and good will."[143]

If Adlai Stevenson appreciated what Harry Truman had done for him, the campaign he was about to run was a funny way of showing it.

4

THE FALL CAMPAIGN

On 26 July, John Foster Dulles, then serving as a foreign policy adviser to the Eisenhower campaign, wired Stevenson: "Tough luck that you have to try to beat the unbeatable." Stevenson scrawled his reply on the telegram: "Dear Foster—My thanks—tell the 'unbeatable' to beware these prairie politicians."[1]

EISENHOWER AS CAMPAIGN MANAGER AND THE "SURRENDER AT MORNINGSIDE HEIGHTS"

Eisenhower began the fall campaign by taking a brief vacation near Fraser, Colorado. In between sessions of fly fishing, Eisenhower's brain trust presented him with a plan for the campaign. The only problem was that they didn't consult Eisenhower—who had planned D-Day and the fall of Nazi Germany—on its contents. After a presentation that, by all accounts, treated the candidate as if he was a rank beginner in politics and knew nothing about the task at hand, Sherman Adams remembered that Eisenhower got up to leave—"his color had heightened somewhat." Adams recalled that Eisenhower later told him: "These people come up here from Washington with a well-laid plan. But I didn't know what the plan was going to be ... until they had it all wrapped up. They didn't ask me if I had a thought or a question. . . . As I sat there I didn't think they had any interest in the fact that I was going to have to win the election for them."[2]

The Denver presentation convinced Eisenhower that he needed an outward sign, both to the nation and to his own staff, that he was running his own campaign. Thus, Eisenhower named himself as his own campaign manager, with Sherman Adams as the campaign's chief of staff and "liaison officer" to the Republican National Committee (RNC).[3] His first decision involved the friction that existed between his political advisers and the Citizens for Eisenhower group. His political advisers counseled that the Citizens should be placed under the control of the regular politicians. Although the Citizens had not drafted Eisenhower, and they were, at best, only marginally responsible for his success to date, they could not be discarded. They had raised a good deal of money, and, more important, Eisenhower respected the work of the amateur politicians who made up this group. Eisenhower spoke to Walter Williams, a Washington state banker who was then serving as cochair of the Citizens, about the need to "articulat[e] all this work with the regular organization so as to minimize friction and any duplication."[4] After some amount of wrangling, on 3 August it was announced that Citizens for Eisenhower would be continued under the leadership of Williams, who would coordinate the group's efforts with Arthur Summerfield, the new chair of the RNC. For the rest of the campaign, the Citizens raised money and did a fair amount of advance work, acting as essentially an independent entry—just as Eisenhower wished.[5]

The early days of Eisenhower's campaign also presented an immediate need to deal with the vanquished Robert Taft. The situation was an extremely sensitive one. Following the Republican Convention—which had been replete with charges of delegate theft and rules violations—relations between the Eisenhower and Taft forces were virtually nonexistent. Everyone in the Eisenhower campaign believed that a rapprochement was necessary. Taft controlled his party's conservative wing, and without its support, Eisenhower's path would be that much more difficult. Moreover, if Eisenhower won the presidency, there was no doubt that Taft would remain the Republican Party's leader in the Senate. Some sort of working relationship had to be developed. There was a chance, of course, that both disaffected conservatives, who were still angry at the manner of Taft's defeat, and disaffected moderates, who did not want to miss their chance to purge their party of Taftian isolationism, would react to any "deal" between the two men with feelings of anger and betrayal. But for Eisenhower, the necessity for gaining Taft's support outweighed any political fallout that might result. On 17 July, he personally wired Taft, making the following request: to "plan a meeting to suit your convenience after your holiday is over."[6]

Taft, who was vacationing at his family's summer home at Murray Bay, Quebec, took his time in responding to Eisenhower's request. Eisenhower's telegram was not unexpected, but Taft was wary. The senator had been badly hurt by his defeat in Chicago, but he held no animus toward Eisenhower. Rather, he held Eisenhower's advisers responsible for the attacks that had been made on his honesty, and he had come to believe that those advisers were planting the seeds for a "New Deal Republican administration, perhaps dominated by Dewey."[7] As he told Indiana senator William Jenner, "I don't see any real bona fide desire on his part, or that of his followers, really to take advice from our wing of the party, or to give them any position in which they will have real influence." Plus, he felt himself in a strong enough position to demand some concessions for his support. If they were not to be met, Taft mused, "I should think it would be better to have no meeting at all."[8]

When Taft finally communicated with the Eisenhower campaign, he did so through Senator Everett Dirksen. Taft had several nonnegotiable demands. First, he required that "no discrimination be exercised against Taft people in the campaign," and that they be "considered for positions in the new administration." Second, Taft made it clear that he would expect the new administration to support a substantial tax cut and promise to defend the Taft-Hartley Act. Finally, Taft made it clear that he would not support a "spender" like Thomas Dewey for secretary of state in an Eisenhower cabinet. Taft promised that "if anything like this could be worked out," he would be glad to have a meeting with Eisenhower and was willing to "campaign vigorously for the ticket, and urge everyone to go along." Taft added, "Otherwise, I will support it, of course, but I think I would confine my speaking to those senators and congressmen in whose election I am interested."[9]

While there is no written record that Eisenhower agreed to Taft's demands as prerequisites for a meeting, he must have done so. A breakfast meeting was scheduled for 12 September at Eisenhower's home on the Columbia University campus at Morningside Heights, and without those assurances, it is unlikely that Taft would have agreed to come. In any case, after the meeting, which lasted only two hours, both Eisenhower and Taft appeared in the doorway for a quick photo, and Taft quickly left. Once away from the meeting, he released a statement saying that all his demands had been met, that he believed Eisenhower "will give this country an administration inspired by the Republican principle of continued and expanding liberty for all as against the growth of New Deal socialism which we would suffer under Governor Stevenson, representative of the left wingerism if not a left winger himself." He also promised that he would campaign actively for the ticket.[10]

Stephen A. Mitchell, the new chair of the Democratic National Committee (DNC), branded the Eisenhower-Taft meeting the "Surrender at Morningside Heights."[11] Stevenson jubilantly repeated the most pointed line of his acceptance address by painting a picture of the Republican party as a "two-headed elephant." To Stevenson, the result of the summit at Morningside was that Eisenhower had lost control of his campaign: "It looks as if Taft lost the nomination but won the nominee."[12] But Taft was satisfied. He wrote a supporter, "I feel confident that in domestic policy at least the general character of this administration will be in accord with the principles in which I believe."[13] Taft had now endorsed Eisenhower and in the final six weeks of the election would campaign for him in twenty states of the Midwest and West—decidedly more campaigning than the Eisenhower staff had dared hope for. Moreover, Taft had walked away from his breakfast at Morningside convinced that even if Eisenhower's advisers were suspect, the general himself was a true conservative.[14]

STEVENSON VERSUS TRUMAN

While Eisenhower took steps to embrace his defeated comrade, Stevenson started his campaign by taking steps to distance himself from his most ardent supporter. In so doing, Stevenson, like Eisenhower, established himself as the head of his own campaign; however, for Stevenson, the costs were high, as his actions continued a pattern that he had begun earlier that January—he infuriated Harry Truman.

Stevenson understood better than any of his advisers that Truman hung over his campaign like the sword of Damocles. In order that he be able to run the kind of campaign that he wanted, as well as gain votes from undecided voters who leaned Democratic but who were sick of war and scandal, Stevenson came to believe that he would have to distance himself from the president. He did so quickly, but he also did so gracelessly, wounding Truman in the process and making for himself an unexpected adversary in the campaign.

Only hours after the Democratic Convention had ended, Stevenson

"The Surrender at Morningside Heights," Robert A. Taft and Dwight D. Eisenhower, 12 September 1952 (Republican National Committee, courtesy of Dwight D. Eisenhower Library)

wrote to his friend Alicia Patterson, "The line to emphasize is that I am not Truman's candidate."[15] He then wrote William McCormack Blair, one of his most trusted advisers, "I mean to . . . run my own campaign my own way for my own objectives. Better to lose than to be a fictitious candidate."[16] Stevenson's first step toward a campaign declaration of independence was to set up his campaign headquarters in Springfield, not in Washington as Truman's advisers had counseled him to do. Stevenson then shocked party stalwarts by dismissing Truman's handpicked chairman of the DNC, Frank McKinney, in favor of Stephen A. Mitchell, one of Stevenson's closest personal advisers. While McKinney had made himself vulnerable as a result of his being linked to the scandals in the Reconstruction Finance Corporation that spring, Truman had made it abundantly clear that he still wanted McKinney to stay.[17] Jake Arvey was also against the move.[18] But Stevenson was adamant. On 20 August, Arvey dutifully presented Mitchell's name to the DNC, which confirmed the choice. The "de-Trumanization" program continued, as Stevenson chose Wilson Wyatt, a former mayor of Louisville, Kentucky, and a co-founder of the liberal Americans for Democratic Action (ADA), and decidedly not a party insider, as his campaign manager.[19] Stevenson also broke with the established DNC donors and struck out on his own (for example, George Ball recruited Roger L. Stevens, a theatrical producer who had recently purchased the Empire State Building, as a key fundraiser).[20] Stevenson also sent Mitchell to ask Truman if he would smooth the way for what promised to be a contentious debate on foreign policy by consenting to have Dean Acheson announce his plans to retire after the election; Truman refused.[21]

Despite his protests to the press that he was just a "buck private in the rear ranks" of the Stevenson campaign,[22] Truman was both surprised and angered by Stevenson's early choices. It is likely that the luncheon meeting at the White House on 12 August among Stevenson, Sparkman, Truman, and their staff was held as much to remind Stevenson of who was still the president as it was to provide the presidential nominee with advice and counsel.[23] But Stevenson was aloof during the interview. Moreover, even though the president made it clear that he was ready to hit the stump, Stevenson did not ask him to campaign until after the meeting, and then only by letter.[24] The strained meeting prompted Roger Tubby, then Truman's assistant press secretary, to remark, "I almost had the feeling that a Republican nominee had come into the house with his team to discuss a takeover."[25]

Stevenson had deliberately bit the hand that fed him. Truman never quite understood this insult—after all, as noted earlier, Truman believed that Stevenson owed his nomination to him. To the feisty and temperamental Truman, Stevenson was guilty of one of the cardinal sins of party politics—ingratitude. Truman's usual therapy when he was upset was to write long letters venting his frustrations, letters that were never sent to the recipient of the diatribe. One such letter to Stevenson shows just how incensed the president really was:

I have come to the conclusion that you are embarrassed by having the President of the United States in your corner in this campaign. Therefore I shall remain silent and stay in Washington until November 4. You were nominated . . . then you proceeded to break up the Democratic Committee, which I spent years in organizing, you called in the former mayor of Louisville [Wyatt] as your personal chairman and fired McKinney, the best chairman of the National Committee in my recollection. Since the convention you have treated the president as a liability. . . . I can't stand snub after snub of you and Mr.

The Democratic nominees meet with the president, 12 August 1952. *Left to right*: Harry S. Truman, John Sparkman, and Adlai E. Stevenson II (National Park Service, Abbie Rowe, courtesy of Harry S. Truman Library)

Wyatt. . . . You and Wilson can now run your campaign without interference or advice.[26]

However, a further Stevenson snub caused Truman to rethink his private promise to be quiet. On 16 August, Stevenson sent a written reply to a question posed by the *Oregon Journal*: "Can Stevenson really clean up the mess in Washington?" In this reply, which was published, Stevenson wrote: "As to whether I can clean up the mess in Washington, I would bespeak the careful scrutiny of what I inherited in Illinois and what has been accomplished in three years. . . . I can only give my best, with ruthless objectivity."[27] By repeating the word "mess," Stevenson was acknowledging that there *was* one in Washington.

Truman groused to an aide, "They are running against me, not Ike. They can't win that way."[28] At his weekly press conference on 21 August, he refused to comment on Stevenson's letter "because I know nothing about any 'mess.'" He also refused to comment on Stevenson's allegation, made the day after the release of the Oregon letter, that corruption in Washington had been "proven" since members of the Truman administration had been indicted and Sparkman's claims that Truman had mishandled the steel strike earlier that year. A furious Truman now wrote another long letter to Stevenson—which was, again, unsent—decrying Stevenson's letter to the *Oregon Herald* and bellowing, "I'm telling you to take your crackpots, your high socialites, with the noses in the air, run your campaign and win if you can. Cowfever could not have treated me any more shabbily than have you. . . . Best of luck to you from a bystander who has become disinterested."[29] In 1960, Truman would remember the 1952 campaign for *Look* magazine in an article under the title "How Stevenson Let Me Down."[30]

Not that he would be expected to, but Eisenhower didn't cooperate with Truman either. On 12 August, Truman informed the general that he had arranged for both candidates to receive weekly intelligence briefings from the CIA; he also invited Eisenhower to a "cabinet luncheon" at the White House. Eisenhower accepted the briefings, but in a telegram released to the press, he passed on the luncheon, explaining to the president, "In my current position as standard bearer of the Republican party . . . it is my duty to remain free to analyze publicly the policies and acts of the present administration whenever it appears to me to be proper and in the country's interests." Truman, who seemed to be both confused and a bit hurt by Eisenhower's public refusal, sent the general a handwritten note, professing—using many of the same words that he had used in his unsent letter to Stevenson—that he was "sorry if I caused you embarrassment. What I've always had in mind was a continuing foreign policy."[31]

Rejected both by the opposition and by the candidate of his own party, and despite the fact that he hadn't been asked, Truman now decided to hit the campaign trail. But Truman would only offer Stevenson his passing support—indeed, the two men did not appear together at any point in the campaign. Rather, in the fall of 1952, over the course of some 215 speeches of varying length and themes, Truman campaigned both against Eisenhower and for himself. The opening moments of Truman's brief speeches usually included references to Stevenson as "the most promising young leader we have had in a generation," and to Sparkman as "the son of a tenant farmer." But after the obligatory endorsements came the litany of Democratic accomplishments since 1932. One brief example from a 29 September Truman whistle-stop in Fargo, North Dakota, will suffice to illustrate:

And you people today—and the historians in the years to come—will find that the record of the administration of Harry S. Truman is a pretty good one. . . . We've crushed the communist conspiracy in this country. And we've stopped the advance of communism all over the globe. . . . The communists have been stopped cold in Korea. . . . We've maintained the prosperity and high standard of living which has become almost synonymous with having Democratic administration in Washington. So the record is good.[32]

Then Truman would light into Eisenhower. His favorite charges were as follows: that Eisenhower was the tool of Taft and the isolationists; that a victory for Eisenhower was a "blank check" for the Republicans to undo all the social gains of the past twenty years; that Eisenhower was unfit for the presidency because he was a military man; that Eisenhower was responsible for wasteful Defense Department spending while at SHAPE; that Eisenhower had agreed with the removal of troops from Korea in 1949; that Eisenhower had changed since Truman had appointed him to NATO ("Something has happened to him . . ."); and the like. Truman's tagline was revealing: "I like Ike too. I like Ike so well that I would send him back to the Army, if I had the chance. And that is what I am trying to do."[33]

The Republican response to Truman came not from Eisenhower but from his running mate. Nixon charged that Truman was "playing cheap, dirty politics" by insulting Eisenhower and predicted that the nation would resent the fact that the president had "gone AWOL" from the Oval Office to campaign when there was so much trouble in the world.[34] Nevertheless, Give-'em-Hell-Harry was still a draw. Truman's crowds greatly outnumbered those of Stevenson, although they usually were not as large as Eisenhower's.[35] When Truman returned home to Independence at the end of the campaign, he must have felt that he had done his best in the campaign to vindicate himself.

STEVENSON'S RHETORIC

The election of 1952 was the last presidential campaign to see wide use of a revered part of political Americana, one that Truman had made legend in 1948—"whistle-stopping." Both candidates spent the majority of their travel time on a train. Stevenson's train, set up much like Eisenhower's, was a completely self-contained presidential election effort. At any given time, the "Democratic Presidential Campaign Special" was home to between eighty-five and a hundred people. Stevenson lived in the rear car, which had an outside speaking platform, five compartments, a shower bath, a dining room that seated twelve, and a tiny kitchen. Directly forward were two club cars that were used for entertaining local politicos. Then came two cars for Stevenson's campaign staff, a press car, two diners, and sleepers for the press.[36] Traveling to and from major speeches, the candidate's train stopped at small towns and junctions. The candidate would emerge at the rear of the train and give a short talk to the crowd assembled at the train station. Lasting only about three minutes, these "back platform talks" paid tribute to the town's major business or crop, spent a moment or two extolling the virtues of the local candidates, and allowed time for local leaders to jump on the train to be photographed with the candidate. The train would then take the candidate to a major city where, more often than not, he would give a speech to a large audience, usually carried on the radio and sometimes broadcast on television. Those who could not hear the speech could read about it the next day in any number of daily newspapers, which, in the manner of the day, printed the candidate's major addresses in their entirety.

It is generally accepted Stevenson's speeches were the greatest legacy of his campaign of 1952. There can be no debate here. Masterpieces of the written word, full of wit and poignancy, Stevenson's speeches still make excellent reading. Stevenson is the only *defeated* presidential candidate who published his campaign speeches and had them become a best seller[37] (one British reporter cooed that Stevenson's speeches were "in the tradition of Lincoln's great and thoughtful speeches").[38] However, to understand fully the impact of Stevenson's speeches on the election, one must look far beyond how well they were written. Both the problems caused by Stevenson's choice of speechwriters and the problems caused by Stevenson's style of delivery contributed to his inability to creep closer to Eisenhower in the polls.

Stevenson's speechwriters took up residence on the third floor of Springfield's tiny Elks Club Lodge. They were young (the average age of the Stevenson staff was 32.7 years), and they ran their operation, according to one reporter, as a "study in informality" with a "homey touch."[39] The most widely known of what was soon dubbed the "Elks Club Group" was Arthur M. Schlesinger Jr. A leading liberal intellectual at age thirty-four (winner of the 1946 Pulitzer Prize for his book *The Age of Jackson*), the former Harriman supporter was personally recruited by Stevenson as a writer of speeches on domestic policy. Schlesinger was joined by David Bell, a White House staffer whom Truman had loaned to the Stevenson campaign; W. Willard Wirtz, who had served on the War Labor Board and the Wage Stabilization Board; and Robert W. Tufts, who had worked in the State Department and was the chief contributor in foreign affairs. Others included poet and former Librarian of Congress Archibald MacLeish; Pulitzer Prize–winning poet and Roosevelt speechwriter Robert Sherwood; historian Bernard DeVoto; Washington journalist Sidney Hyman; former Roosevelt speechwriter Samuel I. Rosenman; Senator Clifford Anderson of New Mexico; Harvard economist John Kenneth Galbraith; *Saturday Evening Post* writer and future Stevenson biographer John Bartlow Martin; and Stevenson confidant George Ball.[40]

However, Stevenson chafed at their drafts, which he believed did not represent his true political philosophy. He believed, and later testimony from the Elks showed him to be correct, that his speechwriters were trying to push him to sound more liberal than he really was (Stevenson to Rosenman: "The fact of the matter is, I must keep in character, and I *am* a moderate, I suppose").[41] Moreover, thanks to their progressive credentials (Schlesinger and Galbraith had been charter members of the ADA), it did not take long for the Eisenhower campaign to set its sights on the Elks Club. Summerfield led the attack in early August when he accused Stevenson of putting together "an organization that would out-Truman the Truman regime in leading the nation down the road to complete socialism."[42]

Stevenson cared very much about the crafting of his speeches. He carefully edited each draft that came from the Elks Club, sometimes revising the talk as he sat on the platform. However, Stevenson showed very little interest in the delivery of his speeches. He would walk onto the podium with his script in a black leather loose-leaf notebook, which close friend Alistair Cooke quipped made the candidate look "like an economics professor on his way to a lecture."[43] Stevenson would then read through his prepared speech—rarely stopping to look up over his glasses at the audience, who were usually struggling to understand his elegant prose and his wry attempts at humor. His speeches were more provocative essays in political affairs than they were pieces of rhetorical persuasion. Extemporizing was an alien talent to Stevenson; he was not good at it, and he rarely tried it.[44] Indeed, these carefully written tracts were read at an audience who simply wanted to be talked to. The problems with Stevenson's speeches are nicely encapsulated in this observation by George Ball, taken from his memoir:

> Reading his speech from manuscript, he often failed to look at the camera, inclining his head so that the light beat glaringly on his shining forehead. . . . In addition, he had a habit that suggested a tic: punctuating his comments by flashing on and off a quick smile, which conveyed the unfortunate impression of artificiality and even insincerity. Nevertheless, as we listened to the speeches we felt enormously proud. Our candidate had "class"; he was not a plodding five star general uttering pedestrian language written by some journalistic hack.[45]

Stevenson knew that he had a problem connecting with his audiences.[46] The solution that both he and his campaign devised was an emphasis on prepared, lengthy speeches and a de-emphasis on impromptu appearances and press conferences. This solution would put Stevenson in the milieu in which he felt the most comfortable.[47] However, this only widened the gap between Stevenson and the electorate. Unlike in 1948, there would be very little hell given from the Democratic candidate in 1952. Perhaps this was the curse that an intellectual in politics carried. Mitchell observed that Stevenson was "enormously informed in national and world affairs, but completely naïve in such popular areas as moving pictures and baseball."[48] Reporter Stewart Alsop noticed the dilemma that Stevenson was creating for himself with his speeches and gave the problem a name that would stick with Stevenson for the rest of his career. To Alsop, the only people who could understand Stevenson's speeches were fellow intellectuals, whom the reporter dubbed "egg-heads," all of whom loved Stevenson. But, as Alsop mused in a column, "How many egg-heads do you think there are?"[49]

EISENHOWER'S RHETORIC

Eisenhower's speeches were born on the ninth floor of the Commodore Hotel in New York. The most influential members of his speechwriting staff were C. D. Jackson and Emmet John Hughes (both of whom were taking a leave of absence from *Time* magazine). They were aided, as schedules permitted, by Herbert Brownell and Harold Stassen. These men drafted the speeches that were sent to the Eisenhower campaign train (the "Look Ahead Neighbor Special") to be vetted and edited by the on-train speech staff. That group included Gabriel Hauge, the research director for Citizens for Eisenhower; Arthur Vandenberg Jr., son of the senator from Michigan and former chairman of the New York branch of Citizens for Eisenhower; Kevin McCann, Eisenhower's former chief of staff at SHAPE and president of Defiance College; Senator Frank Carlson; and Milton Eisenhower, brother of the candidate and president of Pennsylvania State University. Unlike their counterparts at the Springfield Elks Club, Eisenhower's speechwriters showed no ideological enthusiasm. As Hughes remembered it: "Zeal never stirred these councils. Debate was never profound. Panic was unknown. Passion would have seemed strange."[50]

Unlike his opponent, Eisenhower was more interested in crafting a "talk" than he was a "speech." In order to achieve the simplification of language that he desired, he often had staff members read their drafts aloud to him so that he might hear how the speech sounded when delivered.[51] As Hughes would later write, Eisenhower "rebelled against rhetoric. He distrusted abstractions. He shied from generalizations. . . . As the word should be plain, the concept should be concrete."[52]

Eisenhower was far from a sophisticated speaker. Once during the campaign, when a technician scrolled his teleprompter too slowly, the candidate could be heard mumbling, "Go ahead, go ahead, yeah, damn it, I want him to move up!"[53] But ultimately, this didn't matter. Eisenhower strove for, and more often than not achieved, a talk that could be understood by the common voter and did not sound as if it were written by an egghead. This is not to suggest that Eisenhower could not deliver a formal, set speech—he could. Yet he rarely bored, confused, or intimidated an audience. He had a feel for the vernacular that Stevenson neither had nor tried greatly to acquire. For example, during his first southern swing, Eisenhower honed three down-home laugh lines for discussing the economy. The first involved a reference to his wife, claiming she had been "giving me the dickens about prices." Then he explained Democratic taxes to his audience by making fun of their breakfast: "You put a boiled egg on your table . . . and on that egg you are paying 100 taxes that you don't know anything about."[54] The third technique involved a notched board, which was painted to resemble a large dollar bill. As Eisenhower spoke, he knocked off sections of the board to show how the value of the dollar had shrunk.[55] One can hardly imagine Stevenson being comfortable with appearing on the train's back platform in a bathrobe, or singing along with a crowd of Texans who wanted to serenade the candidate at 2:00 a.m.[56] These stunts, which would have been completely foreign to Stevenson—a candidate who once dodged the task of kissing a baby by telling its parent that he had not had the time to wash and that his germs could be harmful to a child[57]—drew laughter, applause, and nods of approval when performed by the general.

THE INVASION OF THE SOUTH

Once he and Taft had buried the hatchet, Eisenhower sought to quell the fears of those, like Taft, who worried that he would run a Deweyesque, "me-too" campaign. Stevenson had decided to concentrate his campaign swings in the West—those states that had bolted their past Republican allegiance and gone for Truman in 1948—and virtually ignore the Northeast and the South, where he felt Democratic influence to be the strongest.[58] Sensing an opening, Eisenhower told his staff that he wanted to, in his words, "invade the so-called 'Solid South.'"[59] He was opposed in his decision by many members of his staff. With the single exception of Hoover's 1928 victory, the South had been solidly Democratic since the Civil War, and they saw any time spent campaigning south of Virginia as wasted. However, Eisenhower knew that there were Dixiecrat votes in the South that were ripe for the picking, a point of view that was seconded by many southern politicians, including Maryland governor Theodore McKeldin, who had placed Eisenhower's name in nomination at the convention ("The ground is still fertile. Discontent with the opposition's policies and behavior in the administration of the nation remains rife. Your prospects for carrying some of the Southern states continues excellent").[60] Eisenhower's instincts prevailed, and on 2–3 September, a Republican candidate for president crossed the Mason-Dixon Line for the first time in decades. It was one of the boldest moves of the campaign on either side, and the one that would have the most far-reaching political consequence.

The four-state tour, the first of three such southern campaign swings for Eisenhower that fall, was a triumph. In Atlanta (the campaign not so coincidentally arrived on the eighty-eighth anniversary of General William T. Sherman's entry into the city in 1864), Eisenhower was greeted by Democratic governor Herman Talmadge and given a ticker tape parade down Peachtree Street.[61] In Jacksonville, Miami, Tampa, Birmingham—the heart of Sparkman country—and Little Rock, the reception was much the same, and the message was the same: that Stevenson, who had yet to schedule a campaign swing in the South, was taking the region's votes for granted.[62] Eisenhower would also deliver a major address in Richmond on 26 September—which was one more address than Dewey gave in the state in 1948.[63]

Campaign stops were not the only thing that Eisenhower did to make inroads in the South. Aside from stating his opposition to a compulsory, federally administered Fair Employment Practice Commission (FEPC), Eisenhower spoke little on civil rights, either in the North or in the South. The one speech in which he dealt with the issue at any length was a talk given in late October outside the Hotel Theresa in Harlem. Eisenhower condescendingly reminded his audience that many blacks had served during World War II, that they fought on the front lines, and that they had "relatively safe billets." Notwithstanding these platitudes, he did not mention civil rights once in the speech.[64] However, Eisenhower did promise that he would accept a qualified African American into his cabinet and stated that he would bar from appointive office in his administration anyone whose actions opposed equality of race or religion.[65] This was more than offset by Eleanor Roosevelt's endorsement of Stevenson, enthusiastically given at a rally in Harlem on 5 October.[66]

In the past, Roosevelt's and Truman's vague promises to blacks had been enough to keep the white southern vote solidly in the Democratic column. But despite entreaties to southern leaders like Virginia's John Battle (where Stevenson argued weakly that a compulsory FEPC "could not be passed anyway"),[67] Stevenson's past support of a permanent FEPC in Illinois unnerved southerners. Put plainly, the South did not trust him, and with good reason. Had Stevenson decided to remain as hazy in his speeches on civil rights as were the civil rights planks of his party's platform, he might have done better in the South. He began in this fashion, at first arguing that the FEPC needed to be a state-controlled, not a federally mandated, organization.[68] This brought howls of derision from the black community; Representative Adam Clayton Powell of New York, for example, called for a black "boycott" of the election unless Stevenson took a more forthright stand on civil rights.[69] Recognizing the significance of the black vote, Stevenson recruited Averell Harriman to help him face down the black community. On 7 August, the two men met with Roy Wilkins, executive secretary of the National Association for the Advancement of Colored People (NAACP), for almost two hours. At the meeting, Stevenson discussed his opposition to the Senate filibuster, as well as how he would potentially use Sparkman to help break Senate Rule 22 on cloture. Wilkins left the meeting believing that Stevenson was "more relaxed than Roosevelt, more in tune with racial issues," and told NAACP president Walter White, whom Wilkins was representing, that Stevenson would make a good president.[70] Satisfied, the NAACP endorsed Stevenson in early September.[71] This, plus Stevenson's opposition to cloture, kept the black vote in the Democratic column. However, his strong civil rights stance stood to cost him in the South.

Stevenson was also hurt in the South by his strong, impolitic stand on the Tidelands oil issue. The main reason for the break between the Shivercrats and the Truman wing of the party was over the question of control of the Tidelands; Truman's two vetoes of bills giving the states control over the offshore oil deposits had angered Texas governor Allan Shivers enough that he considered bolting his party. And Eisenhower, who had already made it clear that he was in favor of the states retaining control of the oil, was waiting with open arms.[72]

Despite the fact that he had ultimately signed the loyalty pledge at the convention, few Democrats fully trusted Shivers. Recognizing the need to keep Shivers in the fold and Texas Democratic in the fall, Stevenson met with Shivers on the issue before the convention adjourned and wrote him in early August, confessing, "I am woefully ignorant about the Tidelands business and would welcome your views."[73] A meeting was set for 23 August. The two men met at the executive mansion in Springfield for four and a half hours. In midafternoon, Shivers emerged, smiled to reporters, and walked off to visit a friend. When he returned to the mansion, Stevenson handed him a statement that said he agreed with the 1950 Supreme Court decision, which said that the Tidelands oil belonged to the federal government. Shivers grumbled to reporters: "This is going to be rough in Texas. I don't know what is going to happen."[74] What happened was that without proclaiming himself a Dixiecrat, Shivers returned to Texas and announced that he was not going to vote for Stevenson and Sparkman.[75] At the Texas Democratic Convention in September, Shivers supported the inclusion of Stevenson and Sparkman on the state ballot but engineered the convention's endorsement of Eisenhower.[76] Shivers, who was running for reelection as governor, cross-filed as a Republican.[77]

For his part, Eisenhower filled the breach nicely, as he announced in his third campaign tour of the South—a 13–15 October swing through Louisiana and Texas—that he would approve any future acts of Congress that would give the states control over the Tidelands.[78] Sam Rayburn, to whom Shivers had promised that if his delegation was seated at the convention, he would support the party's nominee, was furious. The speaker growled, "He lied to me. . . . I don't want the son of a bitch at my funeral."[79]

The South was peeling away from the Democratic Party. The *Richmond Times-Dispatch* was correct in its assessment: "Dixie Leaders Back Stevenson but without Real Enthusiasm."[80] Richard Russell went on a South American vacation in midcampaign; when he returned, he did not campaign for the Democratic ticket. As was his wont, Russell's protégé, Lyndon Johnson, issued a release announcing that he would "support the nominees of the Democratic party," even though "I thoroughly disagree with Governor Stevenson on his views regarding ownership of our Texas Tidelands."[81] Without saying that he was voting for Eisenhower, Harry Byrd of Virginia announced in a 17 October radio address that he could not, "in good conscience, endorse the national Democratic platform or the Stevenson-Sparkman ticket."[82] Other leaders, however, formally abandoned the Democratic ticket for Eisenhower. Chief among these was former secretary of state and South Carolina governor Jimmy Byrnes. On 18 September, Byrnes announced that he was going to "place my loyalty to my country above loyalty to a political party and vote for General Dwight D. Eisenhower";[83] he then proceeded to campaign actively for Eisenhower throughout the South. While there was no organized Dixiecrat opposition in 1952—the defeat of the Northern Coalition over the loyalty pledge had seen to that—it looked like the result might be the same as it had been in 1948.

TELEVISION ADVERTISING

One of the most important legacies of the 1952 election was born in the locker room of the Rhode Island Golf Club. From there, several Eisenhower supporters who were looking for a slogan that was as catchy as Truman's 1948 "You Never Had It So Good!" called Rosser Reeves. Reeves was with the Ted Bates Company, an advertising firm that generally handled accounts for packaged goods such as Carter's Little Liver Pills and Colgate Dental Cream.[84] After testing the early campaign speeches of both Eisenhower and Stevenson, as well as remembering Douglas MacArthur's keynote address (Reeves: "It stank"), Reeves decided to go for broke. Rather than pitch just a slogan, he decided to propose a full television spot campaign to the Citizens for Eisenhower (imaginatively code-named "Operation Spot"). While no American presidential candidate had ever before signed on to a full-fledged television campaign (Dewey had been shown an idea for a television spot campaign by the same Ted Bates Company in 1948),[85] Reeves's arguments were compelling: low cost, high chance of reaching undecided voters, flexible targeting, and, his key argument, "spots were more memorable." The Citizens took Reeves's proposal to the RNC. Robert Humphreys, the RNC's public relations director, presented the plan to both Eisenhower and Nixon on 7 August. Eisenhower approved the plan. Reeves immediately took a six-week leave from Bates and wrote the spots, finishing them on the day they were to begin filming.[86]

Eisenhower hated the idea of making television advertisements, believing them to be demeaning. But he had been sold by Reeves on their potential worth. He would make them, but he would give Reeves only one day of his time. On 11 September, with Milton by his side, Eisenhower came to Manhattan to film a total of thirty-one spots.[87] Eisenhower may have hated doing them, but he was a natural. Each advertisement was entitled "Eisenhower Answers America." These ads were deceptively simple and amazingly effective. An "Everyman" on the street—a trained actor chosen by Reeves—would pose a question, or voice a concern, to Eisenhower. Then in a simple one-shot, Eisenhower would answer that question, looking right into the camera. In one example, a man grabbed the lapel of his suit coat and exclaimed: "General, this suit cost me sixty dollars. I used to buy the same for thirty dollars." Eisenhower responded to the camera: "You paid a hundred and one taxes on that suit, and next year you may pay two hundred, unless you vote for a change."[88] Stevenson was never mentioned in these ads. The "Eisenhower Answers America" ads began to air on Friday, 24 October; they ran through Election Day. The total cost for producing the ads and buying the television time was $2 million.[89]

However, before the spots were scheduled to air, copies of Reeves's advertising plan were leaked. After reading a copy, George Ball pounced; he charged the Republicans with trying to "sell an inadequate ticket to the American people in precisely the way they sell soap, ammoniated toothpaste, hair tonic or bubble gum."[90] Stevenson, who professed not to watch television, was appalled; he told a CBS executive, "This is the worst thing I've ever heard of, selling the presidency like cereal."[91] Indeed, if Stevenson truly believed, as he was to later write, that "people might be better served if a party purchased a half hour of radio and TV silence during which the audience would be asked to think quietly for themselves,"[92] it shows only how little he understood the revolution that was television. But as Stephen C. Wood, a professor of communication, points out in his study of the ad campaign, the whining of the Democrats was disingenuous; they, too, wanted to air spots, but they simply didn't have as much money as the Republicans.[93]

And the money had drastically changed. Between 1940 and 1948, the total advertising costs for the fall presidential campaigns of the two major parties had actually been going *down* (1940: total $6.3 million spent; 1944, $5.0 million; 1948, $4.9 million). The election of 1952 would drastically reverse that trend. A total of $11,640,000 was spent on advertising (Republicans spent $6,610,000; Democrats $5,030,000)—an increase of 138 percent. From that date on, every electoral cycle would see an increase in spending for advertising.[94]

LIBERATION

With the Korean War still white-hot, it is hardly surprising that the Eisenhower campaign chose to lash out at Truman's foreign policy. Yet at the beginning of the campaign, the center of the foreign policy controversy was not the Far East; it was instead Eastern Europe. The first great foreign policy debate centered on the question of the liberation of the people of the Iron Curtain nations from Soviet rule.

The European policy outlined by Eisenhower was one that had been expounded for some time by his newly appointed chief adviser in foreign affairs. John Foster Dulles was born in 1888 in Washington, DC, but was raised in Watertown, New York. He attended Princeton University and George Washington University Law School. Dulles specialized in international law and was a staff attorney at the Versailles Peace Conference following World War I in 1919. As an adviser to Senator Arthur H. Vandenberg (R-MI), he took part in the 1945 San Francisco Conference that created the United Nations and helped draft the UN Charter. A prominent New York attorney, Dulles was a confidant of Dewey's, serving as the governor's foreign policy adviser in both the 1944 and the 1948 presidential campaigns. Dewey appointed his friend to fulfill the unexpired Senate term of Robert Wagner, who resigned in July 1949, but Dulles was defeated by Herbert Lehman in a special election held later that year. Although there was no love lost between Truman and Dulles, the president responded to congressional and public criticism of his foreign policy by bringing Dulles into the administration as a bipartisan foreign policy adviser in 1950. He would resign this position in March 1952 to advise within the Republican Party; on 20 May, he met with Taft to tell him that he was now an Eisenhower man.[95]

Raised in a rigidly Presbyterian home, Dulles had the worldview of a strict Calvinist. For Dulles, the Soviet Union was, in all things, morally wrong. It had, in his words, "trampled [a] moral and natural law," for which it "can and should be made to pay." In the same article, Dulles argued that America should begin to work for the "liberation" of the captive peoples of Eastern Europe, a liberation that would bring about their "separation from Moscow," with the end result being not only their freedom but also a "heavy burden on their jailers."[96]

Both Taft and Eisenhower saw the value of signing on to the policy of liberation. For Taft, it was a strategy made to order to galvanize his conservative base; for Eisenhower, it allowed him to downplay gracefully his views on mutual security—which had so angered the right wing of his party—and adopt a more Taftian view.[97] Both men agreed to the Dulles-written foreign policy plank in the Republican platform, part of which stated that the United States, "as one of its peaceful purposes, looks happily forward to the genuine independence of these captive people [in Eastern Europe]."[98] On 25 August, before the national convention of the American Legion being held in Madison Square Garden, Eisenhower embraced the issue, arguing that the Soviet Union was "attempting to make all human kind [sic] its chattel," challenging the Truman record in attempting to free those nations and promising the cheering audience that "the conscience of America shall never be free until these peoples have the opportunity to choose their own path."[99]

Of course, the liberation policy was, at least in part, designed in the hopes of the Republicans making inroads into the sizable Polish American, Czech American, and Hungarian American vote, which had been a key part of the Roosevelt/Truman coalition. Moreover, as Robert Divine has accurately observed, Stevenson was hardly soft on the issue of communism during the campaign, speaking repeatedly about the differences between the "free world" and the enslaved world.[100] Stevenson, however, believed that Eisenhower's policy of liberation was a very sheer cover for a warmongering desire to send a NATO force to invade Eastern Europe. On Labor Day, Stevenson shot back at Eisenhower in front of a largely Polish American audience at Hamtramck, Michigan:

The cruel grip of Soviet tyranny upon your friends and relatives cannot be loosened by loose talk or idle threats . . . [and] it cannot be loosened by starting a war which would lead to untold suffering. . . . Such a course could liberate only broken, silent, and empty lands. . . . I want to make one thing very plain: even if votes could be won by it, I would not say one reckless word on this matter during this campaign. Some things are more precious than votes.[101]

In Philadelphia, Eisenhower countered by promising that he would only use peaceful means to roll back the Iron Curtain,[102] and the pro-Eisenhower *Time* magazine scoffed at Stevenson's line of argument: "The point: concessions with the Communists have almost always made coexistence with them harder, not easier."[103]

Eisenhower joined liberation with another time-tested campaign theme—that it was "time for a change." By mid-September, he was hammering at the Truman administration, whose members he described as "incompetent fumblers, mossbacks, cronies, crooks, and the disloyal."[104] After he had worked his crowd into a frenzy, he made it clear that it was time for them to go, quoting the book of Ecclesiastes to remind his audience that there was "a time to keep and a time to cast away."[105]

Yet just as the entire issue began to heat up, liberation was pushed to the back burner. For a moment, it was replaced by one of the most famous tempests in a teapot in American political history.

THE NIXON FUND CRISIS

We must begin an analysis of what the press gleefully dubbed the "Nixon Fund Crisis" with an important observation—one that has eluded virtually every analyst of the affair. In the grand scheme of the 1952 campaign, the affair was of little importance. Americans have never voted for a national ticket because of the vice presidential candidate, nor did they do so in 1952. What happened to Richard Nixon was of seminal importance to his later career but in 1952, it meant little to the outcome of the election. What it was, however, was a useful case study in how both Eisenhower and his staff might be expected to manage a political crisis, both as candidate and as president.

Up to mid-September, Nixon's role in the campaign had been the traditional part reserved for the vice presidential candidate. He was expected to quickly take the offensive. This meant a swinging attack on the

The Republican ticket, Dwight D. Eisenhower and Richard M. Nixon,
August 1952 (courtesy of National Archives, White House Photo Office
Collection, Nixon Administration)

Democratic candidates, designed—as had been his congressional and
senatorial campaigns—less to engage his opponents in a serious discussion (or any other kind of discussion) of the issues than to keep them off
balance and continually having to decide whether or not to respond to
Nixon's attacks: attacks that were designed to paint Stevenson as liberal
as possible. Appreciating the moment, Nixon took to the campaign trail
with relish. Moving right into Springfield, within literal earshot of the
Elks Club, Nixon roared, "Adlai Stevenson owes his nomination not to
the people, but to the bosses. . . . I challenge him to be specific and tell
the American people in plain English wherein he disagrees with the
Truman-ADA program."[106]

On Sunday, 14 September, Nixon appeared on NBC's *Meet the Press*,
where he repeated his oft-used line branding Stevenson as a captive
of Truman.[107] After the interview, Nixon was approached by one of the
panelists, syndicated columnist Peter Edson of the Newspaper Enter-
prise Association (NEA). Edson quietly asked Nixon about a story that
had been kicking around since the convention—that Nixon was getting

financial support from a special fund set up by a select group of wealthy Californians. Nixon admitted the existence of the fund to Edson (who would later say that Nixon "didn't attempt to duck the questions in any way")[108] and referred Edson to his personal lawyer, Dana Smith, who willingly explained the fund in greater detail.

Following his discussion with Smith, Edson wrote his story, sending a prepublication proof to Nixon on 17 September (Edson: "Thanks for making this information available to me").[109] The next day, 18 September, Edson's story was carried in NEA affiliate papers around the country with the following lead: "Republican Vice Presidential candidate Richard M. Nixon has been receiving an extra expense allowance from 50 to 100 well-to-do Southern California political angels ever since he entered the Senate in 1951. Over the past two years these contributions have amounted to approximately $17,000."[110] Nixon immediately confirmed the facts of the story but insisted that the fund was used for mailings and other political expenses that he did not feel should be charged to the federal government, and he blamed the communists for the fact that he was being singled out for something that was common practice in Washington.[111]

Most of those who have analyzed the Nixon fund have argued that at this point in the story, both Nixon and Smith were naive to the potential impact of Edson's story. Another, more appropriate way to view the emerging story is that at this point, Edson had unearthed very little of importance. The fund had been the brainstorm of Murray Chotiner and Dana Smith, who proposed that Nixon maintain a year-round campaign chest after his 1950 Senate victory. A man of modest wealth in 1950, Nixon made only $12,500 per annum in salary as a senator, along with about $75,000 for telephone, telegraph, stationery, and staff expenses. The fund would cover transportation to California (Nixon's senatorial allowance covered only one trip home per year), political mailings, radio and television broadcasts, and even Christmas cards. A maximum of $500 per contributor was scrupulously maintained, and the money was put into a trust fund.

The fund was hardly a secret. Virtually everyone in California Republican politics knew about it, but until Edson's "discovery," it was simply not deemed important. Thus, Nixon and Smith reacted properly to Edson's questions. They told him about the fund because there simply was not much of a story there. There was no way they could have known that the tenor of the story was about to change.

But change it did, and literally overnight. Smith had also spoken to Leo Katcher, the West Coast correspondent for the *New York Post*. On Thursday, 18 September, the same day that Edson's story appeared, the *Post* ran a banner headline, blaring "SECRET NIXON FUND." Katcher's story embellished Edson's sober reporting, charging that a "secret" fund (which, as Edson had already reported, it was not) "keeps Nixon in style far beyond his salary" (even a surface examination of the fund showed that it did not).[112] But the truth mattered little. Nixon had been hoisted on his own petard—he had been denigrated; now the question would be, would he respond?

Many scholars have pointed to the obvious—when compared with the colossal sums of money that pass as political contributions today, the Nixon fund was but a drop in the bucket. What is often missed is that even for 1952, the fund was a drop in the bucket. Moreover, it was all accounted for, it paid for minor expenses, and it was perfectly legal. Stevenson even had a personal fund, one that was created from late contributions to his 1948 gubernatorial campaign and had been used to supplement the salaries of some of his staffers.[113] Nixon recognized the story for what it was—hardball politics. He knew just what to do—ignore it, and it would blow over. Thus, he laid low on the issue; all requests for interviews, even those pitched as an opportunity to "explain his side of the story," were refused.[114]

However, the Eisenhower campaign panicked. First, it demanded that Smith release to the press a full list of the donors to the fund. Smith did so on Saturday, 20 September. The list contained seventy-six names, with all but one of the donors contributing between $10 and $100 (one gave $1,000, in two $500 installments). The fund totaled $18,235.[115] Then Sherman Adams initiated and Paul Hoffman supervised a legal and financial investigation of the fund.[116] An independent audit by Price Waterhouse accounted for all but $66.13, noting that the biggest chunk of expense was for Christmas card engraving ($4,237.34). A legal opinion, issued by Gibson, Dunn, and Crutcher of Los Angeles, concluded that the fund was absolutely legal. Both reports were released to a now starving press on Monday, 22 September.[117]

Milton Eisenhower later wrote that his brother was "one of the few prominent Republicans who was not panicked by the story."[118] Eisenhower's own actions suggest otherwise. The order to investigate was in itself a sign of alarm. Moreover, Nixon knew that the entire issue would be defused if Eisenhower simply stated his unqualified trust in his running mate. But to Nixon's exasperation, Eisenhower refused to do so. On the morning of 19 September—before the release of the audits—Eisenhower issued a statement praising Nixon's "American faith and his determination to drive Communistic sympathizers from offices of public trust" and indicating that he "believe[d] Dick Nixon to be an honest man."[119] This fell far short of an unqualified statement of support for Nixon, and Nixon knew it. In fact, the panic was leading the Eisenhower campaign to consider the ultimate act of desperation. Word had leaked that during a supposedly off-the-record conversation with the press, Eisenhower had blurted: "Of what avail is it for us to carry out this crusade against this business of what has been going on in Washington if we, ourselves, aren't as clean as a hound's tooth?"[120] Speculation ran wild; it seemed that the Eisenhower campaign was considering dropping Nixon from the ticket.[121] There was clearly evidence to support this conclusion. William Knowland, the senior senator from California and, according to several accounts, Taft's choice for the vice presidential nomination after Nixon had refused his offer, was summoned from his Hawaiian vacation; he joined the Eisenhower train, and word was leaked that he was about to be named as Nixon's replacement. The *New York Herald Tribune*, whose editor, William Robinson, was a well-known Eisenhower confidant, called for Nixon's resignation on its editorial page. Harold Stassen sent Eisenhower what Stewart Alsop later described as a "long, pompous wire asking him to withdraw."[122] Dewey wanted Nixon off the ticket; Clay wanted Nixon off the ticket. Only Brownell, Summerfield, and Bob Humphreys counseled some amount of patience.[123]

Nixon now felt, quite correctly, that he was campaigning for his political life. He was angry both at Eisenhower's inaction and at the collusion of members of Eisenhower's staff who, now that they had prolonged this crisis, felt that the only way to end it was to end Nixon. Nixon's first conversation with Eisenhower since the appearance of the story served only to convince Nixon that this was true. On the evening of Sunday, 21 September, Eisenhower finally telephoned Nixon. In the course of that conversation, Eisenhower ordered him to appear the following Tuesday night on television and radio and give a speech—a speech that had been Bob Humphreys's idea[124]—and explain his side of the story. For his part, Eisenhower said that he would not issue a statement of support until after Nixon had made his appeal, saying that if he did, "in effect, people will accuse me of condoning wrongdoing." To Nixon, this was an implicit indictment; he was now convinced that Eisenhower himself wanted him off the ticket (as he would later write, "Eisenhower would not have objected if I had told him that I was going to submit a resignation to him").[125] Exhausted, and at his wit's end with Eisenhower, Nixon exploded: "There comes a time like this when you've either got to shit or get off the pot."[126]

Eisenhower immediately got off the pot and increased the pressure on Nixon. The next day, the *New York Times* quoted an unnamed source who claimed that either Nixon or the Eisenhower campaign would soon be releasing an announcement that Nixon was dropping out of the race—a claim that Nixon flatly denied. Then, on 23 September, only moments before Nixon was to deliver his speech, Eisenhower had Dewey call Nixon to tell him that it was the consensus of both Eisenhower and his advisers that upon concluding his speech, Nixon should publicly withdraw from the ticket.[127] Nixon had been given a direct order, and in his pregame state, he detonated, telling Dewey: "Just tell them that I haven't the slightest idea . . . what I'm going to do," and "I know something about politics too!"[128]

What would become known as the "Checkers Speech," which the RNC paid to have broadcast over a national hookup of 64 NBC television stations, 194 CBS radio stations, and all 560 radio stations of the Mutual Network,[129] was not the pioneer use of live television in politics. That honor is reserved for the Kefauver Crime Committee. But the speech saved Nixon's political career. He was clearly a natural in front of the camera, treating it not as an adversary (as he seemed to in 1960 when debating John F. Kennedy) but as a direct conduit to the American people, who would help him convince his adversaries—not the Democrats but now Eisenhower and his advisers—of his innocence. While staring directly into the lone camera at Hollywood's El Capitan Theatre, he looked like any other citizen: respectfully, yet defiantly, pleading his case against the government in court.

Thus, Nixon's speech was deliberately crafted to sound like a bill of particulars—a list of specific shards of evidence designed to show that he had been unfairly maligned both in the press and by the Eisenhower campaign. From the opening sentence—"I have come before you tonight as a candidate for the Vice Presidency and as a man whose honesty and integrity has been questioned"—Nixon set himself up as a hunted man, one who professed not to understand why he was being hunted. Noting that he was taking the effort to explain himself, while the Truman administration's policy toward charges of corruption was to "either ignore them or to deny them without giving details," Nixon announced that he would now give details that would show that the fund was "not a secret," not "morally wrong," and had not padded his own pocket.

In this, Nixon was absolutely accurate. But that fact was well known to Eisenhower and his advisers, who were ready to dump Nixon regardless. Believing that Eisenhower was no longer his ally, Nixon moved to get the American people in his corner. He did so by eliciting the empathy of the audience toward his financial woes. He lamented that like most of them, his salary was small and his expenses were high ("I don't happen to be a rich man"), and that while Sparkman had paid his wife to work in his Senate office (a common practice among congressmen, and true enough in Sparkman's case), Nixon's wife, Pat, had volunteered her time in her husband's office just so he could keep his head above water. He then turned to a classic Horatio Algerish recitation of his middle-class existence ("Our family was of modest circumstances. . . . I worked my way through college. . . . We had a rather difficult time. . . . We've got a house in Washington, which cost $41,000, and on which we owe $20,000. . . . Pat doesn't have a mink coat, but she does have a respectable Republican cloth coat"). But the clincher, which resonated with almost every middle-class family in America, was that Nixon owned a dog—no matter that the little black cocker spaniel was a gift to his two daughters from a political admirer in Texas: "Regardless of what they say about it, we are going to keep it."

Nixon had completely connected with his audience. Like any good advertising copywriter, he now moved to get them to take action. The action he needed was no less than that which would ensure he remain on the ticket despite Dewey's warning. Nixon did so with a gutsy play that was mixed with no small amount of revenge for how he had been treated over the past six days. He began his peroration by demanding that both Stevenson and Sparkman "make a complete financial statement as to their financial history." He suggested, "If they don't, it will be an admission that they have something to hide." Some days earlier, Nixon had become the first candidate for either president or vice president to voluntarily release any part of his financial status. Now, in the first part of the "Checkers Speech," he had released even more personal financial information to the public. If Stevenson and Sparkman agreed to release their information, that, by implication, left only Eisenhower. Instantly picking up on Nixon's challenge, the general, watching the performance from the crow's nest–level office of the manager of the Cleveland

Public Auditorium, where he was scheduled to speak later that evening, rammed his pencil into the legal pad onto which he was taking notes.[130] (It would later be speculated that Eisenhower was particularly upset because releasing his financials would make public the fact that he had claimed the large sum of money he had received for his first memoir, *Crusade in Europe*, as a capital gain, paying only a 25 percent tax on that income rather than the regular income tax rate.)[131] Nixon had made his irritation with Eisenhower absolutely clear; now he would take his fate out of Eisenhower's hands. Nixon pleaded to his audience to call or write the RNC (Eisenhower's name was not mentioned) and "let them decide whether my position on the ticket will help or hurt." Before he could give his viewers the address of the RNC, the network cut him off. Time and money had run out.

At the end of the speech, an exhausted Nixon mumbled, "It wasn't any good."[132] He was not alone in that assessment. A great many contemporary observers agreed with the sentiments of a 24 September 1952 editorial in the pro-Democratic *St. Louis Post Dispatch*: "Mr. Nixon's Performance . . . had many of the elements of a carefully contrived soap opera. . . . He has nerve. Only a man of colossal nerve would undertake to convert the liability of his 'trust fund' into an asset by arguing with a straight face that he needed it to save the taxpayer's money."[133] It is impossible not to agree with these sentiments. But it also worked. Nixon accomplished what he needed to accomplish in the speech. His words clearly resonated with a large portion of Americans. Western Union officials nationwide reached their capacity, and their telephone lines were full; newspaper office telephone lines were jammed with people trying to get the address of the RNC.[134] By the next morning, some 2 million of the 60 million people who had watched the speech had cabled or telephoned the RNC, demanding that Nixon stay on the ticket; the response was much the same at Eisenhower Committee headquarters.[135] There was even a sizable bump in financial contributions to Nixon's campaign.[136] No one now doubted Nixon's fate. The day after the speech, the RNC voted 107 to 0 to keep Nixon on the ticket.[137]

Yet unbelievably, the melodrama rolled on. Eisenhower refused to accede to the inevitable and instead moved to make it absolutely clear that he, not Nixon, was in charge. In a telegram to Nixon that was released to the press, Eisenhower compared Nixon's bravery to that of General Patton; he then said that he had yet to make up his mind regarding Nixon's fate. Then, in a telegram to Nixon, which was released to the press, Eisenhower told him, "To complete the formulation of that personal decision, I feel the need of talking to you and would be most appreciative if you could fly to see me at once."[138] Eisenhower was exacting a pound of flesh; Nixon had been commanded to go to Eisenhower's next campaign stop: Wheeling, West Virginia. Fuming, Nixon dictated a letter of resignation from the ticket. But cooler heads prevailed. Chotiner destroyed the letter,[139] and Nixon was privately assured by a source in the Eisenhower camp that he was still on the ticket. He dutifully flew to Wheeling, where he boarded Eisenhower's campaign plane to meet with the head of the ticket. Moments later, the two men disembarked together, and a condescending Eisenhower proclaimed to the crowd on the tarmac: "You're My Boy."

In what was almost an afterthought, Stevenson, Sparkman, and a still angry Eisenhower (who would tell his brother, "I finally decided that it was better to make the information available than to attempt to explain my refusal")[140] all released their financials.[141]

Eisenhower would later tell his biographer William Bragg Ewald (who was with him in Cleveland the night of the "Checkers Speech"), "One thing I know for sure: it would [have meant] defeat either to throw Nixon off the ticket, or to leave some kind of cloud over the whole episode."[142] Eisenhower was joined in his assessment by none other than Pat Nixon, who has been quoted as telling her husband, "If you withdraw, Ike will lose."[143] They were both wrong. Had Nixon been kicked off the ticket, it is absolutely certain that Eisenhower would still have won. And Nixon's presence on the ticket after the "Checkers Speech" ultimately caused no one to vote for Eisenhower, any more than Nixon's presence on the ticket *before* 23 September would have caused anyone to vote for Eisenhower. The "Checkers Speech" was more important for who Nixon would become rather than as a measure of his worth in 1952. The incident also showed a rather dark side to Eisenhower as a decision maker—slow, petulant, a carrier of grudges. These same qualities would once again be evident as Eisenhower dealt with the problem that was Joe McCarthy.

EISENHOWER, MARSHALL, AND MCCARTHY

One major part of the "mess in Washington" was the perception that the Truman administration had been soft on domestic communists. Both Eisenhower and Stevenson hammered at this issue. But the ubiquitous presence of Joseph McCarthy was a ticking bomb waiting to explode in the laps of both candidates. For Stevenson, even his public agreement that there was a "mess" would not insulate him from attacks on his June 1949 deposition in favor of Alger Hiss—attacks that everyone knew were coming. For Eisenhower, the situation was even trickier as his advisers pressed him to, at the very least, mention the presence of McCarthy, a fellow Republican whom Eisenhower detested.

There is little doubt that Eisenhower found McCarthy's methods repellant. Late in August, while talking to reporters in Denver about the Wisconsin senator, Eisenhower was quoted as saying that he was "not going to support anything that smacks to me of un-Americanism . . . and that includes any kind of thing that looks to me like unjust damaging of reputation."[144] Eisenhower made his feelings toward McCarthy and his followers even clearer when he was forced to share a stage in Indianapolis with Senator William Jenner, one of McCarthy's most enthusiastic disciples. When Jenner jumped up after Eisenhower's speech to put his arm around the general, Eisenhower wriggled away, turned to Representative Charles Halleck, and growled, "Charlie get me out of here!"[145] When Eisenhower told speechwriter Emmet John Hughes that he "felt dirty from the touch" of Jenner, one can easily assume that he would have felt the same way about McCarthy.[146]

Both McCarthy and Jenner had publicly denounced General George Marshall, a man to whom, as we have seen, Eisenhower owed his military career. Both men had characterized Marshall's actions as Truman's secretary of state as traitorous. On the Senate floor on 14 February 1951, McCarthy accused Marshall of being the head of a "great conspiracy" to lose China and Korea and of being "a man steeped in falsehood . . . who has the recourse to lie whenever it suits his convenience."[147] Jenner had simply called Marshall "a front man for traitors."[148]

Eisenhower's first instincts were to publicly defend his friend. In Denver, when reporters reminded Eisenhower about McCarthy's and Jenner's comments, the general snapped: "Now look! General Marshall is one of the patriots of this country. . . . I am not talking about any mistakes in judgment. That was none of my business, and I don't know anything about them."[149] But the issue was too complex to be defused by Eisenhower's annoyance. Running for reelection to the Senate, McCarthy had won the Wisconsin primary on 9 September, and he was set to cruise to a general election victory. Eisenhower endorsed McCarthy's bid for reelection, saying that while he shared the senator's goals, they just differed in their methods.[150] But not to campaign in the state with

McCarthy by his side risked Eisenhower's losing not only the support of the millions of Americans who had come to believe in McCarthy's message but also the twelve electoral votes of Wisconsin, which had gone to Truman in 1948. Virtually all of Eisenhower's advisers—with the notable exception of Dewey—told him he had to campaign in Wisconsin. Eisenhower reluctantly agreed. [151]

According to Eisenhower, the original plan was simple—go into Wisconsin in early October, publicly praise General Marshall, and then deal with the subsequent political fallout, whatever it might be.[152] Eisenhower ordered Hughes to write a defense of Marshall and put it into his talk scheduled to be delivered in Milwaukee at the end of the Wisconsin swing. Hughes did so.[153] As originally written, that speech contained a passage that read:

> Let me be quite specific. I know that charges of disloyalty have, in the past, been levelled against General George C. Marshall. I have been privileged for thirty-five years to know General Marshall personally. I know him as a man and as a soldier, to be dedicated with singular selflessness and the profoundest patriotism to the service of America. And this episode is a sobering lesson in the way that freedom must *not* defend itself.[154]

But the passage was never read. By the time the campaign hit Milwaukee, it had been edited out, replaced with a vague phrase calling for "respect for the integrity of fellow citizens who enjoy their right to disagree with us."[155] Eisenhower's speech, delivered on 3 October, made no reference to Marshall at all.

The story of how the speech was changed, like the story of the Fund Crisis, says much about both Eisenhower and his closest advisers—little of it flattering. The contents of the speech, particularly the defense of Marshall, were to have been a closely held secret. However, the speech was leaked, most likely by Eisenhower's friend General Wilton B. "Jerry" Persons.[156] As had been the case during the Fund Crisis, panic once again swept through the Eisenhower organization. Arthur Summerfield and Thomas Coleman, Taft's Wisconsin adviser who joined the train in Michigan, told Eisenhower that despite what he wanted to do, he should not offend McCarthy, least of all on his home turf.[157] On 2 October, in Peoria, Illinois, Eisenhower met with McCarthy in Summerfield's room. Memories differ as to whether the conversation was cordial or heated, but McCarthy was definitely told about the content of the speech. The next morning, Eisenhower met with McCarthy one more time on the train. McCarthy warned Eisenhower that if he went through with the talk as written, he would be booed. Eisenhower retorted, "I've been booed before, and being booed doesn't bother me."[158] Next up was Wisconsin governor Walter Kohler, who had just read the speech. He told Adams that Taft supporters would abandon Eisenhower if he insulted McCarthy and showed Adams copies of speeches made by McCarthy that purported to show that the senator had never meant to insult Marshall.[159] Kohler's argument convinced Adams, who later explained, "After all, he was the Governor of a state where we were guests and some adjustments had to be made for party harmony."[160] Adams met with Eisenhower; according to Eisenhower's recollection, Adams emphasized that leaving in the reference to Marshall at a huge gathering in McCarthy's home state, particularly when Eisenhower had not yet mentioned Marshall in the campaign, would be an unnecessary pile-on. According to Adams, "Eisenhower thought a minute and then said quickly, 'take it out.'"[161]

The damage was made worse by an Eisenhower staff run amok. Several staffers, including Gabriel Hauge, Robert Cutler, and Fred Seaton, who knew of the content of the original draft but had not been kept deep enough in the loop to know that it had been changed, spent the day whispering to reporters that Eisenhower planned to lambaste McCarthy that evening. William Lawrence of the *New York Times* had been told by one of those staffers that Eisenhower intended in his speech to give Marshall his unqualified endorsement. When the speech was finally given and McCarthy emerged unscathed, the press, particularly the *Times*, had a field day reporting Eisenhower's flip-flop.[162]

Eisenhower's postmortems were both self-effacing and unconvincing. To Stassen, Eisenhower protested, "My staff became practically a unit in recommending it" (a point that was simply not true); "The balance between the hunt for Communism and the methods used in the hunt seemed fairly well preserved without the particular paragraph" (also, given the mealymouthed nature of the speech once edited, highly debatable); and "A considerable amount of argument was presented to show that Senator McCarthy had never made the flat allegation that General Marshall was traitorous in design"—an argument made by Kohler but one that completely ignored the above speeches by McCarthy.[163] As there had been at Morningside Heights, there had definitely been a surrender in Milwaukee. Despite his first instinct to praise Marshall, Eisenhower's decision to edit his own speech hardly showed political courage.

A moment had been missed to go on the record against a demagogue, and Eisenhower had chickened out. Ewald was correct: "However you slice it, it was a mistake."[164]

For Truman, who had already been hurt by Eisenhower's refusal to come to the White House to discuss foreign policy, the Milwaukee speech was the very last straw. In Oakland, California, he called Eisenhower's flip-flop "very sad and pathetic"; in Utica, New York, Truman railed that "[Eisenhower] knows—and he knows today—that General Marshall's patriotism is above question. . . . He ought to despise McCarthy, just as I expected him to—and just as I do. Now, in his bid for votes, he has endorsed Joe McCarthy for reelection—and humbly thanked him for riding on his train."[165] Truman even claimed that Eisenhower's performance in Milwaukee showed that he could not be trusted; therefore, he could not be trusted with the power of the atomic bomb.[166] From that point on, there was not to be even the pretense of amity between the two men; as Clark Clifford remembered, relations between the two men had been "destroy[ed] . . . forever."[167]

Like Truman, Stevenson did not miss the opportunity to draw some blood. And it would not be the first time. From the literal beginning of the campaign, Stevenson, who had called the senator "a sick man,"[168] had struck out at McCarthy with fervor and regularity. Note his first major campaign address at the American Legion on 27 August—a speech he entitled "The Nature of Patriotism":

> What can we say for the man who proclaims himself a patriot—and then for political or personal reasons attacks the patriotism of faithful public servants? I give you, as a shocking example, the attacks which have been made on the loyalty and the motives of our great wartime Chief of Staff, General Marshall. To me this is the type of "patriotism" which is, in Dr. Johnson's phrase, "the last refuge of scoundrels." . . . Surely intolerance and public irresponsibility cannot be cloaked in the shining armor of rectitude and righteousness.[169]

Immediately after Eisenhower delivered his edited Milwaukee address, Stevenson bored in. In Detroit on 7 October: "For all his bragging and fear-mongering the junior senator from Wisconsin has yet to produce evidence leading to the conviction of one single communist agent, either in or out of government."[170] The next day, in Milwaukee: "The pillorying of the innocent has caused the wise to stammer and the timid to retreat."[171]

Compared with Eisenhower, who did nothing during the campaign to challenge McCarthy, Stevenson was a paragon of virtue. However, one notable exception deserves attention. Stevenson had planned a speech in Massachusetts, where Congressman John F. Kennedy was running for the Senate against incumbent Henry Cabot Lodge, that would endorse Kennedy but would also once again denounce McCarthy. However, in the words of reporter Arthur Krock, Kennedy's father, Joseph P. Kennedy Sr., "let it be known that such a speech would hurt his son's chances" by alienating the sizable Catholic vote (McCarthy was Catholic); thus, "the speech was never made."[172] The implication, of course, was that Stevenson had somehow been bought off, a conclusion that has been drawn by several writers. In hindsight, it is tempting to equate Stevenson's refusal to make a speech against McCarthy in Massachusetts with Eisenhower's refusal to make a speech praising Marshall in Milwaukee. While it is true that both men changed a speech to placate Joseph McCarthy, the equation is not apt. Stevenson made many speeches that denounced McCarthy, many of them referring to him by name. Eisenhower made none.

Moreover, after Eisenhower's submission, McCarthy left Eisenhower alone (a state of affairs that would not continue into the Eisenhower administration). After Stevenson's acquiescence in Massachusetts, in contrast, McCarthy turned on him with a vengeance. The primary target was Stevenson's 1949 deposition as a character witness for Alger Hiss (see chapter 2). After several speeches excoriating Stevenson, on 27 October, McCarthy made a televised speech from Chicago's Palmer House Hotel (audience tickets went for $50 apiece; the hall was filled),[173] where he described the politics of "Alger—pardon me, I mean Adlai." McCarthy growled that Stevenson was "part and parcel of the Acheson-Hiss-Lattimore group" and that the governor had "given sympathy and aid to the Communist cause," thereby making him "unfit to be President."[174]

Stevenson tried to extricate himself from McCarthy's constant attacks, but his self-defense was weak. On 23 October, Stevenson spoke in Cleveland, dedicating his entire address to the Hiss case. Trying to use semantics to defend his testimony, Stevenson pointed out, "I said his reputation was 'good,' and it was. I didn't say it was 'very good' . . . I didn't say any of those things the Wisconsin Senator . . . says I said."[175] After McCarthy's television appearance four days later, Stevenson chose not to respond.

"I SHALL GO TO KOREA"

A Harris poll taken in January 1952 showed that 25 percent of Americans felt that Korea was a serious problem. But despite all the news about peace talks and negotiations, nothing seemed to be happening on that front, and the casualties continued to mount. On 12 August, the Selective Service System reported that the manpower shortage at the front was so acute that it might have to begin drafting nineteen-year-olds; eight days earlier, it had floated the idea of drafting young fathers as well as middle-aged doctors.[176] Not only did the war show no signs of ending, but by summer it seemed as if Truman was ready, once again, to escalate. By September, the number of Americans who believed that the war was a problem had risen to 33 percent; in mid-October, 39 percent; and late October, 52 percent.[177]

Not Nixon, not McCarthy, not funds or communists, not liberation or messes in Washington; none of these issues resonated with the American people as did the issue of the war in Korea. By campaign's end, everyone was talking about how Eisenhower and Stevenson proposed to end it. In formulating his strategy on how to address the war, Eisenhower chose not to attack Truman for his decisions following the 1950 invasion. Rather, Eisenhower decided to condemn the president's decisions made regarding the Far East *before* the invasion. At a 4 September rally at Philadelphia's Convention Hall, Eisenhower asked, "Why are we in Korea?" His answer:

> We are in that war because this administration grossly underestimated the actual threat . . . [because] this administration . . . felt compelled to take its forces out of the region. We are in the war because . . . knowing that strength was being massed against the [Korean] republic north of its borders, there was a failure to build up adequate strength in Korea's own defense forces. We are in that war because this administration abandoned China to the Communists. Shall we trust the party which wrote that tragic record to win the peace?[178]

During the next two weeks, Eisenhower referred to the Korean War in almost every speech, emphasizing, as he had done in Philadelphia, "the [Democratic] record of bungling that has trapped us into the Korean War."[179]

On 27 September in Louisville, Stevenson struck back. Point by point, he answered each of the general's criticisms. With regard to the charge that the Truman administration had underestimated the Soviet and Chinese threat to South Korea, Stevenson pointed out that while at SHAPE, Eisenhower had also underestimated the threat. The governor quoted Eisenhower as saying that he saw "no reason" why the Soviets and the Americans "could not live side by side in the world." Stevenson also reminded his audience that *he* had spoken out against the growing Soviet menace as early as March 1946. Stevenson then charged that as army chief of staff, Eisenhower had "recommended the withdrawal of the United States forces from [Korea]." Stevenson argued that there was no way that China could have been saved, and that it was MacArthur who had recommended that Korea not be included in what was termed the American "defense perimeter" in Southeast Asia.

The speech was not, however, an unequivocal defense of Truman's actions before the invasion. In keeping with his strategy of distancing himself from the Truman administration, Stevenson came very close to sounding like Eisenhower:

> Let's admit that mistakes were made. America did mobilize too rapidly and too severely. America did allow the Russians to develop an undue superiority in conventional arms and in ground forces. Perhaps this country should have given a direct military guarantee to the Republic of Korea. And it might well have been wiser if American forces had not crossed the 38th Parallel in the fall of 1950.[180]

Thus, both Eisenhower and Stevenson approached the question of Korea by blaming Truman. Where they diverged in their strategies was that Stevenson blamed Eisenhower as well.

However, Stevenson could get no traction on this issue. This was largely because in early October, Eisenhower changed the tenor of the debate away from the assignment of blame and toward a discussion of finding a solution to the conflict. On 2 October in Champaign, Illinois, Eisenhower called for what can be termed the "Koreanization" of the war. He argued that if there must be a war in Korea, then "that is a job for the Koreans. . . . Let it be Asians against Asians, with our support on the side of freedom."[181] Stevenson attacked Eisenhower's proposal as a thinly veiled American retreat and suggested that any such withdrawal would open the Far East to the threat of communist takeover. When he argued in a televised speech that Korea was an "attack . . . aimed at America and the whole free world," and "world domination is the ultimate target of communist rulers, and world domination includes us,"[182] Stevenson had articulated what would become known as the "domino theory," a year and a half before Eisenhower's famous press conference in which he coined the phrase when talking about the impending collapse of French Indochina.[183] "Koreanization" was hastily conceived, had an obvious political motivation, and was difficult, if not impossible, to put into practice. But Stevenson had offered no idea of his own to end the Korean War.

There the issue might have stayed had it not been for Harry Truman. On 16 October in Hartford, the president directly challenged Eisenhower: "He's made vague promises about how he'll bring the boys back home. . . . He has also stated that he knows a panacea that will cure the Korean situation. . . . I will say to you right here, if he knows a remedy and a method for that situation, it is his duty to come and tell me what it is—and save lives right now."[184] Eisenhower had no such remedy. But the gauntlet had been laid down, and Eisenhower was not about to have Harry Truman have the last word of the campaign on the Korean War. On 24 October, at the Masonic Temple in Detroit, Eisenhower announced that while he was unsure of the solution, at least he would promise to go straight to the source to look for one: "That job requires a personal trip to Korea. I shall make the trip. Only in that way could I learn how to best serve the American people in the cause of peace. I shall go to Korea."[185]

Jake Arvey remembered for an interview, "We were gaining" until Eisenhower's Detroit speech, but there is no statistical evidence of this "gain"—other than Arvey wishing that it were so.[186] An enthusiastic Sherman Adams reportedly gushed, "That does it—Ike is in."[187] But Ike had never been out. The Detroit speech did not put Eisenhower over the top; whether he made the speech or not, he would have comfortably won the election. The overwhelmingly positive response to the speech did, however, demonstrate how much the American public trusted Ike. The hero factor had been latent throughout the campaign. This speech brought it to the surface. Because he had been a soldier, because he had defeated Hitler, because he was a bona fide hero, the American people accepted Eisenhower's promise to look for a solution as being that solution. Stevenson, who had not served in uniform, could never have gotten away with making this vague gesture, even if, as he later claimed, he had thought about making the same promise early in the campaign but had dismissed it[188] (his attempt to laugh off the promise by saying, "If elected, I shall go to the White House," simply sounded foolish).[189] Eisenhower had done nothing more than say that he planned on inspecting the situation, but because it came from Eisenhower, that was more than enough. The *Columbia* (South Carolina) *Record* spoke for many in its editorial of 30 October when it observed that on the "issue of war and peace," Eisenhower was "the one man who is prepared for the task, trained for it."[190]

Perhaps that belief—that the country needed a hero—was the reason Eisenhower won the election of 1952.

5

CONCLUSIONS AND LEGACIES

Looking close to exhaustion, Adlai Stevenson addressed the nation from a Chicago television station on the night before the election. Wearily telling his audience that the fourteen weeks since his nomination had been "a long, long time," the governor admitted, "I have not done as well as I should like to have done, but I have done my best." In an ironic end to a bittersweet campaign, Stevenson's paid broadcast time ran out several minutes before his talk was to end. The last sight that most voters had of Stevenson in 1952 was of him being cut off by the networks.[1]

The next day, 4 November, Stevenson drove seven miles north to his home in Libertyville, Illinois, to vote. Speaking to a crowd of children who had gathered outside the school where he had voted, he joked, "I think you are going to remember today for one thing only, and that is you got a half day off from school." Stevenson and his staff then returned to the governor's mansion in Springfield to await the results that evening.[2]

Dwight Eisenhower spent the last night of his campaign in Boston. Over television and radio, Eisenhower spoke of peace, "the dearest treasure of free men. I have learned this the stern way—from the sight of war." Eisenhower then rode on the "Look Ahead Neighbor Special" to Republican headquarters in New York. As Eisenhower arrived at Grand Central Station at 7:15 a.m., observers noted that he looked fatigued, forgoing his usual military pace for a leisurely stroll to his limousine. The general and his wife voted at 7:38 a.m. in the lobby of an apartment building near their Morningside Heights residence. They then rested most of the day, preparing for the vote watching that would take place that evening at Manhattan's Commodore Hotel.[3]

On election night, Stevenson's supporters gathered at Springfield's Leland Hotel to await the returns. As the polls closed in the East, George Ball put in a call to Connecticut political boss John Bailey to get a first taste of the results. It would not be good. Bailey growled into the phone, "They're murdering us. It's a total disaster."[4]

When the smoke cleared, a defeated Stevenson telegraphed Eisenhower to pledge his support: "The people have made their choice and I congratulate you. That you may be the servant and guardian of peace and make the vale of trouble a door of hope is my earnest prayer."[5] Truman was much less gracious. He telegraphed the president-elect: "Congratulations on your overwhelming victory. The 1954 budget must be presented to Congress before January 15th. All preliminary figures have been made up. You should have a representative meet with the Director of the Bureau of the Budget immediately. The Independence [Truman's official airplane] will be at your disposal if you still desire to go to Korea. HST."[6] Eisenhower ignored the obvious snub (*"if* you still desire to go to Korea") and responded to Stevenson in kind: "I thank you for your courteous and generous message recognizing the intensity of the difficulties that lie ahead."[7] The two men would meet face-to-face for the first time at the White House on 17 February 1953.

The average American, when reflecting on the election, was much less verbose than the principals. Hanging from one brownstone in Boston's Beacon Hill was a banner that read simply, "Thank God."[8]

THE STRUCTURE OF THE VOTE

On 4 November 1952, twenty years of Democratic dominance in national politics came to an end. And by any measure of the record turnout, it was a landslide. In October, Eisenhower had told a crowd that he would need 30 million votes to win the election.[9] He got that, and more (see the appendix). Out of a record 62 million ballots cast (11.2 million more than in 1948, and a record turnout of 63.3 percent of all eligible voters), 34 million Americans (55 percent of the total) voted for Dwight D. Eisenhower, while 27.3 million (44.5 percent of the total) voted for Adlai E. Stevenson II.

Adlai E. Stevenson II and President Dwight D. Eisenhower at the White House, 17 February 1953 (U.S. Army, courtesy of Dwight D. Eisenhower Library)

In the Electoral College, with 270 needed for victory, Eisenhower won 442 electoral votes to 89 for Stevenson.[10]

Eisenhower won more popular votes in 1952 than had any candidate for the presidency to that point in American history. It is easier to note the states that Eisenhower did *not* win: Stevenson won Kentucky, West Virginia, the Carolinas, Georgia, Alabama, Mississippi, Arkansas, and Louisiana; Eisenhower won everything else. This included reversals of Truman's 1948 victories in California, Illinois, and Ohio, as well as victories in key Republican states like Michigan and Ohio with numbers that absolutely transcended Dewey's. Eisenhower ran strongest in the western states, where he captured 57.3 percent of the total vote, as opposed to the 46 percent of Dewey in 1948.[11] Eighteen states that had gone to the Democrats in every election since 1932 now went Republican.

Eisenhower's most impressive victory, however, was in the South. Stevenson's victories in the lower South were by substantial margins. But Eisenhower won 2.5 million more southern votes than had Dewey in 1948, and he won a higher percentage of the vote in the region than had any Republican since Reconstruction.[12] He won Texas with 53.2 percent and Florida with 55 percent of the vote. He also made inroads into the upper South, winning Virginia with 56.5 percent and narrowly winning

Tennessee with 50.1 percent. None of these states had gone Republican since 1938, and Virginia, Texas, and Florida had gone Republican only once since Reconstruction.

Eisenhower also carried several demographic groups that had been carried—by substantial margins—by Franklin Roosevelt in all four of his victories, as well as by Truman in 1948. Since 1932, the Democrats had been able to count on the votes of several white ethnic groups, largely congregated in the big cities of the Northeast. In 1952, Eisenhower won 79 percent of German voters and 53 percent of all Irish voters. Perhaps more surprising was that 50 percent of the Polish voters, who had voted in the 90 percent range for the Democrats since 1932, went for Eisenhower. Eisenhower also won a majority of the vote from women (58.1 percent), Americans over the age of fifty (64 percent), and farmers outside the South (75 percent; indeed, in the twenty-three farm states, Stevenson's total vote was less than Truman's in nineteen of them)—all of whom had been consistent supporters of the Democratic Party since 1932.[13]

Eisenhower also wrested control of the urban vote from the Democrats. In 1952, he carried seventeen out of thirty-five cities with populations greater than 300,000; in 1948, Dewey had carried only three.[14] One of the key reasons that Stevenson did not carry any of the large industrial states was that he lost ground in the major cities of the Northeast and Midwest. In 1948, for example, Truman carried Illinois when Chicago gave 58.6 percent of its vote to him; in 1952, Stevenson got 54 percent of that vote and lost the state. The same pattern followed in Ohio, where Truman carried the state in 1948 in large part thanks to his winning 61 percent of the vote in Cleveland; Stevenson's vote total in that city dropped to 50 percent in 1952, and he lost Ohio as well. Perhaps the most disappointing loss for the Democrats came in New York. Since 1932, Democrats had won between 61 and 75 percent of the New York City vote; in 1952, Stevenson polled only 55 percent in New York City, and he lost the state.[15]

In the end, however, it was the solid support from one group that gave the Eisenhower landslide both its magnitude and its scope. Dwight Eisenhower held a hammerlock on the affections and the votes of the American middle class. Until 1952, it had been a fact of political life that wealthy Americans supported the Republican Party, poorer Americans supported the Democrats, and the growing middle class was fairly evenly divided between the two parties, depending on issues and candidates.[16] There was little surprise when wealthy Americans voted for

Eisenhower—he drew between two-thirds and four-fifths of the upper-income vote in such varied cities as New York, Cleveland, Richmond, Dallas, Miami, and New Orleans. It also came as no surprise that Stevenson kept the loyalty of the majority of lower/working-class voters. What surprised contemporary observers, however, was the magnitude of the shift of the middle-class voter to Eisenhower. On average, an astounding 69 percent of the nation's middle class voted for Eisenhower.[17] These voters were found in the newly populated suburbs, where the urban middle class had been moving in droves since 1945. Eisenhower's voting percentage in the suburbs was an astounding 75 to 90 percent.[18] In 1949, Thomas Dewey had believed that Dwight Eisenhower could carry the middle class, as he had not in 1948. He had been right.

One must look very closely to find anything in the results that was positive toward Stevenson. He carried very few states and even fewer demographic groups. He carried the Jewish vote by a plurality of 70 percent, the Italian vote by 60 percent, the union vote by 60 percent, and voters between the ages of twenty-one and twenty-five by 56 percent.[19] His main bloc of support was the black vote. Blacks were the only major voting group that voted in a higher percentage for Stevenson—79 percent—than they had done for Truman in 1952.[20] Overall, Stevenson ran from four to seventeen points ahead of Truman in terms of the black vote; in the North he won 75 percent of that vote; in the South, he won 59 percent.[21]

However, despite Eisenhower's overwhelming personal victory, as well as his significant inroads into the Democratic base, political scientists Everett Ladd and Charles Hadley are correct when they note that in the wake of the 1952 election, "the ascendant position of the Democratic party remained unshaken."[22] Unlike Truman's 1948 victory, which carried with it a Democratic House and Senate, the Eisenhower landslide of 1952 did not translate itself into an overwhelming Republican victory in the congressional elections. The Republicans only slightly increased the gains they had made in 1950, and their hold on those bodies was precarious at best. In 1952, the GOP made a net gain of only 22 seats in the House—8 fewer than in 1950—controlling that body by a 221–214 edge, and it held the Senate by only one vote, 48–47 (however, since one independent, Oregon's Wayne Morse, would soon switch his party allegiance to the Democrats, the result was a de facto tie). In the Senate, Joseph McCarthy was reelected from Wisconsin, but he ran far behind Eisenhower. William Jenner was reelected in Indiana, but the margin of his victory was razor thin. Victories by Democratic challengers over Republican incumbents included Washington representative Henry "Scoop" Jackson ousting David Cain; former secretary of the air force Stuart Symington defeating Missouri incumbent James Kem; and Congressman John F. Kennedy's victory over Eisenhower's preconvention campaign manager, Henry Cabot Lodge, in Massachusetts. The situation for the Republicans would become more precarious with the 31 July 1953 death of Robert Taft and the appointment of Democrat Thomas A. Burke by the governor of Ohio to serve out Taft's unexpired term. Overall, 359,397 more people voted for Democratic congressional candidates than for Republican candidates.[23]

The results on the local level did little more to comfort the party faithful. A surface view of the gubernatorial elections suggests that the GOP did well: of the thirty-two gubernatorial seats in play in 1952, the Republicans won twenty; they also won seven open seats (where an incumbent was not running) to the Democrats' five. However, those five Democratic victories in open-seat elections, combined with the reelection of five of the eight Democratic incumbents who were up for reelection, muted the Republican gains. Despite Republican victories in the statehouses, the Democrats continued to hold a majority of the nation's governorships, and the party kept an iron control over all forms of local government in the South and in most of the nation's big cities.[24] Political scientist Samuel Lubell explained the rather mauve nature of the Republican victory by observing that the public was continuing to reward the Democratic Party as the party that led the nation out of the Great Depression: "To an appreciable part of the electorate, the Democrats had replaced the Republicans as the party of prosperity."[25] Clearly, while America liked Ike, it didn't necessarily like the Republicans—at least, not quite as much.

WHY IKE?

Then why, despite the fact that the nation was clearly ambivalent about the solutions offered by the Republican Party in 1952, did Dwight D. Eisenhower win? It has almost become a cliché for political historians to label their section on "causes" with a statement reminding the reader of the obvious—that no election on any level is ever decided by just one factor. But in the presidential election of 1952, two factors are, indeed, absolutely clear.

The first was the current of dissatisfaction with the state of the Truman administration—what had been dubbed by both candidates as the "mess in Washington"—and a desire to, in a cliché of its own, "throw the rascals out." Richard Russell, when talking to his sister on the day of Eisenhower's inauguration, quipped, "If I had gotten the nomination, the results would have been the same . . . the country was ready for a change."[26] Russell was right. What one author would call the "tide of revulsion" against "Trumanism" clearly played a large role in Eisenhower's victory.[27] This sentiment, born of corruption, war, inflation, and the general belief that the Democrats had become complacent over the past twenty years, was no more succinctly stated than by the wife of Truman's secretary of the air force: "The people wanted another party in power, no matter what."[28] A clue to this feeling can be seen in this note; 28 percent of those who voted for Truman in 1948 deserted the Democrats and voted for Eisenhower in 1952.[29] Perhaps Harry Truman put it best in a letter to Maury Maverick: "The cards were stacked against us. I don't think [any Democrat] could have won this election."[30]

Yet when reflecting upon whether or not he could have beaten Stevenson in 1952, Robert Taft answered in the positive, suggesting that any *Republican* candidate would have benefited from "the negative enthusiasm about what has been going on in Washington."[31] This does not seem likely. It is arguable that neither Taft, who controlled only the right wing of his party, nor Warren or Stassen, who had little base of support within their party at all, could have done much better than, say, Stevenson. It also downplays the skill with which Eisenhower exploited the public hatred of the Truman administration in his campaign, and it completely ignores the second factor leading to Eisenhower's victory: the fact that the American public truly liked Ike.

This was not a campaign concoction created for a television spot, made more enduring with a strong reaction to a campaign crisis and ensured with a speech. It had long been the case. With a nod to John F. Kennedy and Ronald Reagan, Dwight Eisenhower was clearly the most popular American of the post–World War II period. And Eisenhower was popular with every segment of the American public. He touched a chord in the American people as had no other political leader since Franklin Roosevelt. Eisenhower's military bearing promised security; his unbridled joviality and optimism offered hope; his age—which was never attacked in 1952 by the opposition as being "too old for the job"—offered experience. The tenor of his personality was neatly summarized by journalist and Eisenhower biographer Tom Wicker when he observed that

"Ike was *somebody*. He was a presence—special, not ordinary."[32] Harry Truman could not compete with Eisenhower's popularity, and he knew it—raising the white flag, he had, as we have seen, twice tried to convince Ike to run as a Democrat so that at least he might get some of the credit.

Indeed, despite his obvious political calculations in 1952, Eisenhower was not seen by most Americans as being a politician. He was seen to be somehow above politics, perhaps explaining why so many of his supporters clung to the belief that he was drafted for the nomination when he was actually a declared candidate for that nomination. Of those who voted for Eisenhower, an astounding 89 percent cited a favorable trait in his personality as a reason, whereas only 70 percent of Stevenson voters mentioned their candidate favorably. In the polls, Stevenson simply could not positively compare to Eisenhower except in one area; even Eisenhower voters gave Stevenson favorable marks for his civic experience.[33]

Moreover, it must be remembered that the popular Eisenhower came within an eyelash of never being nominated. For all but forty-eight hours at its convention, the Republican Party clearly liked Bob Taft more than Ike. The creation of the Fair Play Amendment was genius on the part of Herbert Brownell, and it was handled exquisitely by Henry Cabot Lodge. Eisenhower had nothing to do with it, but he reaped the benefits of the political skill of his lieutenants on the floor. Ike's popularity did not win him the nomination; pure power politics did.

And yet, it is clear that once nominated, there was virtually nothing that Eisenhower could have done in the fall to lose the election, short of being caught in a personal scandal (and one wonders if even *that* would have allowed Stevenson to break ahead). Not Stevenson, not any Democrat in the field, not Truman could have beaten Eisenhower in 1952.

So perhaps it is more useful to ask why Eisenhower won so *big*.

Ever the consummate realist, Sam Rayburn blamed the landslide on money: "We had only dollars against their thousands."[34] This statement was actually quite close to the truth, and nowhere was this cost seen more than in the television time bought by the two candidates (as discussed in the previous chapter). A full accounting of the finances of the 1952 election eludes the historian—it would not be until 1975 that federal laws required the level of disclosure that would make a close analysis possible. The nearest figure that we have is that the Republicans raised

$6.6 million (up from \$2.1 million in 1948) to the Democrats' \$5.0 million (up from \$2.7 million in 1948).[35] We also know for a fact that the Republicans vastly outspent the Democrats in 1952—and that money had to come from somewhere.

In terms of the size of Eisenhower's victory, one must also thank Adlai Stevenson. Stevenson also played right into Eisenhower's hands with several decisions that, from the point of view of campaign strategy, were difficult to defend. Most notable was the fact that his decision on the Tidelands delivered Texas to Eisenhower on a silver platter, and his stand on civil rights, particularly on the Fair Employment Practice Commission (FEPC), helped to shatter the solid South. Even Stevenson's most ardent supporters have admitted that he ran a poorly strategized campaign. Many of the letters in Stevenson's postelection correspondence are from Democrats who begged the governor to fire Stephen Mitchell as the chair of the DNC. Truman wholeheartedly agreed; in a 22 December 1952 memo to himself, the president fumed, "When [Frank] McKinney was fired the organization fell apart," and he would later write that "the way the campaign was conducted cost the party at least three to four million votes."[36] This blame was misdirected. Mitchell had decidedly little role in the strategy of the campaign—that role was left to Wilson Wyatt and, ultimately, to the candidate himself. Communication within the campaign was definitely poor; communication between the campaign and the White House was virtually nonexistent.

It should be noted that all too many observers have painted the result of Stevenson's campaign as some kind of moral victory. They agree with Stevenson speechwriter and biographer John Bartlow Martin that while Stevenson "did not win, . . . in losing he won the admiration of millions of people who responded to graceful speeches and ideas."[37] Perhaps. They also agree with Walter Johnson, chairman of the Draft Stevenson Committee, that while Stevenson did not win, "he conducted a campaign that . . . raised American political thinking to a high plane and bequeathed it certain enduring qualities."[38] Perhaps. But a record number of people voted for his opponent. What must be said, in direct defiance of Stevenson's many apologists, was that he was a terrible candidate. He inspired very few people and energized even fewer.

Then what, when all the analyzing is done, should the historian say about the role of the issues in 1952? Eisenhower speechwriter Emmet John Hughes reported that Democratic sage Jim Farley believed that the entire election was won on the issue of the Korean War.[39] Historian

Robert Divine also holds to this belief.[40] Much of the evidence under-pinning this conclusion, however, is found in the public reaction to the Detroit speech; there is very little evidence suggesting that a belief in Eisenhower's "plan" to end the war swayed many votes at all. Indeed, when one looks at members of a group that one might expect would have the war uppermost on their minds when entering the voting booth—women: the mothers, wives, and girlfriends of the soldiers mired on the Korean Peninsula, and the mothers, wives, and girlfriends of potential enlistees and draftees—it was listed as only one of many things that were on women's minds as they cast their votes.[41] Quite simply put, while the issues were discussed, they neither drove nor decided the election.

THE POLITICS OF "MODERATE REPUBLICANISM"

As the Republicans took control of the executive branch in 1953, it was generally assumed that Eisenhower would govern from the right. The conservative wing of the party dominated the cabinet. For example, as part of the deal made at Morningside Heights, Thomas Dewey had been shut out as secretary of state; that position went to conservative John Foster Dulles. On Capitol Hill, the Republican conservatives, now led by Senate Majority Leader Robert Taft and Speaker of the House Joseph Martin of Massachusetts, would organize the Congress. Both Taft and Martin had a long track record of working with southern conservative Democrats to frustrate the aims of Truman's Fair Deal. It was expected that Eisenhower, who had also made a deal with Taft at Morningside Heights to support key parts of the conservative agenda, would govern through this coalition, steadily dismantle what he could of the New/Fair Deal, turn the nation inward toward isolation, and ride the support of a unified Republican Party—something that, as we have seen, he did not have in 1952—to reelection in 1956.

Yet this did not happen. Given the story of the presidential election of 1952, it is difficult to understand why there were so many contemporary commentators who believed Eisenhower to be a closet Taftian conserva-tive. As we have seen, Eisenhower entered the race as much to stop Taft from getting the Republican nomination as he did to stop Truman from being reelected—a point that he made clear both in his correspondence and in his public statements. Taftian conservatism, particularly its belief in international isolation, greatly disturbed Eisenhower. He had spoken often of his preference for internationalism in foreign affairs, and he had aligned himself with Dulles's policy of liberation. Also, Eisenhower disagreed with those conservatives, including Taft, who had long argued for a reduced role for the federal government in both domestic and foreign policy.

Eisenhower termed his governing philosophy the "middle way" or "Moderate Republicanism"—a halfway point between the ideas of the Taftian conservatives and the liberal ideas of the New/Fair Deal. In the domestic policies of his first term, Eisenhower's middle way shaded decidedly to the left. Despite pressure from the right wing of his party—and the expectations of many others—Eisenhower's goal as president was never to overthrow the New/Fair Deal. Indeed, he supported the continuation and expansion of several New Deal programs and advocated for new federal programs when he was convinced that those programs would not significantly add to the financial obligations of the federal government. As he wrote to his brother Edgar on 8 November 1954:

> Should any political party attempt to abolish social security, unemployment insurance and eliminate labor laws and farm programs, you would not hear of that party again in our political history. There is a tiny splinter group, of course, that believes that you can do these things. Among them are a few Texas oil millionaires, and an occasional politician or businessman from other areas. Their number is negligible and they are stupid.[42]

Examples of Eisenhower Republicanism in action offer a mixed bag of success and failure. The St. Lawrence Seaway, first proposed under Warren Harding, began construction in 1954; it would be the largest federal construction project in history (the share of the project paid for by the United States would be $133.8 million) until the advent of the Interstate Highway System, which began construction in 1956. The Housing Act of 1954, while not as extravagant as its liberal supporters had wished, provided for the government construction of 140,000 homes, thus stimulating the public housing boom of the 1960s. And in 1956, the federal minimum wage rose from seventy-five cents to a dollar an hour. None of this came from the mind of a Hooverian/Taftian conservative.

However, as Steven Wagner, the leading scholar of Eisenhower Republicanism, has observed, "More often than not, Eisenhower's legislative proposals were defeated by an unwitting alliance of conservatives, who sought to limit the role of the federal government, and liberals who wanted the federal government to do more than Eisenhower proposed."[43]

While Eisenhower was successful with his proposal to add to the federal bureaucracy by creating the Department of Health, Education, and Welfare (HEW) at the cabinet level (signed by Eisenhower on 11 April 1953; the first secretary of HEW was Eisenhower's longtime Texas supporter Oveta Culp Hobby), his plans for a reinsurance program (where the federal government insured commercial insurance companies and nonprofits against atypical losses) went down to defeat.[44] In the arena of agriculture, Eisenhower was on record during the campaign as being in favor of maintaining price supports at full parity. As president, however, Eisenhower followed the advice of his secretary of agriculture, Ezra Taft Benson, and supported a system of flexible price supports for basic crops, stretching from 75 to 90 percent of parity.[45] He also supported Benson's "Soil Bank" plan, which allowed the farmer to voluntarily choose not to plant a portion of his crop; that acreage would be put into a reserve program for a number of years. This would take some 20 to 25 million acres out of production, thus reducing production and increasing prices. The fact that this was the basic construct of Roosevelt's Agriculture Adjustment Act (AAA) was missed by no one.[46]

In foreign policy, Eisenhower separated himself even more from the Taftian wing of the party. An unabashed internationalist, he planned to fight for foreign aid packages that made sense to him, and against any attempts from any faction to rein in the power of the president to conduct foreign affairs. On the issue of presidential power to conduct foreign policy, Eisenhower clashed openly with the conservative bloc, which wanted to limit the president's power to negotiate treaties and executive agreements, thus limiting his ability to negotiate what had been, for them, another Yalta-like sellout with the Soviets. On 7 January 1953, Senator John Bricker (R-OH) introduced an amendment to the federal Constitution that would end the president's authority to enter into executive agreements, as well as "limit the effect of treaties and executive agreements on U.S. law." The Bricker Amendment was popular in the Senate among both conservative Republicans and Democrats, but Eisenhower threw his immense personal popularity against the measure; on 27 February 1954, it was rejected in the Senate by one vote. Eisenhower also defied the conservative bloc with his support of free trade and his administration's extension of Roosevelt's 1934 Reciprocal Trade Agreement Act.[47] Political scientist Gary Reichard, who observed that only 22.7 percent of House Republicans and 24.4 percent of Republican senators voted against Eisenhower's foreign policy stances, was correct when he observed that by 1954, "the internationalist president had succeeded in altering considerably the foreign policy stance of his party."[48]

THE OFF-YEAR ELECTIONS OF 1954

Eisenhower's "middle way" had borne some successes for the administration. However, the Republican Party as a whole was not the beneficiary of those successes. As the off-year elections crept closer, a sequence of special elections held in 1953 showed just how vulnerable the GOP really was. In Georgia, an election to replace conservative Democrat Eugene Cox, who had died the previous year, was won by Democrat J. L. Pitcher—the Republicans did not even field a candidate. In Illinois, Democrat James Bowler won a special election for the House against his Republican opponent with 85 percent of the vote. Neither of those Democratic wins was a real surprise (the Georgia seat was safely Democratic, and Bowler's opponent hardly campaigned). But two more special elections for the House later that year featured Democratic upsets. A liberal Republican was defeated in Wisconsin (Estes Kefauver had campaigned for the Democratic winner), and Democrat Harrison A. Williams won a seat from a traditionally Republican district in New Jersey.[49]

The reason for these defeats can be found in the convincing research of political scientist Charles A. Moser. He argues that the GOP had spent the years following its 1946 congressional victories concentrating on winning the presidency; thus, it had "failed to establish itself at the grassroots."[50] In other words, everything the party had done to elect Eisenhower in 1952 had distracted it from building the kind of organization that could have lasting success on the state and local levels. This was a reason for the party's middling success in 1952, and the dynamic remained unchanged into the Eisenhower administration. With the notable exception of Nixon, the Eisenhower administration as a whole was more loyal to its president than it was to the party, and it essentially ignored its party duties.[51] In this, Eisenhower must shoulder part of the responsibility. Party regulars bore a grudge toward the Citizens for Eisenhower groups, which had played a role in the election of Eisenhower. However, Eisenhower defended the need for those groups long after the election was over, exploding at critics of the Citizens during a White House meeting. Thus, an opportunity was missed to lessen interparty resentment and build up a stronger party organization.[52] For his part, Stevenson, now the head of the Democratic Party, worked hard following his defeat to strengthen the party at its roots. In the four years between elections, Stevenson kept a particularly high profile, speaking out against the administration on numerous occasions—his March 1954 speech in Miami Beach, scorching Eisenhower for his timidity in handling McCarthy, forced the administration, through Nixon, to reply.[53]

Believing that the country would agree that his first two years in office had produced what he would later label an "excellent legislative record," Eisenhower hoped that he could spare himself the rigor of a national campaign in 1954.[54] But it is not surprising that when the party learned that the number of GOP seats that had initially been deemed to be "safe" was dwindling, Eisenhower was sent on the road. The president's crowds were huge, and his stock speech—on the perils of a divided government, and how it would make his life difficult to work with a Democratic Congress—was met with polite applause. But neither Eisenhower's involvement nor the yeoman efforts of Vice President Nixon, who crisscrossed the country in support of Republican candidates, could stem the Democratic tide.

On 2 November 1954, in what was a very close election across the board, the Democrats took back both houses of Congress. They now controlled the Senate by a one-vote margin, and after a net gain of 17 seats in the House, controlled that body 232–203.[55] Eisenhower would not have a Republican-controlled Congress for the rest of his tenure as president; the Democrats would not relinquish control of the Senate until 1981, and not until 1994 of the House. Thus, Moser argues that 1954 failed to "ratify" the election of 1952; thus 1952 was not a "watershed" election but, at best, a "deviating" election that "did not presage any fundamental reorientation of American politics."[56] However, the Republicans could take some comfort in the fact that the Democrats trailed by some 165,000 total votes in all races for national office outside the South.[57]

THE PRESIDENTIAL ELECTION OF 1956

With the death of Taft, Eisenhower had no challengers for the 1956 Republican nomination. Yet there was considerable drama in the pre-convention Republican maneuvering. It first centered on Eisenhower's health. On 24 September 1955, while vacationing in Denver, Eisenhower suffered what was reported as "digestive upset" but was in reality a massive heart attack. Over the next five months, the party leadership worried that a recovering Eisenhower would not stand for reelection. For his part, a weakened Eisenhower did not want to subject himself to the grueling schedule of another national campaign. He held meetings with his closest advisers where he said as much and offered to them a list of potential successors.[58]

Yet despite coming face-to-face with his own mortality, Eisenhower had also come to believe that his continued service was needed. Key to this was a report he had received in January 1956 from a subcommittee of the National Security Council that had been charged with calculating the destruction that might occur in the early stages of a nuclear war with the Soviet Union. The findings of the committee—a certain economic collapse, the assured death of all government leaders, and the death of about 65 percent of the total population of the United States—sobered Eisenhower. Historian David Nichols observes that Eisenhower came to see the "abyss which he feared the world could sink into without his leadership."[59] On 29 February 1956, Eisenhower announced that he would run again.

The second dramatic interlude involved Richard Nixon. The Fund Crisis had poisoned the relationship between Eisenhower and Nixon. Garry Wills described the relationship well: "They did not forget the night when they touched swords. There would never be any trust between them. And Nixon had begun a tutelage that would gall him and breed resentment through years of friction and slights."[60] While Nixon served the administration well, particularly in the area of keeping the lines of communication open between the White House and the conservatives on Capitol Hill, as well as serving as Eisenhower's surrogate while the president recovered from his heart attack, Eisenhower never fully trusted Nixon, whom he saw to be transparently ambitious. For his part, Nixon never forgot how Eisenhower had treated him in Wheeling. This is the theme of one of the most recent books on the Eisenhower-Nixon relationship; in *The General and the Politician*, historian John W. Malsberger convincingly argues that "neither man wholly liked or understood what he saw in his partner."[61]

Long before Eisenhower's heart attack, a coterie of White House staffers, led by the ever-ambitious Harold Stassen (now the director of the U.S. Foreign Operations Administration), was angling to get Nixon off the ticket. At a 23 July press conference, Stassen took the extraordinary step of proposing that Nixon be replaced by Governor Christian Herter of Massachusetts. At that press conference, Stassen claimed, without sharing how he had come to this conclusion, that "an Eisenhower-Herter ticket will run at least 6 percent stronger than an Eisenhower-Nixon ticket." Herter quickly removed himself from consideration, but that did not deter Stassen, who took a leave of absence to campaign for Herter as Nixon's replacement.[62]

It seems clear that Eisenhower did not want Nixon to stay on the ticket; it seems equally clear that Eisenhower was squeamish about telling Nixon so. Only after Nixon refused to bite at the offer of a cabinet position did Eisenhower finally say that he would be "delighted" if the convention would renominate Nixon. The "Dump Nixon" episode only served to further deteriorate the relationship between the two men and stood to impede Nixon's ambition to earn for himself the Republican nomination in 1960.

There would be no drama surrounding the intentions of Adlai Stevenson in 1956. By 1953, he made it crystal clear in his private correspondence that he wanted a second shot at Eisenhower. His omnipresent campaigning for Democratic candidates in 1954, as well as his pointed criticism of Eisenhower's refusal to publicly castigate Senator Joseph McCarthy, despite the recklessness of his attacks, confirmed his ambition to run again. Stevenson announced his candidacy for the Democratic nomination in November 1955—before his chief rival for the nomination, Estes Kefauver, announced.[63]

But if the election of 1952 had taught him nothing else, it had taught Stevenson that he was not well suited for the grueling day-to-day of the primary trail; pressing the flesh was never his strong suit. It would not be until Kefauver, who had leveled charges that Stevenson was beholden to the Chicago political bosses, handily defeated him in the New Hampshire primary (21,701 to 3,806) and in Minnesota (with 56 percent of the vote) that Stevenson began to campaign with gusto. He defeated Kefauver in Oregon, Florida, and California, and on 31 July Kefauver withdrew from the race.

At the Democratic Convention, held again at the Chicago Amphitheatre, Stevenson easily beat back a Truman-inspired boomlet for now governor of New York Averell Harriman (Truman would tell a jammed press conference at the Blackstone Hotel that Stevenson "lacks the kind of fighting spirit that we need to win").[64] The Stevenson bandwagon engulfed another late candidacy, that of Senate Majority Leader Lyndon Johnson, who had hoped that his high-profile work with the Eisenhower White House would give him a statesmanlike gravitas that would lead the delegates to overlook his less than liberal stand on civil rights.[65] Stevenson was easily nominated on the first ballot.

Neither Johnson nor Harriman expressed any interest in the second spot on the ticket; Kefauver, however, let it be known that he was willing to accept the position. However, thirty-nine-year-old John F. Kennedy, then the junior senator from Massachusetts, had captivated the convention with a strong nominating speech for Stevenson; Kennedy, too, let it be known that he was interested in the second spot. With no obvious choice in sight, and seeking an opportunity to do something unique, Stevenson stunned the party by announcing that he would not interfere at all in its choice for his running mate. This sparked a contest between the well-oiled Kefauver machine and the hastily organized Kennedy candidacy. George Ball would later reveal that Stevenson thought that Kennedy was going to win,[66] but Kefauver prevailed, and Kennedy bowed out gracefully after having learned a valuable lesson in convention floor management—one that would be put to better use four years later.

Stevenson intimate Jacob Arvey would later contend that if Stevenson had outright chosen Kennedy as his running mate in 1956, he might have won.[67] Highly doubtful. Compared with the 1952 campaign, the 1956 contest was a rather dull affair. For his part, Eisenhower chose to do much of his campaigning on radio and television (Truman tried to flush him out but with little success: "The people want to see what you look like, what the feel of you is").[68] The central issue for most of the campaign was Eisenhower's age and health (compounding the political effect of his heart attack, in early June Eisenhower was stricken with ileitis and underwent surgery for a severe intestinal blockage). But Stevenson never gained traction with the argument. To begin with, Stevenson himself had only recently undergone gallbladder surgery. But most important, the American people had spent four years feeling secure under their general-president, and they even liked a rather sick Ike. Indeed, when reporter Tom Wicker, who in 1956 supported Stevenson, tried to make his case to a colleague by observing that Eisenhower had been ill, she responded for millions of like-minded Americans: "Young man, I would vote for Eisenhower if he were dead."[69]

As if this were not enough, two events occurred in the last weeks of the campaign that served to cement in the minds of most Americans how secure they felt with Eisenhower at the helm.

Without access to the Suez Canal, a man-made waterway connecting the Mediterranean and the Red Sea, world trading of Middle Eastern oil would effectively grind to a halt. No one knew this better than the flamboyant Gamel Abdel Nasser, president of Egypt. While Nasser had reacted to the 1948 American recognition of Israel by signing a pact with the Soviet Union, he was more than willing to deal with either nation to further his designs. One such project was the building of a dam on the Nile River to provide cheap hydroelectric power for his people. The Aswan Dam became a symbol of Egyptian modernization, and Nasser had mortgaged much of his popularity toward its success. To finance it, he had borrowed money from the United States, Great Britain, and the World Bank. However, his ideology interfered with his plans. When Nasser recognized the People's Republic of China (PRC) in May 1956, Dulles recommended to Eisenhower that the Americans withdraw their loan offer. Eisenhower agreed, and as soon as Nasser was informed on 26 July, he nationalized the Suez Canal, with the intention of using the tolls he collected to pay for the Aswan Dam.[70]

In the words of David Nichols, the closest student of the Suez Crisis, "The British reaction to the nationalization decree bordered on hysteria."[71] Britain and France (both hoping to reclaim the glory of their pre–World War II empires) and Israel (ready to prove itself as a power to be reckoned with in the Middle East) each used the Suez Crisis as an occasion to flex their muscles. On 31 October, after three months of deliberate deception as to their intent and less than two weeks before the American presidential election, the three nations invaded Egypt, each assuming that their actions would be supported by the United States.

They were not. Through the United Nations, the United States brokered a cease-fire that the Israelis immediately obeyed. The British and the French, however, were not yet ready to stand down. Eisenhower personally called Prime Minister Anthony Eden of Britain and, in the strongest of terms, rebuked him for the invasion and demanded that the British withdraw. Attempting to make political hay, Stevenson charged—correctly—that the Eisenhower administration had kept the gravity of the crisis a secret from the American people and in the process had destroyed our relationship with "our oldest, strongest allies."[72] But Stevenson had run out of time to make his case. While the fighting between the British, French, and Egyptians intensified on 6 November—the day before the election—all parties were sobered by a message from Nikolai Bulganin, then chairman of the Soviet Council of Ministers, that suggested that the Soviets were thinking about sending troops to the region. Eisenhower put American forces on alert, reasoning that "it would be global war if they started it, that's all."[73] Getting the hint, as well as recognizing that the war would quickly bankrupt their treasuries, Britain and France reluctantly began to withdraw their troops as Americans went to the polls.

Playing out concurrently with the Suez Crisis was a bitter reminder of the status of the Cold War. In October 1956, street demonstrations throughout Soviet-occupied Hungary had led to the appointment of communist politician Imre Nagy, a leader of the protests, as prime minister; in an act that stunned the Soviets, Nagy announced that Hungary was withdrawing from the Warsaw Pact. On 4 November—four days after the allied invasion of Egypt and two days before Election Day in the United States—Soviet troops and tanks entered Budapest in an attempt to crush Nagy's revolt. Like the nations that had earlier invaded Egypt, the Hungarian revolutionaries believed they were going to get help from the United States. Indeed, the Central Intelligence Agency (CIA) had played a role in the demonstrations that had put Nagy in power. As soon as the Soviets moved in to suppress the revolt, the CIA pressed Eisenhower to provide covert assistance to Nagy's freedom fighters so that they might resist the Soviet counteroffensive. As he had done with Britain, France, and Israel, Eisenhower refused, and the rebellion was subdued. While the response to this crisis dragged out into early 1957, Eisenhower had once again shown that he could not be counted on to help fight a war of liberation against communism. For his part, Nagy was arrested, tried before a secret tribunal, and executed in June 1958.

The presidential election of 1956 was even more of a validation of Eisenhower's popularity than was 1952. The results of the election, held on 6 November as both the Suez Crisis and the Hungarian revolt were making headlines, revealed a landslide even greater than that of four years earlier. Eisenhower won 457 electoral votes to Stevenson's 73 and captured 57.4 percent of the popular vote—a larger majority than he had won in 1952, out of a larger vote total. Stevenson made no inroads into the "Eisenhower Coalition"—each group that had gone for Eisenhower in 1952 went for him again four years later. Moreover, Eisenhower's popularity had grown so widespread that it had begun to cave in the distinctions between the classes; as political scientist Heinz Eulau noted in his prescient study *Class and Party in the Eisenhower Years*, while Eisenhower had convincingly carried the middle class in 1952, four years later he carried both the middle class and the working class.[74]

Yet Eisenhower's claim that, in 1956, "Modern Republicanism has now proved itself. And America has approved Modern Republicanism" was simply not true.[75] Eisenhower's coattails were no more adherent than they had been in 1952. In the House, Republicans suffered a net loss of 2 seats from 1954, and Democrats retained control of that body, 233–201. They also retained control of the Senate, 49–47. Once again, Eisenhower's popularity outshone the popularity of his party. He ran ahead of the Republican candidate for the House in all but forty-two districts.[76]

There is no doubt that for the next four years, Americans continued to like Ike—this despite the challenges to moderate Republicanism from within his party, led from the left by New York governor Nelson A. Rockefeller and from the right by Arizona senator Barry Goldwater. This, too, despite the events of the Cold War and Eisenhower's often halting response to them. Even a debacle as byzantine as the U-2 Crisis, where Eisenhower was caught in a bold-faced lie to the world, did not destroy the faith that the American people had in him. Most observers agree that had Eisenhower's health prevailed, and had the Twenty-Fourth Amendment to the Constitution not precluded it, Eisenhower would have comfortably won a third term in 1960. Denied the opportunity to once again vote for Eisenhower, the American people had to choose between two extraordinarily young men who were vying for the presidency. They offered radically different perspectives on where the nation should be headed. Republican Richard Nixon argued for the status quo, declaring that under Eisenhower, the nation was still "the strongest nation on earth militarily and economically."[77] Democrat John F. Kennedy called it "a race between the comfortable and the concerned, a race between those who want to be at anchor and those who want to go forward."[78] It would remain for the American people to decide the direction that the country would take as it entered the 1960s.

1952 PRESIDENTIAL GENERAL ELECTION RESULTS

State	Electoral Vote: Eisenhower	Electoral Vote: Stevenson	Total Vote	% Eisenhower	% Stevenson	% Other	Popular: Eisenhower	Popular: Stevenson	Popular: Other
Alabama		11	426,120	35.02	64.55	0.43	149,231	275,075	1,814
Arizona	4		260,570	58.35	41.65		152,042	108,528	
Arkansas		8	404,800	43.76	55.90	0.33	177,155	226,300	1,345
California	32		5,341,603	56.83	42.27	0.91	3,035,587	2,257,646	48,370
Colorado	6		630,103	60.27	38.96	0.76	379,782	245,504	4,817
Connecticut	8		1,096,911	55.70	43.91	0.39	611,012	481,649	4,250
Delaware	3		174,025	51.75	47.88	0.37	90,059	83,315	651
Florida	10		989,337	54.99	44.97	0.04	544,036	444,950	351
Georgia		12	655,803	30.34	69.66	0.00	198,979	456,823	1
Idaho	4		276,231	65.42	34.42	0.16	180,707	95,081	443
Illinois	27		4,481,058	54.84	44.94	0.22	2,457,327	2,013,920	9,811
Indiana	13		1,955,325	58.11	40.99	0.90	1,136,259	801,530	17,536
Iowa	10		1,268,773	63.75	35.59	0.66	808,906	451,513	8,354
Kansas	8		896,166	68.77	30.50	0.73	616,302	273,296	6,568
Kentucky		10	993,148	49.84	49.91	0.24	495,029	495,729	2,390
Louisiana		10	651,952	47.08	52.92		306,925	345,027	
Maine	5		351,786	66.05	33.77	0.18	232,353	118,806	627
Maryland	9		902,074	55.36	43.83	0.81	499,424	395,337	7,313
Massachusetts	16		2,383,398	54.22	45.46	0.32	1,292,325	1,083,525	7,548
Michigan	20		2,798,592	55.44	43.97	0.59	1,551,529	1,230,657	16,406
Minnesota	11		1,379,483	55.33	44.11	0.57	763,211	608,458	7,814
Mississippi		8	285,532	39.56	60.44		112,966	172,566	
Missouri	13		1,892,062	50.71	49.14	0.15	959,429	929,830	2,803
Montana	4		265,037	59.39	40.07	0.54	157,394	106,213	1,430
Nebraska	6		609,660	69.15	30.85		421,603	188,057	
Nevada	3		82,190	61.45	38.55		50,502	31,688	
New Hampshire	4		272,950	60.92	39.08		166,287	106,663	
New Jersey	16		2,419,554	56.81	41.99	1.20	1,374,613	1,015,902	29,039
New Mexico	4		238,608	55.39	44.28	0.33	132,170	105,661	777
New York	45		7,128,241	55.45	43.55	0.99	3,952,815	3,104,601	70,825
North Carolina		14	1,210,910	46.09	53.91		558,107	652,803	
North Dakota	4		270,127	70.97	28.39	0.64	191,712	76,694	1,721
Ohio	25		3,700,758	56.76	43.24		2,100,391	1,600,367	
Oklahoma	8		948,984	54.59	45.41		518,045	430,939	
Oregon	6		695,059	60.54	38.93	0.53	420,815	270,579	3,665
Pennsylvania	32		4,580,969	52.74	46.85	0.41	2,415,789	2,146,269	18,911
Rhode Island	4		414,498	50.89	49.05	0.07	210,935	203,293	270
South Carolina		8	341,086	49.28	50.72		168,082	173,004	
South Dakota	4		294,283	69.27	30.73		203,857	90,426	
Tennessee	11		892,553	49.99	49.71	0.30	446,147	443,710	2,696
Texas	24		2,075,946	53.13	46.69	0.18	1,102,878	969,228	3,840
Utah	4		329,554	58.93	41.07		194,190	135,364	
Vermont	3		153,557	71.45	28.23	0.32	109,717	43,355	485

1952 Presidential General Election Results (*continued*)

State	Electoral Vote: Eisenhower	Electoral Vote: Stevenson	Total Vote	% Eisenhower	% Stevenson	% Other	Popular: Eisenhower	Popular: Stevenson	Popular: Other
Virginia	12		619,689	56.32	43.36	0.32	349,037	268,677	1,975
Washington	9		1,102,708	54.33	44.69	0.98	599,107	492,845	10,756
West Virginia		8	873,548	48.08	51.92		419,970	453,578	
Wisconsin	12		1,607,370	60.95	38.71	0.34	979,744	622,175	5,451
Wyoming	3		129,251	62.71	37.09	0.21	81,047	47,934	270
Total	442	89	61,751,942	55.18	44.33	0.49	34,075,529	27,375,090	301,232

Source: http://uselectionatlas.org/RESULTS/.

NOTES

All public statements made by Franklin D. Roosevelt, Harry Truman, or Dwight Eisenhower while president can be found in *The Public Papers of the President*, searchable at the American Presidency Project of the University of California, Santa Barbara: http://www.presidency.ucsb.edu/ws/. Thus, speeches and proclamations by these three presidents are not cited in this book unless a videotape or script of a specific speech was consulted.

ACRONYMS AND SHORT TITLES

AES	Adlai E. Stevenson II
AESP	Adlai E. Stevenson II, Papers, Seeley G. Mudd Library, Princeton University.
DDE	Dwight D. Eisenhower
DDEL	Dwight D. Eisenhower Presidential Library, Abilene, Kansas
EPPP	Dwight D. Eisenhower, Pre-Presidential Papers, DDEL
HST	Harry S. Truman
HSTL	Harry S. Truman Library, Independence, Missouri
HSTP	Harry S. Truman Papers, HSTL, Independence, Missouri
LOC	Library of Congress
NYT	*New York Times*
OTR	Robert H. Ferrell, ed., *Off the Record: The Private Papers of Harry S. Truman*. New York: Harper & Row, 1980.
Papers of AES	Walter Johnson, ed., *The Papers of Adlai E. Stevenson*. Vol. 3, *Governor of Illinois: 1949–1953*. Boston: Little, Brown, 1973. Vol. 4, *"Let's Talk Sense to the American People,"* 1952–1955. Boston: Little, Brown, 1974.
Papers of DDE	Louis Galambos, *The Papers of Dwight D. Eisenhower*. Vols. 12 and 13, *NATO and the Campaign of 1952*. Baltimore: Johns Hopkins University Press, 1989.
PNP	Paul T. David, Malcolm Moos, and Ralph Goldman, *Presidential Nominating Politics in 1952*. Vol. 1, *The National Story*; vol. 2, *The Northeast*; vol. 3, *The South*; vol. 4, *The Middle West*; vol. 5, *The West*. Baltimore: Johns Hopkins University Press, 1954.
PSF	President's Secretary's File
RMN	Richard M. Nixon
RMNPPC	Richard M. Nixon Pre-Presidential Collection, Campaign 1952, Vice Presidential Series, Richard M. Nixon Library, Laguna Niguel, California
RTP	Clarence E. Wunderlin, ed., *The Papers of Robert A. Taft*. Vol. 4, *1949–1953*. Kent, OH: Kent State University Press, 2006.
SGML	Seeley G. Mudd Library, Princeton University

Speeches of AES   Adlai E. Stevenson, *Major Campaign Speeches of Adlai Steven-son, 1952*. New York: Random House, 1953.

USN&WR   *U.S. News & World Report*

PREFACE AND ACKNOWLEDGMENTS

1. Lanham, MD: University Press of America, 1985.

INTRODUCTION. TRUMAN'S TROUBLES, 1949–1951

1. HST to Bess Truman, 29 June 1949, *OTR*, 159. Also in Robert H. Ferrell, ed., *Dear Bess: The Letters from Harry to Bess Truman, 1910–1959* (New York: Norton, 1983), 558.

2. Truman diary entry, 16 April 1950, in *OTR*, 177–178. Truman paraphrases this entry in *Memoirs*, vol. 2, *Years of Trial and Hope* (Garden City, NY: Doubleday, 1956), 488.

3. David McCullough, *Truman* (New York: Simon & Schuster, 1992), 873–874.

4. Truman diary entry, 30 January 1952, in HSTP, PSF, Longhand Notes File, dated folder.

5. HST to Martha Ellen and Mary Jane Truman, 20 September 1946, *OTR*, 97.

6. Quoted in Michael R. Gardner, *Harry Truman and Civil Rights: Moral Courage and Political Risks* (Carbondale: Southern Illinois University Press, 2002), 12.

7. Lucius Jefferson Barker, "Offshore Oil Politics: A Study in Public Policy Making" (PhD diss., University of Illinois, 1954), 7–12.

8. *NYT*, 28 March 1952, 22.

9. Alfred Steinberg, *Sam Rayburn: A Biography* (New York: Hawthorn Books, 1975), 273.

10. Kirk H. Porter and Donald B. Johnson, *National Party Platforms: 1840–1960* (Urbana: University of Illinois Press, 1961), 435.

11. For a good summary of the fight over the civil rights plank, see Gardner, *Harry Truman and Civil Rights*, 97–99.

12. The standard treatment of the 1948 election is Andrew E. Busch, *Truman's Triumphs: The 1948 Election and the Making of Postwar America* (Lawrence: University Press of Kansas, 2012).

13. Ibid., 162.

14. A useful summary of the fate of Truman's Fair Deal legislation can be found in Andrew J. Dunar, *America in the Fifties* (Syracuse, NY: Syracuse University Press, 2006), 31–33.

15. Andrew J. Dunar, *The Truman Scandals and the Politics of Morality* (Columbia: University of Missouri Press, 1984), 158. See also Sean J. Savage, "Truman in Historical, Popular, and Political Memory," in David S. Margolies, ed., *A Companion to Harry S. Truman* (Oxford: Blackwell, 2012), 16.

16. Quoted in Robert H. Ferrell, *Harry S. Truman and the Modern American Presidency* (Boston: Little, Brown, 1983), 144.

17. Elmo Roper, *You and Your Leaders: Their Actions and Your Reactions* (New York: William Morrow, 1957), 146.

18. Alonzo L. Hamby, *Man of the People: A Life of Harry S. Truman* (New York: Oxford University Press, 1995), 534–539 ("sons of bitches" quote on p. 534).

19. Quoted in Walter LaFeber, *America, Russia, and the Cold War, 1945–1980* (New York: Wiley, 1980), 117.

20. Taft to Leroy E. Smith, 23 May 1951, *RTP*, vol. 4, 287.

21. Chester J. Pach and Elmo Richardson, *The Presidency of Dwight D. Eisenhower*, rev. ed. (Lawrence: University Press of Kansas, 1991), 21.

22. Dennis Merrill, ed., *Documentary History of the Truman Presidency*, vol. 30, *The Constitutional Crisis over President Truman's Seizure of the Steel Industry in 1952* (New York: University Publications of America, 2001), xxx–xxxi.

23. Hamby, *Man of the People*, 595.

24. The standard treatment of the subject is Maeva Marcus, *Truman and the Steel Seizure Case: The Limits of Presidential Power* (New York: Columbia University Press, 1977), 3.

25. *NYT*, 9 April 1952.

26. *NYT*, 27 May 1952.

27. *NYT*, 20 April 1952; 29 May 1952.

28. Taft speech, Pittsburgh, Pennsylvania, 15 April 1952, *RTP*, vol. 4, 368; *NYT*, 18 April 1952.

29. *NYT*, 10 May 1952.

30. Kevin Mattson, *Just Plain Dick: Richard Nixon's Checkers Speech and the "Rocking, Socking" Election of 1952* (New York: Bloomsbury, 2012), 15.

31. 343 U.S. 579 (1951).

32. 341 U.S. 494 (1951).

33. Quoted in Edwin R. Bayley, *Joe McCarthy and the Press* (Madison: University of Wisconsin Press, 1981), 36.

34. Quoted in Steinberg, *Rayburn*, 265.

CHAPTER 1. THE REPUBLICAN PRECONVENTION CAMPAIGNS

1. John Fousek, *To Lead the Free World: American Nationalism and the Cultural Roots of the Cold War* (Chapel Hill: University of North Carolina Press, 2000), 7.

2. Quoted in Geoffrey Kabaservice, *Rule and Ruin: The Downfall of Moderation and the Destruction of the Republican Party, from Eisenhower to the Tea Party* (New York: Oxford University Press, 2012), 8.

3. Ibid.

4. See, for example, Taft to Herbert C. Hoover, 5 February 1952, *RTP*, vol. 4, 353.

5. William S. White, *The Taft Story* (New York: Harper, 1954), 51; Russell Kirk and James McClellan, *The Political Principles of Robert A. Taft* (New York: Fleet Press, 1967), 13.

6. Quoted in James T. Patterson, *Mr. Republican: A Biography of Robert A. Taft* (Boston: Houghton Mifflin, 1972), 135.

7. Kabaservice, *Rule and Ruin*, 5.

8. Taft to James M. Hutton Jr., 7 February 1952, *RTP*, vol. 4, 355.

9. Jeff Broadwater, *Eisenhower and the Anti-Communist Crusade* (Chapel Hill: University of North Carolina Press, 1992), 29.

10. Taft to Chase Mellon Jr., 1 January 1952, in *RTP*, vol. 4, 338–339.

11. Patterson, *Mr. Republican*, 185.

12. Taft to C. F. Wurster, 19 February 1952, *RTP*, vol. 4, 356–357.

13. Quoted in Robert A. Divine, *Foreign Policy and U.S. Presidential Elections: 1952–1960* (New York: New Viewpoints, 1974), 8–9.

14. Taft to Merryle S. Rukeyser, 28 July 1951, *RTP*, vol. 4, 304.

15. Taft to Bertha H. Putnam, 19 February 1951, *RTP*, vol. 4, 261.

16. Taft to Marilyn Lifschitz, 3 January 1952, *RTP*, vol. 4, 345.

17. Taft to Benjamin S. Hubbell Jr., 17 August 1951, *RTP*, vol. 4, 312.

18. Quoted in Merle Miller, *Plain Speaking: An Oral Biography of Harry S. Truman* (New York: Berkeley Books, 1973), 122.

19. Patterson, *Mr. Republican*, 214.

20. Taft to J. B. Martin Jr., 27 October 1951, *RTP*, vol. 4, 323.

21. Editor's comments, *RTP*, 337–338.

22. *NYT*, 17 October 1951.

23. HST to Taft, 17 October 1951; Taft to HST, 29 October 1951, HSTP, PSF, box 50, Taft folder.

24. Quoted in Piers Brendon, *Ike: His Life and Times* (New York: Harper & Row, 1986), 202.

25. Peter Lyon, *Eisenhower: Portrait of a Hero* (Boston: Little, Brown, 1974), 51.

26. Marquis Childs, *Eisenhower: Captive Hero* (New York: Harcourt, Brace, & World), 1958), 39.

27. Lyon, *Eisenhower*, 80.

28. Travis Beal Jacobs speculates that the way that Eisenhower went about accepting this appointment, "being persuaded that it was his duty and that his selection received unanimous support," was the way that Eisenhower went after the Republican nomination in 1952 ("Eisenhower, the American Assembly, and 1952," *Presidential Studies Quarterly* 22 [Summer 1992]: 455–456).

29. Quoted in James Reston, *Deadline: A Memoir* (New York: Random House, 1991), 191.

30. Public Information Office, Columbia University (undated), EPPP: Principal File, box 4, American Assembly folder.

31. Jacobs, "American Assembly," 464.

32. See Brendon, *Ike*, 200.

33. See, for example, DDE to Philip Young, 24 February 1951, *Papers of DDE*, vol. 12, 69–70.

34. Jacobs, "American Assembly," 462–463. The best summary of Eisenhower and the American Assembly can be found in Travis Beal Jacobs, *Eisenhower at Columbia* (New Brunswick, NJ: Transaction, 2001), 238–269. See also

William B. Pickett, *Eisenhower Decides to Run: Presidential Politics and Cold War Strategy* (Chicago: Ivan R. Dee, 2000), 28–29.

35. Jacobs, "American Assembly," 462.

36. DDE diary entry, 5 March 1951, *Papers of DDE*, vol. 12, 91.

37. DDE diary entry, 27 April 1951, *Papers of DDE*, vol. 12, 245.

38. DDE to Kenneth Claiborne Royall, 7 April 1951, *Papers of DDE*, vol. 12, 199–200.

39. Editor's introduction, *Papers of DDE*, vol. 12, xiv. To suggest, as did Joseph M. Dailey, that Eisenhower was "avoiding politics at NATO" is simply nonsense ("The Reluctant Candidate: Dwight D. Eisenhower in 1951," in Joann P. Krieg, ed., *DDE: Soldier, President, and Statesman* [Westport, CT: Greenwood Press, 1987], 2).

40. For a sample of this correspondence, see DDE to Harriman, 2 March 1951; DDE to Harriman, 8 March 1951; DDE to Harriman, 4 May 1951; DDE to Harriman, 1 June 1951, *Papers of DDE*, vol. 12, 88–90, 104–106, 262–266, 315–319.

41. Quoted in Tom Wicker, *Dwight D. Eisenhower* (New York: Times Books, 2002), 137.

42. DDE diary entry, 15 March 1951, in Tyler Abell, ed., *The Drew Pearson Diaries, 1949–1959* (New York: Holt, Rinehart, and Winston, 1974), 152.

43. Wicker, *Eisenhower*, 137–138.

44. The quote comes from an interview with PBS's Bill Moyers, found at http://www.mythsdreamssymbols.com/herojourney.html.

45. Quoted in Herbert S. Parmet, *Eisenhower and the American Crusades* (New York: Collier Macmillan, 1972), 7.

46. David McCullough, *Truman* (New York: Simon & Schuster, 1992), 429–430; Stanley M. Rumbough Jr., *Citizens for Eisenhower: The 1952 Presidential Campaign—Lessons for the Future?* (McLean, VA: International Publishers, 2013), 26.

47. Rumbough, *Citizens for Eisenhower*, 24.

48. Ibid., 26.

49. Quoted in ibid., 26–27.

50. Quoted in Pickett, *Eisenhower Decides to Run*, 44. Pickett interprets this second letter as follows: "It is not clear that he intended to remain in the political arena" (44). See also Andrew E. Busch, *Truman's Triumphs: The 1948 Election and the Making of Postwar America* (Lawrence: University Press of Kansas, 2012), 83–84.

51. *NYT*, 3 August 1951; DDE to Bernard Baruch, 23 August 1951, *Papers of DDE*, vol. 12, 485, 486n2.

52. DDE diary entry, 7 July 1949, in Robert H. Ferrell, ed., *The Eisenhower Diaries* (New York: Norton, 1981), 162.

53. Dewey to DDE, 27 December 1949, EPPP: Principal File, box 34, Dewey folder.

54. Herbert Brownell, conference panelist, "The Great Crusade," DDEL,

November 1992. Eisenhower reminisced on this moment in DDE to Thomas Dewey, 1 August 1952, EPPP, Ann Whitman File, Administration Series, box 11, Dewey folder; also in *Papers of DDE*, vol. 13, 1303–1304.

55. DDE to Thomas E. Dewey, 19 March 1951, *Papers of DDE*, vol. 12, 142–143, 143n2.

56. DDE diary entry, 1 January 1951, *Papers of DDE*, vol. 12, 5–6.

57. DDE to William Alexander Hewitt, 2 August 1951, *Papers of DDE*, vol. 12, 456 (emphasis in original), 456.

58. DDE to Sigfrid B. Unander, 17 April 1951, *Papers of DDE*, vol. 12, 216.

59. DDE diary entry, 13 March 1951, *Papers of DDE*, vol. 12, 123.

60. Thus, those who claim, as does Piers Brendon, that "the Eisenhower boom . . . was being deliberately orchestrated and conducted by Ike's backers, with the tacit connivance of the General himself," make their claims in the face of overwhelming evidence to the contrary (Brendon, *Ike*, 209).

61. Rumbough, *Citizens for Eisenhower*, 3.

62. Ibid.

63. Ibid., 19–30.

64. Clay to DDE, 16 October 1951, EPPP: Principal File, box 24, Clay folder (6).

65. Jean Edward Smith, *Lucius D. Clay: An American Life* (New York: Henry Holt, 1990), 582.

66. Clay to DDE, 18 May 1951, EPPP: Principal File, box 24, Clay folder (6). See also *Papers of DDE*, vol. 12, 308n3.

67. DDE to Clay, 20 May 1951, EPPP: Principal File, box 24, Clay folder (6; emphasis in original); also in *Papers of DDE*, vol. 12, 306–310.

68. Clay to DDE, 13 August 1951, EPPP: Principal File, box 24, Clay folder (6). Eisenhower would finally request that Clay drop the code (DDE to Clay, 27 September 1951, EPPP: Principal File, box 24, Clay folder [5]; also in *Papers of DDE*, vol. 12, 580–581).

69. Clay to DDE, 22 August 1951, Eisenhower PPP: Principal File, box 24, Clay folder (6).

70. Steve M. Barkin, "Eisenhower and Robinson: The Candidate and the Publisher in the 1952 Campaign," in Krieg, *DDE*, 13.

71. DDE to Bert Andrews, 31 August 1951, *Papers of DDE*, vol. 12, 507.

72. Herbert Brownell, *Advising Ike: The Memoirs of Attorney General Herbert Brownell* (Lawrence: University Press of Kansas, 1993), 95–96; Milton Eisenhower, *The President Is Calling* (Garden City, NY: Doubleday, 1974), 243–245; Brendon, *Ike*, 204; Divine, *Foreign Policy and U.S. Presidential Elections*, 13. Later, Eisenhower told his brother Milton, who had been present at the meeting, "In the absence of the assurance I had been seeking, it would be silly for me to throw away whatever political influence I might possess to help keep us on the right track" (quoted in Eisenhower, *The President Is Calling*, 245).

73. Robert F. Burk, *Dwight D. Eisenhower: Hero and Politician* (Boston: G. K. Hall, 1986), 119.

74. Herbert Brownell, conference panelist, "The Great Crusade," DDEL, November 1992.
75. Quoted in Divine, *Foreign Policy and U.S. Presidential Elections*, 31.
76. DDE diary entry, 4 October 1951, *Papers of DDE*, vol. 12, 608–609.
77. From Clark memoir, quoted in Pickett, *Eisenhower Decides to Run*, 128–129. The same story, without quoting from the letter, is found in William Bragg Ewald, *Eisenhower the President: Crucial Days, 1951–1960* (Englewood Cliffs, NJ: Prentice-Hall, 1981), 38–41. According to Clark, he showed the letter to John Hay "Jock" Whitney, the publisher of the *New York Herald-Tribune*; businessman James Brownlee; and Nelson A. Rockefeller, then serving as the chairman of the International Development Advisory Board.
78. DDE to E. E. Hazlett, 14 November 1951, EPPP: Principal File, box 56, Hazlett folder (3); also in *Papers of DDE*, vol. 12, 712–716.
79. DDE to Edgar Eisenhower, 6 December 1951, *Papers of DDE*, vol. 12, 757 (emphasis in original).
80. Smith, *Clay*, 583–584.
81. Quoted in Pickett, *Eisenhower Decides to Run*, 115.
82. George Lodge (of the *Boston Herald*), "The Campaign to Win the Republican Nomination for Dwight D. Eisenhower: November 16, 1951–July 12, 1952," EPPP, box 23, Lodge Campaign Memo folder.
83. Quoted in Smith, *Clay*, 585. In error, Arthur Krock wrote in his memoir that in December 1951, a "three-man board of strategy"—Clay, George Allen, and Sid Richardson—was "established to promote Eisenhower as the Republican candidate for President" (Arthur Krock, *Memoirs: Sixty Years on the Firing Line* [New York: Funk & Wagnalls, 1968], 284).
84. Lodge letter quoted in *Papers of DDE*, vol. 12, 779n2.
85. "Who's Who in the GOP: Stassen," *Time*, 26 April 1948, 22; Richard Norton Smith, *Thomas E. Dewey and His Times* (New York: Simon & Schuster, 1982), 483–485.
86. Shanley Diaries, DDEL, box 1, p. 6.
87. Ibid., p. 29.
88. DDE to Clay, 3 October 1951, EPPP: Principal File, box 24, Clay folder; also in *Papers of DDE*, vol. 12, 606.
89. Clay to DDE, 7 December 1951, EPPP: Principal File, box 24, Clay folder (5).
90. DDE diary entry, 21 December 1951, *Papers of DDE*, vol. 12, 809, 809n2; Shanley Diaries, DDEL, box 1, p. 177; *NYT*, 28 December 1951; 7 January 1952.
91. Taft to Hugh A. Butler, 28 December 1951, *RTP*, vol. 4, 331.
92. DDE diary entry, 11 December 1951, *Papers of DDE*, vol. 12, 772.
93. DDE to Lodge, 12 December 1951, *Papers of DDE*, vol. 12, 778.
94. Lodge letter quoted in *Papers of DDE*, vol. 12, 829n1.
95. DDE to Lodge, 29 December 1951, *Papers of DDE*, vol. 12, 829.
96. HST to DDE, 28 December 1951; DDE to HST, 1 January 1952, *Papers of DDE*, vol. 12, 830–831, 831n1; also in *OTR*, 220.
97. He would later write of his announcement in the press statement he felt

"forced to make" (DDE to Edward John Bermingham, 7 January 1952, *Papers of DDE*, vol. 121, 855). See also DDE diary entry, 10 January 1951, *Papers of DDE*, vol. 13, 870; and DDE to Clifford Roberts, 11 January 1952, *Papers of DDE*, vol. 13, 874 (Lodge's announcement "caused me a bit of bitter resentment").

98. *NYT*, 8 January 1952; see also *Papers of DDE*, vol. 13, 836n2.
99. *NYT*, 9 January 1952.
100. George Lodge (of the *Boston Herald*), "The Campaign to Win the Republican Nomination for Dwight D. Eisenhower: November 16, 1951–July 12, 1952), EPPP, box 23, Lodge Campaign Memo folder, 11–12.
101. *NYT*, 28 January 1952; Joseph Reuben Churgin, "Anatomy of a Presidential Primary: An Analysis of New Hampshire's Impact on American Politics" (PhD diss., Brown University, 1970), 62–63.
102. Allen to DDE, 8 January 1952, EPPP: Principal File, box 4, Allen folder.
103. DDE to Edward John Bermingham, 7 January 1952, *Papers of DDE*, vol. 12, 855.
104. DDE diary entry, 7 January 1952, in C. L. Sulzberger, *A Long Row of Candles: Memoirs and Diaries, 1934–1954* (New York: Macmillan, 1969), 715.
105. *NYT*, 2 January 1952.
106. Patterson, *Mr. Republican*, 161.
107. Ibid., 511; Karl A. Lamb, "The Opposition Party as Secret Agent: Republicans and the Court Fight, 1937," *Papers of the Michigan Academy of Science, Arts, and Letters* 46 (1961): 539–550.
108. Patterson, *Mr. Republican*, 512; memo from Coleman, 17 March 1952, Taft Papers, LOC, Political File, 1952, box 327, Arizona folder.
109. Taft speech, Portland, Oregon, 13 February 1952, Robert A. Taft Papers, LOC, Speech File, box 1337, dated folder.
110. Taft speech, New York City, 26 January 1952, Robert A. Taft Papers, LOC, Speech File, box 1337, dated folder.
111. Quoted in *NYT*, 1 March 1952.
112. Quoted in *NYT*, 23 February 1952; and Marty Snyder, *My Friend Ike* (New York: Frederick Fell, 1956), 119.
113. Taft to George H. Hall, 28 February 1951, and Taft to Paul W. Shafer, 5 November 1951, *RTP*, 265n, 324; Broadwater, *Eisenhower and the Anti-Communist Crusade*, 30; A. M. Sperber, *Murrow: His Life and Times* (New York: Freundlich Books, 1986), 383–384.
114. DDE to Edwin Clark, 9 January 1952, *Papers of DDE*, vol. 13, 870.
115. DDE to Clay, 23 January 1952, *Papers of DDE*, vol. 13, 909–910; Clay to DDE, 1 February 1952, EPPP: Principal File, box 24, Clay folder (4).
116. See DDE to Paul Hoffman, 24 January 1952, *Papers of DDE*, vol. 13, 912.
117. For but one example, see DDE to Albert John Hayes, 31 January 1952, *Papers of DDE*, vol. 13, 937–938.
118. DDE to Paul Hoffman, 9 February 1952, EPPP: Principal File, box 57, Hoffman folder (2); also in *Papers of DDE*, vol. 13, 954–957.
119. *Chicago Tribune*, 8 January 1952, quoted in *Papers of DDE*, vol. 13, 934n1.

120. DDE to Clay, 28 January 1952, EPPP: Principal File, box 24, Clay folder (4); also in *Papers of DDE*, vol. 13, 926.

121. Smith, *Clay*, 593; Dewey quoted in Snyder, *My Friend Ike*, 107.

122. Quoted in Smith, *Clay*, 593.

123. *NYT*, 8 and 9 February 1952; Rumbough, *Citizens for Eisenhower*, 47–51; Snyder, *My Friend Ike*, 112.

124. Dwight D. Eisenhower, *The White House Years*, vol. 1, *Mandate for Change: 1953–1956* (Garden City, NY: Doubleday, 1963), 20.

125. DDE diary entry, 12 February 1952, *Papers of DDE*, vol. 13, 971.

126. DDE to E. E. Hazlett, 12 February 1952, EPPP: Principal File, box 56, Hazlett folder (2); also in *Papers of DDE*, vol. 13, 977–981; and Robert W. Griffith, *Ike's Letters to a Friend, 1941–1958* (Lawrence: University Press of Kansas, 1984), 97–101.

127. Eisenhower, *Mandate for Change*, 21.

128. Quoted in Smith, *Clay*, 590.

129. Eisenhower, *Mandate for Change*, 21.

130. DDE to George Sloan, 21 February 1952, *Papers of DDE*, vol. 13, 107; also in Robert L. Branyan and Lawrence H. Larsen, eds., *The Eisenhower Administration, 1953–1961: A Documentary History*, vol. 1 (New York: Random House, 1971), 21–22.

131. Eisenhower diary entry, 28 February 1952, *Papers of DDE*, vol. 13, 1026–1027.

132. Lyn Ragsdale, ed., *Vital Statistics on the Presidency*, 3rd ed. (Washington, DC: CQ Press, 2008), 40; *NYT*, 10 February 2008.

133. Lodge memorandum, 31 January 1952, Lodge Papers, Eisenhower Campaign, 1952, box 2, New Hampshire folder.

134. *NYT*, 27 February 1952.

135. *NYT*, 8 March 1952.

136. "New Hampshire Primary," *Time*, 11 February 1952, 17.

137. Ibid.; *NYT*, 31 January 1952; Churgin, "Anatomy of a Presidential Primary," 66.

138. Taft speech, Manchester, New Hampshire, Taft Papers, Box 1330, Speeches, 1952 folder.

139. Ibid.

140. *NYT*, 4 March 1952.

141. "Techniques and Tactics," *Time*, 24 March 1952, 19–20.

142. *NYT*, 10 March 1952; 12 March 1952; "What New Hampshire Really Means," *USN&WR*, 21 March 1952, 24–26; Churgin, "Anatomy of a Presidential Primacy," 80; Patterson, *Mr. Republican*, 523.

143. *NYT*, 13 March 1952.

144. Ibid.

145. Ibid.

146. *NYT*, 17 March 1952.

147. *NYT*, 16 March 1952; Donald H. Ackerman Jr., "The Write-In Vote for Dwight D. Eisenhower in the Spring 1952 Minnesota Primary: Minnesota Politics on the Grass-Roots Level" (PhD diss., Syracuse University, 1954),

122; "The Minnesota Explosion," *Time*, 31 March 1952, 19. See also Jacobs, *Eisenhower at Columbia*, 277.

148. *NYT*, 14 March 1952; Ackerman, "Minnesota," 123–124.

149. *NYT*, 16 March 1952.

150. *NYT*, 21 March 1952; 22 March 1952; "Minnesota Explosion," 20; Ackerman, "Minnesota," 120.

151. Sulzberger diary entry, 20 March 1952, in Sulzberger, *A Long Row of Candles*, 738.

152. Quoted in *NYT*, 19 March 1952.

153. Brownell, *Advising Ike*, 95–100; Herbert Brownell, conference panelist, "The Great Crusade," DDEL, November 1992. When panel chair Ray Scherer (formerly of *NBC News*) suggested that Eisenhower "almost played this reluctant thing out too long," Brownell nodded his head in agreement.

154. *NYT*, 27 March 1952.

155. *NYT*, 9 April 1952.

156. Taft statement, 9 April 1952, *RTP*, 366.

157. *NYT*, 1 April; 2 April; 3 April; 9 April; "Taft Makes It a Battle," *USN&WR*, 11 April 1952, 18–20; Miles McMillan, "How Taft Was Saved," *New Republic*, 14 April 1952, 16–17.

158. *NYT*, 8 April 1952; 11 April 1952.

159. DDE to HST, 2 April 1952, EPPP, box 116, Truman, January 1951–April 1952 folder; also in *Papers of DDE*, vol. 13, 1154–1156.

160. HST to DDE (handwritten), 6 April 1952, EPPP, box 116, Truman, January 1951–April 1952 folder. Eisenhower discusses the exchange of letters in *Mandate for Change*, 23. Clay biographer Jean Edward Smith errantly reports that Eisenhower wrote to Truman on 12 April. Smith implies that this decision was caused by a 6 April handwritten letter that Dewey sent to Eisenhower, telling him that MacArthur would sweep the convention—according to Smith, no copy of the letter was kept (Smith, *Clay*, 594–596). Even if such a letter *had* existed, it was written *after* Eisenhower had written Truman asking to be relieved of his command. David Halberstam repeats this error in *The Fifties* (New York: Villard Books, 1993), 211.

161. *NYT*, 11 April 1952; 12 April 1952; 13 April 1952.

162. *NYT*, 16 April 1952.

163. *NYT*, 7 January 1952; Paul Casdorph, *A History of the Republican Party in Texas, 1865–1965* (Austin, TX: Pemberton Press, 1965), 174–176.

164. Casdorph, *Republican Party in Texas*, 179–180; O. Douglas Weeks, *Texas Presidential Politics in 1952* (Washington, DC: Institute of Public Affairs, 1953), 51; "Steamroller in Texas," *Time*, 9 June 1952, 20.

165. Parmet, *Eisenhower and the American Crusades*, 76; Patterson, *Mr. Republican*, 539.

166. Don E. Carleton, *Red Scare! Right-Wing Hysteria, Fifties Fanaticism, and Their Legacy in Texas* (Austin: Texas Monthly Press, 1985), 319.

167. *NYT*, 5 May 1952; *PNP*, vol. 3, 321.

168. Merlo Pusey, *Eisenhower the President* (New York: Macmillan, 1956), 15; Casdorph, *Republican Party in Texas*, 184.

169. *NYT*, 27 May 1952; 28 May 1952; Brownell, *Advising Ike*, 112–113; Casdorph, *Republican Party in Texas*, 184; George H. Mayer, *The Republican Party, 1854–1964* (New York: Oxford University Press, 1964), 488, Weeks, *Texas Presidential Politics in 1952*, 60–65; "Steamroller," 21.

170. Quoted in Casdorph, *Republican Party in Texas*, 185.

171. Quoted in "Steamroller," 21.

172. Quoted in Patterson, *Mr. Republican*, 544.

173. *NYT*, 28 May 1952.

174. Earl Warren, *The Memoirs of Earl Warren* (Garden City, NY: Doubleday, 1977), 249.

175. *Sacramento Bee*, 17 March 1974.

176. *NYT*, 1 March 1952; 10 April 1952.

177. Warren, *Memoirs*, 249.

178. Ibid., 228, 253; Ed Cray, *Chief Justice: A Biography of Earl Warren* (New York: Simon & Schuster, 1997), 223.

179. Tate to Taft, 19 November 1951, Taft Papers, Political File, 1952, box 465, Tate folder.

180. *PNP*, vol. 5, 229.

181. Herbert Brownell, conference panelist, "The Great Crusade," DDEL, November 1992.

182. Quoted in *NYT*, 6 June 1952.

183. Transcript, Press Conference, Abilene, Kansas, 5 June 1952, EPPP, Ann Whitman File—Speeches, box 1, book 2.

184. Poll in Kevin Mattson, *Just Plain Dick: Richard Nixon's Checkers Speech and the "Rocking, Socking" Election of 1952* (New York: Bloomsbury, 2012), 45.

185. *Washington Times-Herald*, 10 June 1952.

186. Quoted in George Lodge (of the *Boston Herald*), "The Campaign to Win the Republican Nomination for Dwight D. Eisenhower: November 16, 1951–July 12, 1952), EPPP, box 23, Lodge Campaign Memo folder, p. 21.

CHAPTER 2. THE DEMOCRATIC PRECONVENTION CAMPAIGNS

1. *NYT*, 24 January 1952; 13 February 1952.

2. Among the more severe heresies to southerners were decisions such as those that ruled that restrictive racial covenants (agreements among neighbors to sell their homes only to whites) violated the Fourteenth Amendment (*Shelley v. Kraemer*, 334 U.S. 1, 1948), which invalidated racial discrimination in railroad cars (*Henderson v. U.S.*, 339 U.S. 816, 1950), and ruled that denying a black student the right to apply to an Oklahoma law school also violated the Fourteenth Amendment (*Sipuel v. Board of Regents of University of Oklahoma*, 332 U.S. 631, 1948).

3. See Frederick M. Vinson Papers, Margaret I. King Library, University of Kentucky, Personal File, box 553, Truman, General folder. See also Harry S.

Truman, *Memoirs*, vol. 2, *Years of Trial and Hope* (Garden City, NY: Doubleday, 1956), 489–490; Michael R. Gardner, *Truman and Civil Rights: Moral
Courage and Political Risks* (Carbondale: Southern Illinois University Press,
2002), 164.

4. Truman, *Memoirs*, vol. 2, 489–490.

5. Clark Clifford, *Counsel to the President: A Memoir* (New York: Random
House, 1991), 282. The story of the courting of Vinson would not find its
way to the press until February (see *Washington Post*, 21 February 1952).
Vinson would die in September 1953 at age sixty-three; President Eisen-
hower would replace him as chief justice by nominating Earl Warren of
California.

6. David McCullough, *Truman* (New York: Simon & Schuster, 1992), 887–888.

7. *NYT*, 9 November 1951; DDE to Sulzberger, 10 November 1951, *Papers of
DDE*, vol. 12, 701; Arthur Krock, *Memoirs: Sixty Years on the Firing Line*
(New York: Funk & Wagnalls, 1968), 267–269; Sulzberger diary entry, 16
November 1951, in C. L. Sulzberger, *A Long Row of Candles: Memoirs and
Diaries, 1934–1954* (New York: Macmillan, 1969), 693.

8. DDE Diary entry, 25 September 1951, *Papers of DDE*, vol. 12, 565.

9. Jack Anderson and Fred Blumenthal, *The Kefauver Story* (New York: Dial
Press, 1956), 28.

10. "Bosses Are Icy to Kefauver; Truman Wants No Part of Him," *Newsweek*, 4
February 1952, 20; *NYT*, 4 February 1952; Anderson and Blumenthal, *The
Kefauver Story*, 129–131; "What Kefauver Would Be Like," *USN&WR*, 22
February 1952, 13–14.

11. Joseph Bruce Gorman, *Kefauver: A Political Biography* (New York: Oxford
University Press, 1981), 53.

12. Eric Goldman, *The Crucial Decade and After, 1945–1960* (New York: Vintage
Books, 1960), 194.

13. Anderson and Blumenthal, *The Kefauver Story*, 154, 172–174; Gorman,
Kefauver, 81–84; William Howard Moore, *The Kefauver Committee and the
Politics of Crime: 1950–1952* (Columbia: University of Missouri Press, 1974),
236.

14. Anderson and Blumenthal, *The Kefauver Story*, 166–167; Charles L. Fontenay, *Estes Kefauver: A Biography* (Knoxville: University of Tennessee Press,
1980), 177–179; Gorman, *Kefauver*, 81–84; Moore, *Kefauver Committee*,
157–158; William S. White, *Citadel: The Story of the U.S. Senate* (New York:
Harper & Bros., 1956), 260–263.

15. Paul H. Douglas, *In the Fullness of Time: The Memoirs of Paul H. Douglas*
(New York: Harcourt Brace Jovanovich, 1972), 220, 232.

16. Clinton P. Anderson, *Outsider in the Senate: Senator Clinton Anderson's
Memoirs* (New York: World, 1970), 107.

17. Truman, *Memoirs*, vol. 2, 494.

18. Memorandum, 7 July 1952, HSTP, PSF, Longhand Notes File, dated folder;
also in *OTR*, 261 (misdated here as 6 July).

19. *NYT*, 5 December 1951.

20. "Bosses Are Icy to Kefauver," 20. Kefauver wrote to Truman as soon as the *Newsweek* story came out, protesting that he had "never made such a statement." Truman responded: "I paid no attention whatever to it" (Kefauver to HST, 31 January 1952; HST to Kefauver, 4 February 1952, HSTP, PSF: Political File, box 46, Kefauver folder).

21. *NYT*, 24 January 1952.

22. Truman recounted for his diary the story of one such meeting to attempt to sway him to become a candidate; see Truman diary entry, 18 February 1952, HSTP, PSF, Longhand Notes File, dated folder. Clifford, who was present at that meeting, remembers it in *Counsel to the President*, 283.

23. Truman private memorandum, 8 May 1950, HSTP, PSF, box 333, 1950 File; quoted in Truman, *Memoirs*, vol. 2, 491.

24. Hermon Dunlop Smith Reminiscences, in Edward P. Doyle, ed., *As We Knew Adlai: The Stevenson Story by Twenty-Two Friends* (New York: Harper & Row, 1966), 28–29.

25. Jacob Arvey Reminiscences in Doyle, *As We Knew Adlai*, 50–51.

26. Radio Report from AES to People of Illinois, 23 May 1949, *Papers of AES*, vol. 3, 91.

27. Statement, 30 July 1949, *Papers of AES*, vol. 3, 136.

28. Veto Message (Broyles Bill), 26 June 1951, *Papers of AES*, vol. 3, 414, 418.

29. Quoted in editor's comments, *Papers of AES*, vol. 3, 413.

30. The full text of Stevenson's deposition can be found in *NYT*, 15 October 1952. See also Confidential Memorandum on the Hiss Issue, AESP, box 267; "The Alger Hiss Issue," *Time*, 3 November 1952, 20.

31. AES, letter to the editor (*Chicago Tribune*), 27 August 1951, *Papers of AES*, vol. 3, 445–446.

32. AES to Alicia Patterson, late November or early December 1951, *Papers of AES*, vol. 3, 472.

33. AES to Porter McKeever, 2 April 1951, *Papers of AES*, vol. 3, 378.

34. John Bartlow Martin, *It Seems Like Only Yesterday: Memoirs of Writing, Presidential Politics, and the Diplomatic Life* (New York: William Morrow, 1986), 141–143; Adlai E. Stevenson, *Adlai's Almanac: The Wit and Wisdom of Stevenson of Illinois* (New York: Henry Schuman, 1952).

35. David Halberstam, *The Fifties* (New York: Villard Books, 1993), 220.

36. Stevenson's letters are rife with complaints. For one example, see AES to Mrs. Edison Dick, 21 April 1949, *Papers of AES*, vol. 3, 71.

37. John Patrick Clancy, "Adlai Ewing Stevenson and the Bureaucracy of the Democratic Party in the 1950s" (PhD diss., United States International University, 1975), 1.

38. Stewart Alsop, *Nixon and Rockefeller: A Double Portrait* (New York: Doubleday, 1960), 21.

39. Bert Cochran, *Adlai Stevenson: Patrician among the Politicians* (New York: Funk & Wagnalls, 1969), chap. 2 heading.

40. Kenneth S. Davis, *The Politics of Honor: A Biography of Adlai E. Stevenson* (New York: Putnam, 1967), 12.

41. George W. Ball, *The Past Has Another Pattern: Memoirs* (New York: Norton, 1982), 112; John Kenneth Galbraith, *Annals of an Abiding Liberal* (New York: Plume, 1980), 297.

42. *New York Herald Tribune*, 24 October 1949; reprinted in *Papers of AES*, vol. 3, 176–180.

43. Martin, *It Seems Like Only Yesterday*, 143.

44. John Kenneth Galbraith, *A Life in Our Times: Memoirs* (Boston: Houghton Mifflin, 1981), 287–288.

45. "Sir Galahad," *Time*, 28 January 1952, 19.

46. Ball, *Past Has Another Pattern*, 113–114; James Reston, *Deadline: A Memoir* (New York: Random House, 1991), 274–275; Truman, *Memoirs*, vol. 2, 491; Jeff Broadwater, *Adlai Stevenson and American Politics: The Odyssey of a Cold War Liberal* (New York: Twayne, 1994), 107.

47. Truman diary entry, 4 March 1952, HSTP, Longhand Notes File, dated folder; also in *OTR*, 244–245. See also Ball, *Past Has Another Pattern*, 117–118.

48. AES to Archibald MacLeish, 29 February 1952, *Papers of AES*, vol. 3, 527.

49. AES to Alicia Patterson, 29 January 1952, *Papers of AES*, vol. 3, 509.

50. Quoted in Merle Miller, *Plain Speaking: An Oral Biography of Harry S. Truman* (New York: Berkeley Medallion Books, 1973), 117.

51. AES to Ball, 21 February 1952, AESP, Series 1, Correspondence, box 9, Ball folder; Ball, *Past Has Another Pattern*, 115–116.

52. "Stevenson of Illinois: Who Is He?," pamphlet printed by the Illinois Committee for Stevenson for President, 27 February 1952, Leo Lerner Papers, George Arents Research Library, Syracuse University, box 51; Walter Johnson, *How We Drafted Adlai Stevenson* (New York: Knopf, 1955), 18–25; Broadwater, *Adlai Stevenson and American Politics*, 107; "How and Why Stevenson?," *Newsweek*, 28 July 1952, 17.

53. Broadwater, *Adlai Stevenson and American Politics*, 108.

54. See, for example, Johnson to AES, 28 February 1951; Draft of Speech on States Rights Issue (undated); AES to Johnson, 6 March 1952; Johnson to AES, 6 June 1952; AES to Johnson, 14 June 1952; Johnson to AES, 8 July 1952; in AESP, Series 1, Correspondence, box 45, folder 3, Johnson folder.

55. The section in Ball's memoirs (*Past Has Another Pattern*) on all this is entitled "Adlai Plays Hamlet."

56. Carl Rowan, *Breaking Barriers: A Memoir* (Boston: Little, Brown, 1991), 216.

57. Robert A. Caro, *The Years of Lyndon Johnson: Master of the Senate* (New York: Knopf, 2002), 177.

58. The very best short biography of Richard Russell can be found in Caro, *Master of the Senate*, 164–196. See also "The Negative Power," *Time*, 19 May 1952.

59. Gilbert C. Fite, *Richard B. Russell, Jr., Senator from Georgia* (Chapel Hill: University of North Carolina Press, 1991), 271–274.

60. *NYT*, 29 February 1952; Fite, *Russell*, 274.

61. Quoted in *St. Louis Post-Dispatch*, 2 March 1952.

62. *NYT*, 1 February 1952; Jonah Reuben Churgin, "Anatomy of a Presidential Primary: An Analysis of New Hampshire's Impact on American Politics" (PhD diss., Brown University, 1970), 78.

63. *NYT*, 1 February 1952.

64. Quoted in Gorman, *Kefauver*, 119.

65. NYT, 6 February 1952; Churgin, "Anatomy of a Presidential Primary," 79.

66. Kefauver speech, Nashua, 10 February 1952, Estes Kefauver Papers, University of Tennessee (Knoxville), Speeches and News Releases File, dated folder (the emphasized phrase was underlined in Kefauver's podium copy).

67. Quoted in *NYT*, 12 March 1952.

68. *NYT*, 12 March 1952; *PNP*, vol. 2; "Labor By-passes Truman," *USN&WR*, 21 March 1952, 25.

69. "The Rise of Senator Legend," *Time*, 24 March 1952, 20.

70. Hubert H. Humphrey, *The Education of a Public Man: My Life and Politics* (Garden City, NY: Doubleday, 1976), 179; Fontenay, *Estes Kefauver*, 198; Gorman, *Kefauver*, 135.

71. AES to Alicia Patterson, 13 March 1952, *Papers of AES*, vol. 3, 531.

72. AES to Charles Murphy, 17 March 1952, *Papers of AES*, vol. 3, 533–534.

73. Such a defeat had happened only a handful of times since the primary system had been initiated. In 1912, Theodore Roosevelt defeated incumbent William Howard Taft in Oregon, California, South Dakota, Nebraska, Illinois, Ohio, Maryland, and New Jersey; Robert LaFollette defeated Taft in North Dakota and Wisconsin. In 1924, LaFollette defeated incumbent Calvin Coolidge in Wisconsin, and Hiram Johnson won in California. In 1932, incumbent Herbert Hoover lost Maryland to Joseph I. France, Nebraska to George Norris, Ohio to Jacob Coxey, and South Dakota to Royal C. Johnson. In 1936, Franklin D. Roosevelt lost New York to Henry Breckinridge.

74. *NYT*, 15 January 1952.

75. *NYT*, 30 March 1952; "Exit Smiling," *Time*, 7 April 1952, 19–20; "I Shall Not Accept," *Life*, 37; Rudy Abramson, *Spanning the Century: The Life of W. Averell Harriman, 1891–1986* (New York: William Morrow, 1992), 485–487; *PNP*, vol. 1, 40; Robert F. Stinnett, *Democrats, Dinners, and Dollars: A History of the Democratic Party, Its Dinners, Its Rituals* (Ames: Iowa University Press, 1967), 168–188.

76. Preston C. King Jr. to George E. Allen, 1 April 1952, EPPP, Principal File, box 4, Allen folder.

77. John Bartlow Martin, *Adlai Stevenson of Illinois* (New York: Anchor Books, 1977), 547–548. The *New York Times* reported a surge in Stevenson's poll numbers in the days after Truman's announcement (*NYT*, 6 April 1952).

78. For background on Kerr, see a biography of his son, written by Ronn Cupp and Bob Burke, *Robert S. Kerr, Jr.: Mr. Water* (Oklahoma City: Oklahoma Heritage Association, 2005), 7–85.

79. Ann Hodges Morgan, *Robert S. Kerr: The Senate Years* (Norman: University of Oklahoma Press, 1977), 22.

80. Ibid.

81. Ibid., 32.
82. Clifford, *Counsel to the President*, 275.
83. "High Rise for Gas," *Time*, 10 April 1950, 20.
84. Morgan, *Kerr*, vii; *NYT*, 5 January 1951.
85. "Wildcatter," *Time*, 25 February 1952, 25.
86. Quoted in Morgan, *Kerr*, 37.
87. Quoted in "Death of a Senator," *Time*, 11 January 1963, 23.
88. *NYT*, 7 February 1952.
89. Truman, *Memoirs*, vol. 2, 494.
90. *NYT*, 6 February 1952; 8 March 1952; Morgan, *Kerr*, 117–118.
91. Morgan, *Kerr*, 117–120.
92. Anderson, *Outsider in the Senate*, 117; *PNP*, vol. 4, 295–296; Fontenay, *Estes Kefauver*, 198–199; Gorman, *Kefauver*, 136; Morgan, *Kerr*, 118–120.
93. AES to Mrs. Edison Dick, 15 March 1952, *Papers of AES*, vol. 3, 532.
94. Abramson, *Spanning the Century*, 487–489.
95. "Patrician," *Time*, 26 May 1952, 23.
96. *NYT*, 5 May 1952; Alonzo L. Hamby, *Beyond the New Deal: Harry S. Truman and American Liberalism* (New York: Columbia University Press, 1973), 485.
97. Quoted in *NYT*, 16 May 1952.
98. Truman private memorandum, 6 July 1952, *OTR*, 261.
99. *NYT*, 23 April 1952; Abramson, *Spanning the Century*, 492.
100. Envelope found in Election File, Leo Lerner Papers, box 57.
101. *PNP*, vol. 2, 314–315.
102. Ibid., 332.
103. Abramson, *Spanning the Century*, 491–492.
104. Ibid., 495.
105. Truman, *Memoirs*, vol. 2, 494.
106. HST to Vivian Truman, 26 May 1952, HSTP: PSF, box 295, Vivian Truman folder.
107. Stevenson statement, 31 March 1952, *Papers of DDE*, vol. 3, 540; *NYT*, 31 March 1952.
108. AES to HST, HSTP: PSF, Personal File, box 274, Stevenson folder; also in *Papers of AES*, vol. 3, 540.
109. HST to AES, 4 April 1952, HSTP: PSF, Personal File, box 274, Stevenson folder.
110. AES Statement, 16 April 1952, *Papers of AES*, vol. 3, 551–552.
111. AES to HST, 16 April 1952, HSTP: PSF, Personal File, box 274, Stevenson folder; also in *Papers of AES*, vol. 3, 552–553.
112. HST to AES, 22 April 1952, HSTP: PSF, Personal File, box 274, Stevenson folder.
113. Stevenson speech, 17 April 1952, *Papers of AES*, vol. 3, 553–555. See also Abramson, *Spanning the Century*, 490.
114. Quoted in editor's comments, *Papers of AES*, vol. 3, 562.
115. AES to Alicia Patterson, 18 April 1952, *Papers of AES*, vol. 3, 556.
116. Quoted in editor's comments, *Papers of AES*, vol. 3, 563n105.

117. William Carl Zehnder, "The 1952 Presidential Election in the State of Florida" (master's thesis, Florida Atlantic University, 1973), 74.

118. Copy of handbill in John S. Battle Executive Papers (Executive Department), Virginia State Library, Richmond, VA; General Correspondence File, box 134, Democratic National Committee folder.

119. *NYT*, 5 May 1952.

120. Quoted in Zehnder, "1952 Presidential Election in the State of Florida," 74–75.

121. William C. Berman, *The Politics of Civil Rights in the Truman Administration* (Columbus: Ohio State University Press, 1970), 199; Fite, *Russell*, 286.

122. Quoted in Zehnder, "1952 Presidential Election in the State of Florida," 78; "Duel in the South," *Time*, 5 May 1952, 25.

123. Quoted in Fontenay, *Estes Kefauver*, 203.

124. *PNP*, vol. 3, 134–137.

125. Caro, *Master of the Senate*, 467.

126. *Atlanta Constitution*, 8 May 1952.

127. *PNP*, vol. 3, 226.

128. Ibid.

129. Ibid., 228–229.

130. Quoted in Ricky F. Dobbs, *Yellow Dogs and Republicans: Allan Shivers and Texas Two-Party Politics* (College Station: Texas A&M University Press, 2005), 80. See also Sean P. Cunningham, *Cowboy Conservatism: Texas and the Rise of the Modern Right* (Lexington: University Press of Kentucky, 2010), 29.

131. Caro, *Master of the Senate*, 463–470; Dobbs, *Yellow Dogs*, 82.

132. O. Douglas Weeks, *Texas Presidential Politics in 1952* (Washington, DC: Institute for Public Affairs, 1953), 16–17.

133. *PNP*, vol. 3, 334–336; Weeks, *Texas Presidential Politics in 1952*, 25–38.

134. *PNP*, vol. 3, 337; Dobbs, *Yellow Dogs*, 83–84.

135. Dobbs, *Yellow Dogs*, 83–84.

136. Maverick to Truman, 29 May 1952, HSTP, Official File, box 61, Texas folder; Truman to Maverick, 2 June 1952, HSTP, PSF, box 290, Maverick folder.

137. AES to Alicia Patterson, 15 May 1952, *Papers of AES*, vol. 3, 564.

138. Stevenson Statement, 30 June 1952, *Papers of AES*, vol. 3, 576–577.

139. "The Tie That Binds," *Time*, 28 July 1952, 11.

140. Ibid., 12.

141. Alben Barkley, *That Reminds Me* (Garden City, NY: Doubleday, 1954), 224.

142. Transcripts of Sidney Shallett's interviews with Alben W. Barkley, HSTL, box 1, reel 6, side 6, pp. 12–14. There is a somewhat muted discussion of this incident in Barkley, *That Reminds Me*, 227.

143. Barkley, *That Reminds Me*, 227.

144. Ibid., 229; *PNP*, vol. 1, 68.

145. Truman diary entry, 11 July 1952, HSTP, PSF, Longhand Notes File, 11 July 1952, dated folder; Barkley, *That Reminds Me*, 230–231. See also Truman, *Memoirs*, vol. 2, 495.

146. Truman private memorandum, 6 July 1952, *OTR*, 261.

147. HST to Thomas Gavin, 16 July 1952, Alben W. Barkley Correspondence with HST (microfilm), HSTL, reel 1. The letter is reproduced in the photograph section of Barkley, *That Reminds Me.*

CHAPTER 3. THE CONVENTIONS

1. Memorandum to Members of Executive Committee, 10 November 1951, HSTP, Official File, box 942, Democratic National Convention folder 1; *NYT*, 7 July 1952.

2. Andrew E. Busch, *Truman's Triumphs: The 1948 Election and the Making of Postwar America* (Lawrence: University Press of Kansas, 2012), 189.

3. Eric Barnouw, *Tube of Plenty: The Evolution of American Television* (New York: Oxford University Press, 1975), 7, 99–134; Charles A. H. Thomson, *Television and Presidential Politics: The Experience in 1952 and the Problems Ahead* (Washington, DC: Brookings Institution, 1956), 7.

4. Democratic National Committee Records: 1932–1964, John F. Kennedy Library, Publicity Division. See Charles Van Devanter to Fry, 6 February 1952, box 360, Sponsorship of Convention folder; Charles Van Devanter to Thomas Velotta, 13 February 1952, box 368, Sponsorship of Convention—Code folder; Fry to Van Devanter, 21 February 1952, box 367, Interoffice Memos folder; Fry File Memo, 28 February 1952, box 365, ABC folder.

5. In addition to the sources in note 4, see Fry to Thomas Velotta, 16 May 1951 and 14 April 1952, box 365, ABC folder.

6. *NYT*, 9 March 1952.

7. Lyn Ragsdale, ed., *Vital Statistics on the Presidency*, 3rd ed. (Washington, DC: CQ Press, 2008), 69.

8. *NYT*, 22 August 2012.

9. "Eve of the Big Show," *Time*, 7 July 1952, 15; *NYT*, 2 July 1952.

10. "Eve of the Big Show," 13.

11. *NYT*, 3 July 1952.

12. Marty Snyder, *My Friend Ike* (New York: Frederick Fell, 1956), 16–17; David Halberstam, *The Fifties* (New York: Villard Books, 1993), 212.

13. For a full text of the Republican platform, see Kirk H. Porter and Donald B. Johnson, *National Party Platforms: 1840–1960* (Urbana: University of Illinois Press, 1961), 497–505; and *NYT*, 11 July 1952.

14. *NYT*, 2 July 1952; Thompson, *Television*, 28–29.

15. Katherine Graham Howard, *With My Shoes Off* (New York: Vantage Press, 1977), 132; *NYT*, 4 July 1952.

16. *NYT*, 2 July 1952.

17. *Atlanta Constitution*, 3 July 1952.

18. *NYT*, 1 July 1952.

19. For his view on how the Eisenhower forces exploited this decision, see Herbert Brownell, *Advising Ike: The Memoirs of Attorney General Herbert Brownell* (Lawrence: University Press of Kansas, 1993), 115.

20. *NYT*, 4 July 1952; "Contests," *Time*, 14 July 1952, 18–20; *PNP*, vol. 1, 69.

21. *Papers of DDE*, vol. 13, 1245n2.

22. *NYT*, 3 July 1952; "Marching through Georgia," *Time*, 14 July 1952, 18–19; *PNP*, vol. 1, 69; *PNP*, vol. 3, 100–102.

23. *NYT*, 3 July 1952.

24. *NYT*, 24 June 1952.

25. "The Texas Steal," *Time*, 14 July 1952, 20–21.

26. Henry Cabot Lodge, *The Storm Has Many Eyes* (New York: Norton, 1973), 114.

27. Brownell, *Advising Ike*, 116; Herbert Brownell, conference panelist, "The Great Crusade," DDEL, November 1992.

28. George Lodge (of the *Boston Herald*), "The Campaign to Win the Republican Nomination for Dwight D. Eisenhower: November 16, 1951–July 12, 1952), EPPP, box 23, Lodge Campaign Memo folder, 27–29.

29. *NYT*, 5 July 1952; *PNP*, vol. 1, 69–70.

30. Herbert J. Brownell, conference panelist, "The Great Crusade," November 1992; George Lodge, "The Campaign to Win the Republican Nomination for Dwight D. Eisenhower," 22.

31. Brownell, *Advising Ike*, 114.

32. *NYT*, 7 July 1952; "The Men Who Did It," *Time*, 21 July 1952, 12; Lodge, *Storm Has Many Eyes*, 107; Richard Norton Smith, *Thomas E. Dewey and His Times* (New York: Simon & Schuster, 1982), 589–590.

33. Poster, Young and Rubicam, Inc., Records of "Citizens for Eisenhower," DDEL, box 2, Ad Proofs for Eisenhower folder (all emphasis in original).

34. *Chicago Daily News*, clipping (undated), Young and Rubicam Papers, DDEL, box 2, Ad Proofs for Taft folder.

35. George Lodge, "The Campaign to Win the Republican Nomination for Dwight D. Eisenhower," 30–33; Howard, *With My Shoes Off*, 137–138; Lodge, *Storm Has Many Eyes*, 115–118; *NYT*, 8 July 1952.

36. *NYT*, 8 July 1952; "The Men Who Didn't," *Time*, 21 July 1952, 12–13; *PNP*, vol. 1, 74–75; Howard, *With My Shoes Off*, 140–141.

37. *Official Report of the Proceedings of the Twenty-Fifth Republican National Convention* (Washington, DC: Judd & Detweiler, 1952), 26–27.

38. Ibid., 28–29.

39. James T. Patterson, *Mr. Republican: A Biography of Robert A. Taft* (Boston: Houghton Mifflin, 1972), 554.

40. *Proceedings of the Republican Convention*, 30–52; *PNP*, vol. 1, 75.

41. *NYT*, 8 July 1952.

42. Quoted in Howard, *With My Shoes Off*, 142.

43. Quoted in *PNP*, vol. 1, 78.

44. Jeff Broadwater, *Eisenhower and the Anti-Communist Crusade* (Chapel Hill: University of North Carolina Press, 1992), 33.

45. William Manchester, *American Caesar: Douglas MacArthur, 1880–1964* (Boston: Little, Brown, 1978), 820; Earl Warren, *The Memoirs of Earl Warren*

(Garden City, NY: Doubleday, 1977), 252. Warren remembered that Taft came to the governor's hotel room to negotiate for California's seventy votes. Taft promised Warren any position in the administration but said that the vice presidency might be a bit difficult because he had already promised it to MacArthur. This brings up a story that has received wide, if uncredited, play—that at the convention, Eisenhower promised Warren the first available seat on the Supreme Court if he would only shift his support to Eisenhower. Brownell argues quite vociferously that no deal was made at the convention, pointing out that Warren never *did* switch his votes to Eisenhower, even after Eisenhower had secured the nomination (Brownell, *Advising Ike*, 118).

46. *The Influence of Television on the 1952 Election* (Crosby Broadcasting Study, Miami University, 1953). Out of the total national television audience, 59 percent of those watching television at the time of the speech watched MacArthur's keynote; 53 percent saw Alben Barkley's "Farewell Address," 49 percent watched Eisenhower's acceptance address, and a mere 35 percent saw Stevenson's acceptance address.

47. *Proceedings of the Republican Convention*, 67–76; *NYT*, 8 July 1952.

48. Quoted in Manchester, *American Caesar*, 820–821.

49. Sulzberger diary entry, 7 July 1952, in C. L. Sulzberger, *A Long Row of Candles: Memoirs and Diaries, 1934–1954* (New York: Macmillan, 1969), 769.

50. *NYT*, 1 August 1952.

51. The Christian Nationalist Party was on the ballot only in Washington, Missouri, Arkansas, and Texas.

52. *PNP*, vol. 4, 137.

53. *Proceedings of the Republican Convention*, 144. For a good short analysis of this speech, see Broadwater, *Eisenhower and the Anti-Communist Crusade*, 34.

54. *Proceedings of the Republican Convention*, 178; "Keep It Clean," *Time*, 21 July 1952, 15–16; Neil MacNeil, *Dirksen: Portrait of a Public Man* (New York: World, 1970), 103–104; Smith, *Dewey*, 593.

55. *Proceedings of the Republican Convention*, 179–180. The case cited by Eastvold was *Colegrove v. Green* (328 U.S. 549, 1946); any reading of the case finds Eastvold's use of *Green* as a precedent for his argument to be a tremendous stretch.

56. *PNP*, vol. 1, 214–215.

57. Quoted in *NYT*, 10 July 1952.

58. Quoted in "The Nominating Ballot," *Time*, 21 July 1952, 16.

59. Shanley Diaries, DDEL, box 1, p. 449; *NYT*, 9 July 1952.

60. *NYT*, 12 July 1952; Patterson, *Mr. Republican*, 563.

61. *NYT*, 12 July 1952.

62. Garry Wills, *Nixon Agonistes: The Crisis of the Self-Made Man* (New York: New American Library, 1969), chap. 4.

63. Richard M. Nixon, *The Memoirs of Richard Nixon* (New York: Grosset & Dunlap, 1978), 81–82.

64. Ibid., 83; Stewart Alsop, *Nixon and Rockefeller: A Double Portrait* (Garden City, NY: Doubleday, 1960), 68; Jack Harrison Pollack, *Earl Warren: The Judge Who Changed America* (New York: Prentice Hall, 1979), 135–136.

65. Memo (signed by Dana Smith), undated, Lodge Papers, Eisenhower Campaign, 1952, box 2, California folder.

66. See Robert F. Agnew to Republican National Committee, 6 June 1952; Kenneth Keating et al. to Guy Gabrielson, 7 June 1952 (congressmen signed this letter supporting Nixon for the keynote, including Michigan congressman Gerald R. Ford; Robert B. Ladd to Guy Gabrielson, 9 June 1952; and Nixon to Robert Agnew, 9 June 1952; all in RMNPPC, box 1, 1952, June 1–10 folder.

67. Nixon to California Delegates, 11 June 1952, Nixon Pre-Presidential Papers, Series 320, Name File, box 123, California Campaigns File.

68. Ed Cray, *Chief Justice: A Biography of Earl Warren* (New York: Simon & Schuster, 1997), 229–235; Pollack, *Warren*, 136.

69. On 8 May 1952, Nixon spoke at the annual meeting of the New York State Republicans at New York City's Waldorf Astoria Hotel. His usual communism/corruption speech was, once again, a hit. After the speech, Thomas Dewey invited Nixon to his suite for dinner and offered him the vice presidential nomination on an Eisenhower-led ticket. Most observers agree that the conversation took place, but there is no evidence that Dewey was acting with Eisenhower's knowledge. There are also discrepancies as to Nixon's response—Dewey remembered Nixon saying that he would be "greatly honored," Nixon did not record his response, Nixon hagiographer Earl Mazo remembered Nixon telling him in astonishment that he couldn't believe that Dewey was actually serious, and Brownell remembered unreservedly that Nixon had accepted Dewey's offer. Despite Dewey's and Herbert Brownell's memories, it seems unlikely that Nixon accepted the offer of the vice presidency right on the spot. To begin with, it runs contrary to Nixon's political character to believe that he closed off all other options a full two months before the convention. And secondly, in the immediate hours following his nomination, Eisenhower was not behaving like a man who already had a running mate in his pocket. Indeed, the evidence points to a confused and confusing process for choosing a running mate, one that revealed that Eisenhower himself did not even know his own role in that process. See Herbert Brownell, conference panelist, "The Great Crusade," DDEL, November 1992; Earl Mazo, *Richard Nixon: A Political and Personal Portrait* (New York: Harper & Brothers, 1959), 84; Smith, *Dewey*, 584; Nixon, *Memoirs*, 84.

70. *NYT*, 12 July 1952; Dwight D. Eisenhower, *The White House Years*, vol. 1, *Mandate for Change: 1953–1956* (Garden City, NY: Doubleday, 1963), 46–47; Nixon, *Memoirs*, 86–88.

71. Jean Edward Smith, *Lucius D. Clay: An American Life* (New York: Henry Holt, 1990), 600–602. In his memoirs, Brownell tells essentially this story, only remembering that list had five or six names on it, including Nixon's (Brownell, *Advising Ike*, 120).

72. Nixon, *Memoirs*, 88–89.

73. *Proceedings of the Republican Convention*, 431–432.

74. Ibid., 432; *NYT*, 12 July 1952.

75. John S. D. Eisenhower, *Strictly Personal* (Garden City, NY: Doubleday, 1974), 134.

76. HST to Ethel Noland, 11 July 1952, *OTR*, 261.

77. *St. Louis Post-Dispatch*, 20 July 1952.

78. Flyer, "The People Speak: Kefauver," undated, AESP, Series 1, Correspondence, box 46, folder 7.

79. Quoted in editor's comments, *Papers of AES*, vol. 3, 580.

80. Quoted in *NYT*, 19 July 1952.

81. Interview notes, Arvey (1966), John Bartlow Martin Papers, SGML, box 6, Arvey folder.

82. Elmo Roper, *You and Your Leaders: Their Actions and Your Reactions* (New York: William Morrow, 1957), 207–208.

83. Interview notes, Arvey (1966), Martin Papers, box 6, Arvey folder.

84. The five drafts of the preliminary platform are in Charles Murphy Papers, HSTL, box 2, Democratic Platform 1952, folders 1 and 2. See also memorandum, Murphy to HST, 16 July 1952, Murphy Papers, box 2, Democratic Platform 1952, folder 1; and memorandum, Neustadt to Murphy, 20 May 1952, Richard E. Neustadt Papers, HSTL, Chronological File, box 2, May 1952 folder.

85. Quoted in *NYT*, 17 July 1952.

86. John Sparkman to Harold D. Cullen, 3 June 1952, John J. Sparkman Papers, William Stanley Hoole Library, University of Alabama, Political File, box 168, folder 44-2.

87. John Sparkman to Thomas O. Brown, 14 June 1952, Sparkman Papers, Political File, box 168, folder 44-2.

88. John Sparkman to H. Coleman Long, 6 June 1952, Sparkman Papers, Political File, box 168, folder 44-1.

89. Porter and Johnson, *National Party Platforms*, 487.

90. *NYT*, 25 July 1952.

91. Memorandum, Neustadt to Murphy, 20 May 1952, Neustadt Papers, HSTL, Chronological File, box 2, May 1952 folder.

92. John J. Sparkman Reminiscences in Edward P. Doyle, ed., *As We Knew Adlai: The Stevenson Story by Twenty-Two Friends* (New York: Harper & Row, 1966), 119; William C. Berman, *The Politics of Civil Rights in the Truman Administration* (Columbus: Ohio State University Press, 1970), 119; *PNP*, vol. 1, 132.

93. *NYT*, 17 July 1952.

94. *NYT*, 19 July 1952.

95. Quoted in *NYT*, 20 July 1952.

96. *NYT*, 19 July 1952; O. Douglas Weeks, *Texas Presidential Politics in 1952* (Washington, DC: Institute of Public Affairs, 1953), 78.

97. Kefauver to HST, 20 July 1952, HSTP, PSF, box 46, Kefauver folder.

98. Ricky F. Dobbs, *Yellow Dogs and Republicans: Allan Shivers and Texas Two-Party Politics* (College Station: Texas A&M University, 2005), 86; D. B. Hardeman and Donald C. Bacon, *Rayburn: A Biography* (Austin: Texas Monthly Press, 1987), 363.

99. *NYT*, 19 July 1952; 20 July 1952.

100. Ibid.

101. Ibid.

102. Rudy Abramson, *Spanning the Century: The Life of W. Averell Harriman, 1891–1986* (New York: William Morrow, 1992), 496.

103. Harry S. Truman, *Memoirs*, vol. 2, *Years of Trial and Hope* (Garden City, NY: Doubleday, 1956), 495; Alben Barkley, *That Reminds Me* (Garden City, NY: Doubleday, 1954), 237–238.

104. Truman, *Memoirs*, vol. 2, 495; Barkley, *That Reminds Me*, 241–242; statement, 21 July 1952, Alben Barkley Papers, University of Kentucky, Speech File, box 22, dated folder.

105. Walter Reuther to AES, 29 July 1952, AESP, Series 1, Correspondence, box 66, folder 9 (Reuther); Frank Cormier and William J. Eaton, *Reuther* (Englewood Cliffs, NJ: Prentice-Hall, 1970), 287–289.

106. Truman, *Memoirs*, vol. 2, 495.

107. Barkley, *That Reminds Me*, 236–237.

108. *Speeches of AES*, 3–6.

109. John Bartlow Martin, *It Seems Like Only Yesterday: Memoirs of Writing, Presidential Politics, and the Diplomatic Life* (New York: William Morrow, 1986), 145.

110. *Chicago Daily News*, 21 July 1952.

111. *Official Report of the Proceedings of the Democratic National Convention, 1952* (n.p.: Democratic National Committee Publication, 1952), 43–54; "We Shall Triumph Again," *Time*, 28 July 1952, 9.

112. *Proceedings of the Democratic Convention*, 55; *NYT*, 22 July 1952.

113. *Proceedings of the Democratic Convention*, 57.

114. Ibid., 58.

115. Ibid., 73–76; *PNP*, vol. 1, 126–127.

116. *PNP*, vol. 1, 131; Weeks, *Texas Presidential Politics in 1952*, 80.

117. Walter Johnson, *How We Drafted Adlai Stevenson* (New York: Knopf, 1955), 137–141; Johnson to Brookings Institution Project, 13 November 1953, reprinted in part in *PNP*, vol. 1, 137–138.

118. Johnson, *How We Drafted Adlai Stevenson*, 140. See also *NYT*, 17 July 1952.

119. Abramson agrees with this assessment (*Spanning the Century*, 498).

120. Truman private memorandum, 24 July 1952, OTR, 262; Truman, *Memoirs*, vol. 2, 496–497.

121. *Proceedings of the Democratic Convention*, 334.

122. Ibid., 339; Hardeman and Bacon, *Rayburn*, 365; L. Vaughan Howard and David R. Deener, *Presidential Politics in Louisiana, 1952* (New Orleans: Tulane University Press, 1954), 76–77.
123. *Proceedings of the Democratic Convention*, 347.
124. Ibid., 363; Philip A. Grant, "Eisenhower and the 1952 Invasion of the South: The Case of Virginia," *Presidential Studies Quarterly* 20 (1990): 285–286.
125. Hardeman and Bacon, *Rayburn*, 364. Humphrey does not mention this, or his support of the coalition, in his memoir (*The Education of a Public Man: My Life and Politics* [Garden City, NY: Doubleday, 1976]).
126. David McCullough, *Truman* (New York: Simon & Schuster, 1992), 904.
127. Harriman substantiates this account in an interview cited in Robert J. Donovan, *Tumultuous Years: The Presidency of Harry S. Truman, 1949–1953* (New York: Norton, 1982), 397. See also interview notes, Arvey (1966), John Bartlow Martin Papers, SGML, box 6, Arvey folder; "The Big Battle," *Time*, 4 August 1952, 10. Interestingly, although Harriman agrees with this assessment, both his biographer and Truman's main biographer do not, arguing that Harriman dropped out of the race before Truman had a chance to tell him to do so (Abramson, *Spanning the Century*, 501–502; McCullough, *Truman*, 905).
128. Quoted in Alfred Steinberg, *Sam Rayburn: A Biography* (New York: Hawthorn Books, 1975), 275.
129. Kefauver press release, 29 July 1952, Estes Kefauver Papers, University of Tennessee, Speech File.
130. *Proceedings of the Democratic Convention*, 536; Paul H. Douglas, *In the Fullness of Time: The Memoirs of Paul H. Douglas* (New York: Harcourt Brace Jovanovich, 1972), 566–567; Charles L. Fontenay, *Estes Kefauver: A Biography* (Knoxville: University of Tennessee Press, 1980), 227–228; Joseph Bruce Gorman, *Kefauver: A Political Biography* (New York: Oxford University Press, 1981), 155; Hardeman and Bacon, *Rayburn*, 367–368.
131. *Proceedings of the Democratic Convention*, 538.
132. *Speeches of AES*, 7–10.
133. "Richard Russell, Georgia Giant," unedited transcript, bound copy in Richard B. Russell Library, University of Georgia, reel 24.
134. Margaret Rutledge Shannon interview (1971), Richard Russell Oral History Project, Richard B. Russell Library, University of Georgia, 25.
135. John T. Carleton interview, Richard B. Russell Oral History Project, Richard B. Russell Library, University of Georgia, 7.
136. Gilbert C. Fite, *Richard B. Russell, Jr., Senator from Georgia* (Chapel Hill: University of North Carolina Press, 1991), 295.
137. Quoted in *NYT*, 1 July 1952.
138. Truman, *Memoirs*, vol. 2, 497. Russell's biographer claims that it was Russell who suggested Sparkman, and the other leaders went for it; there is no evidence of this (Fite, *Russell*, 296).
139. John J. Sparkman Reminiscences, in Doyle, *As We Knew Adlai*, 119.

140. Steinberg, *Rayburn*, 276

141. "Prize Specimen," *Time*, 4 August 1952, 15; "Sparkman's Role," *USN&WR*, 1 August 1952, 16.

142. HST to AES (handwritten), in HSTP, PSF, Personal File, box 274, Stevenson folder. Also in *OTR*, 263.

143. AES to HST, 29 July 1952, HSTP, PSF, Personal File, box 274, Stevenson folder. Also in *Papers of AES*, vol. 4, 20 (here, the date of the letter—dated as 27 July—is in error).

CHAPTER 4. THE FALL CAMPAIGN

1. John Foster Dulles to Stevenson (with handwritten reply), 26 July 1952, AESP, Series 1, Correspondence, box 25, folder 17, Dulles folder.

2. Quoted in Sherman Adams interview, in Kenneth W. Thompson, ed., *The Eisenhower Presidency: Eleven Intimate Perspectives of Dwight D. Eisenhower* (Lanham, MD: University Press of America, 1984), 183–184.

3. Herbert S. Parmet, *Eisenhower and the American Crusades* (New York: Collier Macmillan, 1972), 108.

4. DDE to Arthur Summerfield, 15 July 1952, *Papers of DDE*, vol. 13, 1273.

5. Memorandum of agreement between DDE, RMN, Arthur Summerfield, Sherman Adams, Walter Williams, and Wesley Roberts (undated), Robert Humphreys Papers, DDEL, box 10, 1952: Campaigns and Elections folder (2); *Papers of DDE*, vol. 13, 1320n1; Marty Snyder, *My Friend Ike* (New York: Frederick Fell, 1956), 165–167; Parmet, *Eisenhower and the American Crusades*, 111.

6. DDE to Taft, 17 July 1952, *Papers of DDE*, vol. 13, 1278–1279.

7. Taft memorandum on General Eisenhower, July 1952, *RTP*, vol. 4, 403. See also Taft to Prescott Bush, 4 August 1952, *RTP*, vol. 4, 406; and Taft to Vincent Starzinger, 11 August 1952, *RTP*, vol. 4, 412–413.

8. Taft to William Jenner, 4 August 1952, *RTP*, vol. 4, 407.

9. Taft to Everett Dirksen, 6 August 1952, *RTP*, vol. 4, 412; Taft memorandum (undated), Taft Papers, Subject File, box 1107, 1952—Eisenhower folder; James T. Patterson, *Mr. Republican: A Biography of Robert A. Taft* (Boston: Houghton Mifflin, 1972), 572–576.

10. Taft statement, 12 September 1952, *RTP*, vol. 4, 416; *NYT*, 13 September 1952; Dwight D. Eisenhower, *The White House Years*, vol. 1, *Mandate for Change: 1953–1956* (Garden City, NY: Doubleday, 1963), 64; "Taft," *USN&WR*, 19 September 1952, 50–51, 90–91; "Bob the Bugler," *Time*, 22 September 1952, 24; Patterson, *Mr. Republican*, 576–577.

11. *NYT*, 13 September 1952.

12. Quoted in *NYT*, 13 September 1952.

13. Taft to John Meyer, 5 October 1952, Robert A. Taft Papers, LOC, Political File—1952, box 326, Alabama folder.

14. Editor's comments in *RTP*, vol. 4, 396.

15. AES to Alicia Patterson, 27 July 1952, *Papers of AES*, vol. 4, 21.

16. AES to Blair, 30 July 1952, Adlai E. Stevenson Gubernatorial Papers, Illinois State Historical Library, Springfield, Illinois, Personal Correspondence File, box 89-2, "B" folder.

17. Memorandum from Frank McKinney, 4 January 1952; Frank McKinney to Howard McGrath, 16 February 1952, HSTP, Official File, D(299-A), box 941, 1952–1953 folder; Steven Mitchell Reminiscence in Edward P. Doyle, ed., *As We Knew Adlai: The Stevenson Story by Twenty-Two Friends* (New York: Harper & Row, 1966), 82–83.

18. Interview notes, Jacob Arvey (1966), John Bartlow Martin Papers, Seeley G. Mudd Manuscript Library, SGML, box 6, Arvey folder.

19. *NYT*, 2 August 1952; "Campaign Manager," *Time*, 11 August 1952, 17.

20. James A. Bill, *George Ball: Behind the Scenes in U.S. Foreign Policy* (New Haven, CT: Yale University Press, 1997), 44.

21. David McCullough, *Truman* (New York: Simon & Schuster, 1992), 906.

22. *NYT*, 3 August 1952.

23. For the letters of invitation to this meeting, as well as a discussion of the preliminary agenda, see HST to AES, 4 August 1952, and AES to HST, 6 August 1952, HSTP, PSF, Personal File, box 274, Stevenson folder (Stevenson letter to Truman also in *Papers of AES*, vol. 4, 36).

24. AES to HST, 13 August 1952, *Papers of AES*, vol. 4, 42. It should be noted that Stevenson was upset that he be seen as under *anyone's* thumb; he would write to Mrs. Edison Dick in exasperation that some in the press had called him the "puppet" of both Wyatt and his own speechwriters (AES to Mrs. Edison Dick, 8 August 1952, *Papers of AES*, vol. 4, 37).

25. Quoted in Bert Cochran, *Harry Truman and the Crisis Presidency* (New York: Funk & Wagnall's, 1969), 381.

26. HST to AES, unsent and undated, in *OTR*, 266–267.

27. Quoted in "The Key to the Campaign," *Time*, 1 September 1952, 11.

28. Quoted in Robert Donovan, *Tumultuous Years: The Presidency of Harry S. Truman, 1949–1953* (New York: Norton, 1982), 398.

29. HST to AES, unsent and undated, in *OTR*, 268–269.

30. Harry S. Truman, "How Stevenson Let Me Down," *Look*, 7 June 1960.

31. Telegram, HST to DDE, 12 August 1952, EPPP, Ann Whitman File, Administration Series, Truman folder, 12 August 1952–15 January 1953; telegram, DDE to HST, 14 August 1952, ibid. (also in *Papers of DDE*, vol. 13, 1322–1323); HST to DDE, 16 August 1962, ibid. (also in *OTR*, 263–364). See also *NYT*, 15 August 1952.

32. Rear Platform Talk, Fargo, North Dakota, 29 September 1962, HSTP, PSF, Speech File, box 16, dated folder.

33. For examples of Truman's campaign rhetoric, see *NYT*, 2 October 1952; 3 October 1952; 5 October 1952; and 8 October 1952.

34. Quoted in *NYT*, 7 October 1952.

35. William C. Meulemans, "The Presidential Majority: Presidential Campaigning in Congressional Elections (PhD diss., University of Idaho, 1970), 237.

36. Jane Dick, *Whistlestopping with Adlai* (Chicago: October House, 1952), 122–123.

37. That work was *Speeches of AES*.

38. Quoted in *NYT*, 1 September 1952.

39. *NYT*, 1 September 1952.

40. "Stevenson's Ghost Writers," *USN&WR*, 16 September 1952, 57–58; John Kenneth Galbraith, *A Life in Our Times: Memoirs* (Boston: Houghton Mifflin, 1981), 292–293; John Bartlow Martin, *It Seems Like Only Yesterday: Memoirs of Writing, Presidential Politics, and the Diplomatic Life* (New York: William Morrow, 1986), 146–147.

41. AES to Samuel I. Rosenman, 21 August 1952, *Papers of AES*, vol. 4, 46. See also Martin, *It Seems Like Only Yesterday*, 148; and Jeff Broadwater, *Adlai Stevenson and American Politics: The Odyssey of a Cold War Liberal* (New York: Twayne, 1994), 119.

42. "Campaign Manager," *Time*, 11 August 1952, 117; Clifton Brock, *Americans for Democratic Action: Its Role in National Politics* (Washington, DC: Public Affairs Press, 1962), 140; Broadwater, *Adlai Stevenson and American Politics*, 119.

43. Alistair Cooke, *Six Men* (New York: Knopf, 1977), 136.

44. For but one testimony to this, see Martin, *It Seems Like Only Yesterday*, 156. See also Broadwater, *Adlai Stevenson and American Politics*, 120.

45. George W. Ball, *The Past Has Another Pattern: Memoirs* (New York: Norton, 1982), 125.

46. See, for example, *NYT*, 2 September 1952.

47. *NYT*, 14 September 1952.

48. Steven Mitchell Reminiscences, in Doyle, *As We Knew Adlai*, 66.

49. Joseph Alsop and Stewart Alsop, *The Reporter's Trade* (New York: Reynal, 1958), 188–190. Alsop took great pains to make it clear to Stevenson that his sobriquet should be taken as a compliment: "Just to keep the record straight, I didn't say that only egg-heads could understand your speeches; I said that all the egg-heads were for you. . . . At any rate, I'd like to say that this particular egg-head deeply admires the quality of the campaign you have been waging" (Stewart Alsop to AES, 9 October 1952, AESP, Series 1, Correspondence, box 2, folder 17).

50. Emmet John Hughes, *Ordeal of Power: A Political Memoir of the Eisenhower Years* (New York: Atheneum, 1963), 23.

51. Ibid., 24.

52. Ibid., 116.

53. Quoted in Evan Thomas, *Ike's Bluff: President Eisenhower's Secret Battle to Save the World* (New York: Little, Brown, 2012), 117.

54. Eisenhower speech, Atlanta, 2 September 1952, and Eisenhower speech, Birmingham, 3 September 1952, EPPP, Ann Whitman Files, box 1, book 2; *NYT*, 3 September 1952; 4 September 1952.

55. Merlo J. Pusey, *Eisenhower the President* (New York: Macmillan, 1956), 26.

56. Eisenhower, *Mandate for Change*, 63.

57. *NYT*, 2 September 1952.
58. *NYT*, 4 September 1952.
59. Eisenhower, *Mandate for Change*, 54.
60. Theodore McKeldin to DDE, 8 August 1952, EPPP, Ann Whitman File, Administration Series, box 23, McKeldin folder.
61. *NYT*, 3 September 1952.
62. *NYT*, 4 September 1952; "New Accent," *Time*, 15 September 1952, 23–24.
63. *NYT*, 27 September 1952.
64. Eisenhower speech, Harlem, 25 October 1952, Benedict Papers, DDEL, box 5, dated folder; *NYT*, 26 October 1952.
65. *NYT*, 6 September 1952.
66. Ibid.
67. AES to John Battle, 23 August 1952, *Papers of AES*, vol. 4, 47–48.
68. *NYT*, 31 July 1952.
69. Quoted in *NYT*, 5 August 1952.
70. Roy Wilkins, *Standing Fast: The Autobiography of Roy Wilkins* (New York: Viking Press, 1982), 212; William C. Berman, *The Politics of Civil Rights in the Truman Administration* (Columbus: Ohio State University Press, 1970), 220–221.
71. *NYT*, 10 September 1952.
72. See DDE to H. J. (Jack) Porter, 28 March 1952, *Papers of DDE*, vol. 13, 1143; DDE to Swede Hazlett, 12 July 1952, in Robert W. Griffith, ed., *Ike's Letters to a Friend, 1941–1948* (Lawrence: University Press of Kansas, 1984), 102–103.
73. AES to Allan Shivers, 3 August 1952, *Papers of AES*, vol. 4, 32.
74. Interview notes, Arvey (1966), Martin Papers, SGML, box 6, Arvey folder; Ricky F. Dobbs, *Yellow Dogs and Republicans: Allan Shivers and Texas Two-Party Politics* (College Station: Texas A&M University Press, 2005), 89; "Trouble with Texas," *Time*, 1 September 1952, 12.
75. *NYT*, 25 August 1952.
76. *NYT*, 10 September 1952; O. Douglas Weeks, *Texas Presidential Politics in 1952* (Washington, DC: Institute of Public Affairs, 1953), 85–91.
77. Sean P. Cunningham, *Cowboy Conservatism: Texas and the Rise of the Modern Right* (Lexington: University Press of Kentucky, 2010), 29. In November, Shivers the Democrat defeated Shivers the Republican by more than 900,000 votes.
78. Eisenhower speech, New Orleans, 13 October 1952, Benedict Papers, DDEL, box 4, dated folder; L. Vaughan Howard and David R. Deener, *Presidential Politics in Louisiana, 1952* (New Orleans: Tulane University Press, 1954), 89.
79. Quoted in Dobbs, *Yellow Dogs*, 86.
80. *Richmond Times Dispatch*, 8 August 1952.
81. Press release from Office of Lyndon B. Johnson, 28 August 1952, HSTP, PSF, Political File, box 49, Mitchell folder.
82. Quoted in Philip A. Grant, "Eisenhower and the 1952 Invasion of the South: The Case of Virginia," *Presidential Studies Quarterly* 20 (1990): 288.
83. Byrnes statement, 18 September 1952, James Byrnes Papers, Clemson University, Speech File, dated folder.

84. John E. Hollitz, "Eisenhower and the Admen: The Television 'Spot' Campaign of 1952," *Wisconsin Magazine of History* 66 (1982): 31.

85. In 1936, Republican candidate Alf Landon became the first presidential candidate to utilize a *radio* spot ad campaign.

86. Stephen C. Wood, "Television's First Political Spot Ad Campaign: 'Eisenhower Answers America,'" *Presidential Studies Quarterly* 20 (1990): 267–271.

87. Ibid., 271.

88. Advertisement quoted in Hollitz, "Eisenhower and the Admen," 25; storyboards for the ad can be found in ibid., 32–33, 36. See also Stanley M. Rumbough Jr., *Citizens for Eisenhower: The 1952 Presidential Campaign: Lessons for the Future?* (McLean, VA: International Publishers, 2013), 95–114.

89. See the sources in note 88, as well as David Halberstam, *The Fifties* (New York: Villard Books, 1993), 228.

90. Quoted in Wood, "Television's First Political Spot Ad Campaign," 272.

91. Quoted in Halberstam, *The Fifties*, 232.

92. *Speeches of AES*, xxiv.

93. Wood, "Television's First Political Spot Ad Campaign," 275.

94. Burton A. Abrams and Russel F. Settle, "The Effect of Political Campaign Broadcasting on Political Campaign Spending: An Empirical Investigation," *Journal of Political Economics* 84 (1976): 1095–1097.

95. *NYT*, 23 March 1952; Dulles to DDE, 20 May 1952, EPPP, Principal File, box 36, Dulles folder.

96. John Foster Dulles, "A Policy of Boldness," *Life*, 19 May 1952, 146, 154. An excellent analysis of this article can be found in Townsend Hoopes, *The Devil and John Foster Dulles* (Boston: Little, Brown, 1973), 126–128.

97. For a discussion of this, see DDE to John Foster Dulles, 20 June 1952, *Papers of DDE*, vol. 13, 1254–1255.

98. Kirk H. Porter and Donald B. Johnson, *National Party Platforms: 1840–1960* (Urbana: University of Illinois Press, 1961), 497–499. See also Robert A. Divine, *Foreign Policy and U.S. Presidential Elections: 1952–1960* (New York: New Viewpoints, 1974), 26–27.

99. Eisenhower speech, New York City, 25 August 1952, in Robert L. Branyan and Lawrence H. Larsen, eds., *The Eisenhower Administration, 1953–1961: A Documentary History*, vol. 1 (New York: Random House, 1971), 32–36.

100. Divine, *Foreign Policy and U.S. Presidential Elections*, 67.

101. *NYT*, 2 September 1952; *Speeches of AES*, 53–56.

102. *NYT*, 5 September 1952.

103. "Foreign Policy Debate," *Time*, 22 September 1952, 25–26.

104. Quoted in *NYT*, 18 September 1952.

105. Quoted in *NYT*, 19 September 1952.

106. Excerpts from speech of RMN, 13 August 1952, AESP, box 222, Nixon folder 2; quoted in *NYT*, 14 August 1952.

107. Nixon interview, *Meet the Press*, 14 September 1952, Lawrence Spivak Papers, LOC, box A-36, dated folder.

108. Quoted in Earl Mazo, *Richard Nixon: A Political and Personal Portrait* (New York: Harper & Brothers, 1959), 107.

109. Edson to RMN, 17 September 1952, RMNPPC, box 173, 1952, 16–19 September folder.

110. Clipping, Peter Edson story (filed as NEA Washington correspondent), 18 September 1952, RMNPPC, box 173, 1952, 16–19 September folder.

111. *NYT*, 19 September 1952; Halberstam, *The Fifties*, 237–238.

112. *New York Post*, 18 September 1952.

113. See *NYT*, 22 September 1952; 25 September 1952; Steven A. Mitchell Reminiscence, in Doyle, *As We Knew Adlai*, 79; editor's comments, *Papers of AES*, vol. 3, 9–10; Galbraith, *A Life in Our Times*, 301; Broadwater, *Adlai Stevenson and American Politics*, 123.

114. See, for example, T. Wells Church to RMN, 19 September 1952, RMNPPC, box 173, 1952, 16–19 September folder. Church offered Nixon three minutes of airtime on the *Robert Trout World News Program*, just to explain his side of the fund story. There was no response.

115. Of the many places that this list is available, see "The Remarkable Tornado," *Time*, 29 September 1952, 12; and Appendix, *USN&WR*, 3 October 1952, 62.

116. Hoffman to James Blaine, 29 September 1952, Paul Hoffman Papers, DDEL, box 20, Personal Chronological File, dated folder; Sherman Adams, *Firsthand Report: The Story of the Eisenhower Administration* (New York: Popular Library, 1962), 45.

117. The original reports of these investigations are in Eisenhower Papers, Official File, box 712, folder 138-C-4 (Republican Campaign Folder 2); and in AESP, box 268, Nixon–General folder. The results of both these investigations can be found in Appendix, *USN&WR*, 3 October 1952, 62–66.

118. Milton S. Eisenhower, *The President Is Calling* (Garden City, NY: Doubleday, 1974), 251.

119. Eisenhower press release, 19 September 1952, EPPP, Ann Whitman Files, Speeches, box 1, book 4.

120. Richard M. Nixon, *The Memoirs of Richard Nixon* (New York: Grosset & Dunlap, 1978), 96; Richard M. Nixon, *Six Crises* (Garden City, NY: Doubleday, 1962), 93; "The Remarkable Tornado," 12.

121. See *NYT*, 21 September 1952.

122. Stewart Alsop, *Nixon and Rockefeller: A Double Portrait* (New York: Doubleday, 1960), 61.

123. Ibid., 69; William Bragg Ewald, *Eisenhower the President: Crucial Days, 1951–1960* (Englewood Cliffs, NJ: Prentice Hall, 1981), 51; Jean Edward Smith, *Lucius D. Clay: An American Life* (New York: Henry Holt, 1990), 606.

124. The story of Humphreys's sales pitch on the speech to the Eisenhower staff, particularly to a doubting Sherman Adams, is well told in John W. Malsberger, *The General and the Politician: Dwight Eisenhower, Richard Nixon, and American Politics* (New York: Rowman & Littlefield, 2014), 10. See also Kevin Mattson, *Just Plain Dick: Richard Nixon's Checkers Speech*

and the *"Rocking, Socking" Election of 1952* (New York: Bloomsbury, 2012), 119.

125. Nixon, *Memoirs*, 98.

126. Ibid., 97–98; Nixon, *Six Crises*, 99–101.

127. Adams, *Firsthand Report*, 47; Nixon, *Memoirs*, 102–103; Nixon, *Six Crises*, 109–111.

128. Quoted in Nixon, *Six Crises*, 127–129.

129. Halberstam, *The Fifties*, 239.

130. Alsop, *Nixon and Rockefeller*, 64–65; Ewald, *Eisenhower the President*, 55; Parmet, *Eisenhower and the American Crusades*, 139.

131. *NYT*, 28 September 1952. This conclusion has been reached by virtually every biographer of both Eisenhower and Nixon.

132. "The Trial," *Time*, 6 October 1952, 20.

133. *St. Louis Post-Dispatch*, 24 September 1952.

134. *NYT*, 24 September 1952.

135. Hundreds of these letters and telegrams are found in EPPP, White House Central File, folder 3-A-2, Vice President of the United States folder 2; and EPPP, Official File 109, box 465, Nixon Speech, three folders. One such telegram came from Eisenhower's brother Edgar, who gave some unsolicited advice: "If you don't unqualifiedly endorse Nixon after that talk last night, you might as well fold your tent and fade away." Eisenhower scribbled on the telegram: "No answer" (Edgar Eisenhower to DDE, 25 September 1952, EPPP, Ann Whitman File, Administration Series, box 11, Edgar Eisenhower folder, 1952 [3]).

136. One folder of Nixon's papers is full of post-Checkers donations (see RMNPPC, box 185, 1952, July–September folder). One donor wrote, "I have $25 to donate to contribute towards any sort of coat Pat would like to have"; another enclosed "a small check for the little faithful wife to use as she sees fit." See also Dana Smith to Murray Chotiner, 2 October 1952, RMNPPC, box 185, 1952, 2–20 October folder.

137. *NYT*, 25 September 1952.

138. DDE to RMN, 23 September 1952, *Papers of DDE*, vol. 13, 1361–1362.

139. Nixon, *Memoirs*, 106; Nixon, *Six Crises*, 120–121.

140. DDE to Edgar Eisenhower, 21 October 1952, *Papers of DDE*, vol. 13, 1393. For the order to release the financials, see DDE to Arthur H. Vandenberg Jr., 11 October 1952, ibid., 1378.

141. *NYT*, 29 September 1952; 5 October 1952; 11 October 1952; Wilson W. Wyatt, *Whistle Stops: Adventures in Public Life* (Lexington: University Press of Kentucky, 1985), 102.

142. Ewald, *Eisenhower the President*, 49.

143. Quoted in Alsop, *Nixon and Rockefeller*, 61.

144. Quoted in Michael O'Brien, *McCarthy and McCarthyism in Wisconsin* (Columbia: University of Missouri Press, 1980), 137.

145. Adams, *Firsthand Report*, 41–42; Parmet, *Eisenhower and the American Crusades*, 127–128.

146. Quoted in Hughes, *Ordeal of Power*, 38.
147. Quoted in Richard Rovere, *Senator Joe McCarthy* (New York: Harcourt Brace, 1959), 15.
148. Quoted in Parmet, *Eisenhower and the American Crusades*, 127.
149. Quoted in "The McCarthy Problem," *Time*, 1 September 1952, 10.
150. *NYT*, 4 October 1952.
151. Jeff Broadwater, *Eisenhower and the Anti-Communist Crusade* (Chapel Hill: University of North Carolina Press, 1992), 44.
152. Eisenhower, *Mandate for Change*, 317.
153. Hughes, *Ordeal of Power*, 41–42.
154. Quoted in ibid., 39.
155. Eisenhower speech, Milwaukee, Steven Benedict Papers, DDEL, box 2, dated folder; Eisenhower speech, Milwaukee, EPPP, Ann Whitman Files, box 2, speech books.
156. Broadwater, *Eisenhower and the Anti-Communist Crusade*, 45.
157. Ibid.
158. Quoted in ibid.
159. Ibid.
160. Adams, *Firsthand Report*, 41.
161. Sherman Adams interview, in Thompson, *Eisenhower Presidency*, 187.
162. Broadwater, *Eisenhower and the Anti-Communist Crusade*, 46–47.
163. DDE to Harold Stassen, 5 October 1952, *Papers of DDE*, vol. 13, 1372.
164. Ewald, *Eisenhower the President*, 58.
165. All speeches quoted in McCullough, *Truman*, 910–911.
166. *NYT*, 8 October 1952.
167. Clark Clifford, *Counsel to the President: A Memoir* (New York: Random House, 1991), 284–285.
168. Quoted in Broadwater, *Eisenhower and the Anti-Communist Crusade*, 39.
169. *Speeches of AES*, 20.
170. Ibid., 217.
171. Stevenson speech, 8 October 1952, Milwaukee, AESP, Speeches and Statements File, box 39, dated folder.
172. Arthur Krock, *Memoirs: Sixty Years on the Firing Line* (New York: Funk & Wagnalls, 1968), 342.
173. McCarthy advertised his talk through mass mailings; see Robert Wood to "Dear Friend," 15 October 1952, AESP, Series 6, Subject Files, box 379, folder 8, McCarthy folder.
174. The complete speech is reprinted in Allen J. Matusow, ed., *Joseph McCarthy* (Englewood Cliffs, NJ: Prentice Hall, 1970), 61–64. See also *NYT*, 28 October 1952.
175. *Speeches of AES*, 271.
176. Mattson, *Just Plain Dick*, 81.
177. Louis Harris, *Is There a Republican Majority? Political Trends: 1952–56* (New York: Harper & Bros., 1956), 25–56; Ronald J. Caridi, *The Korean War and*

American Politics: The Republican Party as a Case Study (Philadelphia: University of Pennsylvania Press, 1968), 211.

178. NYT, 2 September 1952.
179. Eisenhower speech, 9 September 1952, Indianapolis, Stephen Benedict Papers, DDEL, box 2, dated folder.
180. Speeches of AES, 181–188.
181. Eisenhower speech, 2 October 1952, Champaign, Benedict Papers, box 2, dated folder.
182. Speeches of AES, 251–259; Divine, Foreign Policy and U.S. Presidential Elections, 73.
183. Divine makes this point in Foreign Policy and U.S. Presidential Elections, 73. The press conference where Eisenhower coined the term "domino theory" was held on 7 April 1954.
184. Quoted in NYT, 17 October 1952.
185. NYT, 25 October 1952. The speech went through three separate drafts; they are available, with Hughes's editing marks, in Emmett John Hughes Papers, SGML, box 1, folder 7.
186. Interview notes, Jacob Arvey (1966), Martin Papers, SGML, box 6, Arvey folder.
187. Adams, Firsthand Report, 51. Other such observations: Arthur Krock wrote that Eisenhower "cinch[ed] his victory" with the speech (Memoirs, 272); Jacob Arvey remembered saying to his wife, "That's the speech that will beat us" (Jacob Arvey Reminiscence in Doyle, As We Knew Adlai, 64).
188. Speeches of AES, xxvii; John Sparkman Reminiscence in Doyle, As We Knew Adlai, 212–122.
189. Quoted in Joseph C. Goulden, Korea: The Untold Story of the War (New York: Times Books, 1982), 613.
190. Columbia Record, 30 October 1952.

CHAPTER 5. CONCLUSIONS AND LEGACIES
1. "A Good Loser," Time, 10 November 1952, 25.
2. NYT, 7 November 1952, 16; John Bartlow Martin, Adlai Stevenson of Illinois (New York: Anchor Books, 1977), 754–757.
3. "A Place to Start," Time, 10 November 1952, 22–23.
4. Quoted in George W. Ball, The Past Has Another Pattern: Memoirs (New York: Norton, 1982), 130.
5. Quoted in Martin, Adlai Stevenson of Illinois, 758.
6. Telegram, HST to DDE, undated, EPPP, Ann Whitman File, Administration Series, box 33, Truman folder, 12 August 1952–15 January 1953 (1).
7. Quoted in Martin, Adlai Stevenson of Illinois, 758.
8. Chester J. Pach and Elmo Richardson, The Presidency of Dwight D. Eisenhower, rev. ed. (Lawrence: University Press of Kansas, 1991), 27.
9. NYT, 8 October 1952.

10. Lyn Ragsdale, ed., *Vital Statistics on the Presidency*, 3rd ed. (Washington, DC: CQ Press, 2008), 136.

11. Alfred deGrazia, *The Western Public: 1952 and Beyond* (Stanford, CA: Stanford University Press, 1954), 7.

12. Timothy N. Thurber, *Republicans and Race: The GOP's Frayed Relationship with African-Americans, 1945–1974* (Lawrence: University Press of Kansas, 2013), 46.

13. Election Report: CIO Analysis, AESP, Presidential Campaign Staff Files, box 291, Election Analysis folder; Angus Campbell, Gerald Gurin, and Warren E. Miller, *The Voter Decides* (Evanston, IL: Row, Peterson, 1954), 70; Louis Harris, *Is There a Republican Majority? Political Trends: 1952–56* (New York: Harper & Bros., 1956), 87, 92, 101, 108–113, 173; Earl Roger Kruschke, *The Woman Voter: An Analysis from Personal Interviews* (Washington, DC: Public Affairs Press, 1955), 2.

14. Samuel Lubell, *The Future of American Politics* (New York: Harper & Row, 1965), 44n.

15. "What Won for Ike," *USN&WR*, 14 November 1952, 21.

16. There are as many definitions of the American "middle class" as there are observers. Choosing to see it holistically, sociologist C. Wright Mills defined it as a new class of white-collar workers, tied together by a "marketing mentality" (*White Collar: The American Middle Classes* [New York: Oxford University Press, 1951], 182). Choosing to see it as a function of income, the U.S. Department of Commerce defined the middle class as those families whose income hovered around $3,900—the median income for all families in 1952 (U.S. Department of Commerce, "Current Population Reports: Consumer Income," 27 April 1954, 2). All agreed on one point—in the early 1950s, the number of those who fit the profile of a member of the American middle class was rapidly rising (see Harris, *Is There a Republican Majority?*, 125).

17. Heinz Eulau, *Class and Party in the Eisenhower Years* (New York: Free Press of Glencoe, 1962), 2; Ragsdale, *Vital Statistics on the Presidency*, 119.

18. Lubell, *Future of American Politics*, 6; Samuel Lubell, *The Revolt of the Moderates* (New York: Harper, 1956), 245; Morris Janowitz and Dwaine Marvick, *Competitive Pressure and Democratic Consent: An Interpretation of the 1952 Presidential Election* (Chicago: Quadrangle Books, 1964), 28.

19. Harris, *Is There a Republican Majority?*, 77, 99, 101, 147, 160.

20. Lubell, *Future of American Politics*, 101n5; Ragsdale, *Vital Statistics on the Presidency*, 119.

21. Harris, *Is There a Republican Majority?*, 77, 101, 156–159; Lubell, *Revolt of the Moderates*, 245.

22. Everett Carl Ladd Jr. and Charles D. Hadley, *Transformations of the American Party System: Political Coalitions from the New Deal to the 1970s* (New York: Norton, 1975), xx.

23. Herbert S. Parmet, *Eisenhower and the American Crusades* (New York: Macmillan, 1972), 145.

24. Michael J. Dubin, *United States Gubernatorial Elections, 1932–1952: The Official Results by State and County* (Jefferson, NC: McFarland, 2014), 14–15.
25. Lubell, *Future of American Politics*, 62–63.
26. Mrs. Ina Russell Stacy interview (1971), Richard B. Russell Oral History Project, Richard B. Russell Library, University of Georgia, 13.
27. Malcolm Moos, *The Republicans: A History of Their Party* (New York: Random House, 1956), 494.
28. Gay Finletter to AES, 6 November 1952, AESP, Subseries 1A, Office Correspondence, Finletter folder.
29. Campbell, Gurin, and Miller, *The Voter Decides*, 16.
30. HST to Maury Maverick, 7 November 1952, HSTP, PSF: Personal File, box 269, Maverick folder.
31. Quoted in James T. Patterson, *Mr. Republican: A Biography of Robert A. Taft* (Boston: Houghton Mifflin, 1972), 580.
32. Tom Wicker, *Dwight D. Eisenhower* (New York: Times Books, 2002), 137.
33. Campbell, Gurin, and Miller, *The Voter Decides*, 53–58.
34. Rayburn to Oscar Chapman, 10 November 1952, Oscar Chapman Papers, HSTL, box 87, Political-General folder.
35. Ragsdale, *Vital Statistics on the Presidency*, 146.
36. Memorandum, 22 December 1952, *OTR*, 282; Harry S. Truman, *Truman Speaks His Mind* (original title, *Mr. Citizen*; New York: Popular Library, 1960), 44.
37. John Bartlow Martin, *It Seems Like Only Yesterday: Memoirs of Writing, Presidential Politics, and the Diplomatic Life* (New York: William Morrow, 1986), 141.
38. Walter Johnson, *How We Drafted Adlai Stevenson* (New York: Knopf, 1955), 17.
39. Emmet John Hughes, *The Ordeal of Power: A Political Memoir of the Eisenhower Years* (New York: Atheneum, 1963), 43.
40. Robert A. Divine, *Foreign Policy and U.S. Presidential Elections: 1952–1960* (New York: New Viewpoints, 1974), 84–85; Robert A. Divine, *Eisenhower and the Cold War* (New York: Oxford University Press, 1981), 18–19.
41. Harris, *Is There a Republican Majority?*, 21–44.
42. DDE to Edgar Eisenhower, 8 November 1954, *Papers of DDE*, vol. 15, doc. 1147.
43. Steven Wagner, *Eisenhower Republicanism: Pursuing the Middle Way* (DeKalb: Northern Illinois University Press, 2006), 5.
44. Andrew J. Dunar, *America in the Fifties* (Syracuse, NY: Syracuse University Press, 2006), 103.
45. Wagner, *Eisenhower Republicanism*, 49–50.
46. Ibid., 55.
47. Ibid., 91–96.
48. Gary W. Reichard, *The Reaffirmation of Republicanism: Eisenhower and the Eighty-Third Congress* (Knoxville: University of Tennessee Press, 1975), 88, 96.

49. Charles A. Moser, "Watershed and Ratifying Elections: A Historical View of the 1934 and 1954 Congressional Elections" (Washington, DC: Free Congress Research and Education Foundation, 1982), 17–18, 20.

50. Ibid., 29.

51. Charles A. H. Thomson and Frances M. Shattuck, *The 1956 Presidential Campaign* (Washington, DC: Brookings Institution Press, 1960), 5.

52. Dwight D. Eisenhower, *The White House Years*, vol. 1, *Mandate for Change, 1953–1956* (Garden City, NY: Doubleday, 1963), 429; Moser, "Watershed and Ratifying Elections," 19.

53. Ball, *Past Has Another Pattern*, 132–133.

54. Quoted in Eisenhower, *Mandate for Change*, 431.

55. "Statistics of the Congressional Election of November 2, 1954" (Washington, DC: U.S. Government Printing Office, 1956).

56. Moser, "Watershed and Ratifying Elections," vi.

57. Thomson and Shattuck, *1956 Presidential Campaign*, 5.

58. Richard L. Guylay, "Eisenhower's Two Presidential Campaigns," in Joann P. Krieg, *DDE: Soldier, President, and Statesman* (Westport, CT: Greenwood Press, 1987), 27–29; David A. Nichols, *Eisenhower, 1956* (New York: Simon & Schuster, 2011), 49–51; Thomson and Shattuck, *1956 Presidential Campaign*, 20–23.

59. Nichols, *Eisenhower, 1956*, 64.

60. Garry Wills, *Nixon Agonistes: The Crisis of the Self-Made Man* (New York: New American Library, 1969), 113–114.

61. John W. Malsberger, *The General and the Politician: Dwight Eisenhower, Richard Nixon, and American Politics* (Lanham, MD: Rowman & Littlefield, 2014), 2. Irwin Gellman argues that "Nixon had, at least, a very good, if not an excellent, relationship with Eisenhower." Irwin F. Gellman, "The Richard Nixon Vice Presidency: Research without the Nixon Manuscripts," in Melvin Small, ed., *A Companion to Richard M. Nixon* (West Sussex: Blackwell, 2011), 111.

62. Thomson and Shattuck, *1956 Presidential Campaign*, 81–87. In his memoir, Stassen does not even mention the episode (Harold Stassen and Marshall Houts, *Eisenhower: Turning the World towards Peace* [St. Paul, MN: Merrill/Magnus, 1990]).

63. Thomson and Shattuck, *1956 Presidential Campaign*, 29.

64. Quoted in David McCullough, *Truman* (New York: Simon & Schuster, 1992), 1135.

65. See Robert A. Caro, *The Years of Lyndon Johnson: Master of the Senate* (New York: Knopf, 2002), 801–830.

66. Ball, *Past Has Another Pattern*, 141.

67. Interview notes, Jacob Arvey (1966), John Bartlow Martin Papers, SGML, box 6, Arvey folder.

68. Quoted in Nichols, *Eisenhower, 1956*, 175.

69. Quoted in Wicker, *Eisenhower*, 1.

70. Nichols, *Eisenhower, 1956*, 108–131.

71. Ibid., 133–134.
72. Quoted in ibid., 213.
73. Quoted in Divine, *Eisenhower and the Cold War*, 87.
74. Eulau, *Class and Party in the Eisenhower Years*, 93.
75. Quoted in Lewis L. Gould, *Grand Old Party: A History of the Republicans* (New York: Random House, 2003), 339.
76. Thomson and Shattuck, *1956 Presidential Campaign*, 355.
77. Quoted in Malsberger, *The General and the Politician*, 182.
78. Kennedy speech, Libertyville, Illinois, 25 October 1960, John F. Kennedy Library, Columbia Point, Massachusetts, http://www.jfklibrary.org/Research/Research-Aids/JFK-Speeches/Libertyville-IL_19601025.aspx.

Both Dwight Eisenhower and Adlai Stevenson were prodigious letter writers. Eisenhower's letters were longer; Stevenson's were wittier; both men were thoughtful observers of the chaos that surrounded their respective political fates. The historian is well served by their correspondence, and both are housed in extraordinarily rich collections. The Principal File in the Dwight D. Eisenhower, Pre-Presidential Papers (DDEL) is *the* file for correspondence relating to Eisenhower's protests and decision making on entering the 1952 race. Particularly helpful was his correspondence with General Lucius Clay, his brother Milton, and his friend "Swede" Hazlett. There are also several useful nuggets in Eisenhower's Pre-Presidential Papers (EPPP), particularly the files of his secretary, Ann Whitman. The papers of Adlai E. Stevenson II (Seeley G. Mudd Manuscript Library, Princeton University; SGML) are also a valuable source. Aside from the voluminous correspondence files are subject files on the 1952 campaign that guide the researcher through Stevenson's numerous refusals to run. His personal files have one folder of diary entries for the years 1944–1964, but there are none for 1952. Less helpful are the Adlai E. Stevenson Gubernatorial Papers (Illinois State Historical Library, Springfield, Illinois). The papers of Harry S. Truman (Harry S. Truman Library, Independence, Missouri) have a useful system called the "B-File," which contains material pulled from the holdings that is of importance to a topic. The B-File entitled "The Old President as Political Campaigner: 1952–1972" was particularly helpful, as were the President's Secretary's Files (PSF)—files that Truman's secretary, Rose Conway, kept close to the Oval Office because of their significance.

Other useful manuscript sources include George W. Ball, Papers (SGML); Alben Barkley, Papers (University of Kentucky); John S. Battle, Executive Papers (Executive Department; Virginia State Library, Richmond, Virginia); Stephen Benedict, Papers (DDEL); Paul G. Hoffman, Papers (DDEL); the Carol Evans Papers on Adlai Stevenson (SGML); Emmet John Hughes, Papers (SGML); Robert Humphreys, Papers (DDEL); the Walter Johnson Papers on Adlai Stevenson (SGML); Estes Kefauver, Papers (University of Tennessee, Knoxville); John Bartlow Martin, Papers (SGML); Richard M. Nixon Pre-Presidential Collection, Campaign 1952, Vice Presidential Series (Richard M. Nixon Library, Laguna Niguel, California); Bernard M. Shanley, Diaries (DDEL); John J. Sparkman, Papers (William Stanley Hoole Library, University of Alabama); and Frederick M. Vinson, Papers (Margaret I. King Library, University of Kentucky).

The Eisenhower Papers Project at Johns Hopkins University has produced one of the most useful editions of a manuscript corpus presently available—the twenty-one-volume *Papers of Dwight David Eisenhower*. Relevant for this work are Louis Galambos, ed., *The Papers of Dwight D. Eisenhower*, vols. 12 and 13, *NATO and the Campaign of 1952* (Baltimore: Johns Hopkins University Press,

1989). The entire project is a masterpiece of documentary editing. The editors are particularly sage and subtle observers of the Eisenhower career—more so than *any* writer of *any* secondary work. Their mastery of the detail and their often probing annotation are beyond critique, and their incredibly detailed explanatory footnotes completely flesh out the entire chain of correspondence. Walter Johnson, ed., *The Papers of Adlai E. Stevenson*, vol. 3, *Governor of Illinois: 1949–1953* (Boston: Little, Brown, 1973); vol. 4, *"Let's Talk Sense to the American People,"* 1952–1955 (Boston: Little, Brown, 1974), is much less satisfying. The choice of letters (when compared with the breadth of the correspondence in the Stevenson Papers, SGML, above) is disappointing. Many of the letters chosen are chatty, almost casual responses of little consequence, and the annotations both are thin and tend to lean toward hero worship of their subject. The single most self-revelatory material included is the correspondence between Stevenson and his friends Alicia Patterson and Mrs. Edison Dick. A large number of Stevenson's speeches, all of which had already been published in Stevenson, *Major Campaign Speeches of 1952* (below; twenty-five of the fifty speeches published in this volume are included in Johnson's volume; he even kept the same subtitles and labels for his edition), are included in vol. 4 of the *Papers of AES*; if they were *not* included, it would be a thin volume, indeed. Robert H. Ferrell, ed., *Off the Record: The Private Papers of Harry S. Truman* (New York: Harper & Row, 1980), is a highly selective, highly entertaining, and ultimately quite useful collection, as it contains the key letters in the Truman-Stevenson correspondence of 1952, as well as Truman's lethal and insightful unsent letters, where he lays bare his unvarnished opinion of Stevenson. Clarence E. Wunderlin, ed., *The Papers of Robert A. Taft*, vol. 4, 1949–1953 (Kent, OH: Kent State University Press, 2006), is very well annotated (it offers useful secondary and newspaper sources in the annotations), includes a selection of Taft's speeches, and is neutral in its editorial presentation.

Unique in this regard is Adlai E. Stevenson, *Major Campaign Speeches of Adlai Stevenson, 1952* (New York: Random House, 1953). An instant best seller, this collection of fifty of Stevenson's best-known speeches from the 1952 campaign, offered without annotation, is a useful source for those analyzing Stevenson's rhetoric. In addition, the introduction to this book is the only place where Stevenson, who did not leave behind a memoir or a diary, writes about any portion of his life. Here, he writes about the election of 1952. He comments on the speechwriting process, describes his political philosophy, and lightly fleshes out his role in the election. Adlai E. Stevenson, *Adlai's Almanac: The Wit and Wisdom of Stevenson of Illinois* (New York: Henry Schuman, 1952), features an eclectic collection of Stevenson's bon mots.

Other useful published collections include Robert L. Branyan and Lawrence H. Larsen, eds., *The Eisenhower Administration, 1953–1961: A Documentary History*, 2 vols. (New York: Random House, 1971); Robert H. Ferrell, ed., *Dear Bess: The Letters from Harry to Bess Truman, 1910–1959* (New York: Norton, 1983); Robert W. Griffith, ed., *Ike's Letters to a Friend, 1941–1958* (Lawrence: University Press of Kansas, 1984—the correspondence is with "Swede" Hazlett); Dennis Merrill, ed., *Documentary History of the Truman Presidency*, vol. 30, *The Constitutional*

Crisis over President Truman's Seizure of the Steel Industry in 1952 (New York: University Publications of America, 2001); and Harry S. Truman and Dean Acheson, *Affection and Trust: The Personal Correspondence of Harry S. Truman and Dean Acheson* (New York: Knopf, 2010).

Lyn Ragsdale, ed., *Vital Statistics on the Presidency*, 3rd ed. (Washington, DC: CQ Press, 2008), is indispensable. Other specialty primary sources of value include Kirk H. Porter and Donald B. Johnson, *National Party Platforms: 1840–1960* (Urbana: University of Illinois Press, 1961); *Official Report of the Proceedings of the Twenty-Fifth Republican National Convention* (Washington, DC: Judd & Detweiler, 1952); and *Official Report of the Proceedings of the Democratic National Convention, 1952* (n.p.: Democratic National Committee Publication, 1952). The published papers from a conference on the Eisenhower presidency, held at Hofstra University in March 1984 and published as Joann P. Krieg, ed., *DDE: Soldier, President, and Statesman* (Westport, CT: Greenwood Press, 1987), hold several essays of value.

The researcher of the election of 1952 is helped by several useful bibliographies: Robert D. Bohanan, comp., "Dwight D. Eisenhower: A Selected Bibliography of Periodical and Dissertation Literature," DDEL, National Archives and Records Service, General Services Administration, 1981; John Robert Greene and Allan Metz, comps., *Richard M. Nixon: A Bibliography* (Middletown, CT: Godfrey Memorial Library, 2006); R. Alton Lee, *Dwight D. Eisenhower: A Bibliography of His Times and Presidency* (Wilmington, DE: Scholarly Resources, 1991); and Elizabeth R. Snoke, *Dwight D. Eisenhower: A Centennial Bibliography* (Fort Leavenworth, KS: U.S. Army Command and General Staff College, 1990).

Several published diaries were helpful: Tyler Abell, ed., *The Drew Pearson Diaries, 1949–1959* (New York: Holt, Rinehart, and Winston, 1974); Robert H. Ferrell, ed., *The Eisenhower Diaries* (New York: Norton, 1981), although this diary contained precious little on 1952; Arthur M. Schlesinger Jr., *Journals, 1952–2000* (New York: Penguin Books, 2007); and C. L. Sulzberger, *A Long Row of Candles: Memoirs and Diaries, 1934–1954* (New York: Macmillan, 1969).

The memoir and autobiographical literature that pertains to the 1952 election is vast—save for the fact that neither Stevenson nor Taft wrote a memoir of his own. Of the candidates, Dwight D. Eisenhower, *The White House Years*, vol. 1, *Mandate for Change: 1953–1956* (Garden City, NY: Doubleday, 1963), is a slow read, pedantically written and with notable omissions. However, in his opening section on 1952, he underscores the message that his letters corroborate—he did nothing to aid those who, in 1951, touted him for the presidency. Earl Warren, *The Memoirs of Earl Warren* (Garden City, NY: Doubleday, 1977), offers little on 1952. The same cannot be said for Richard M. Nixon, *Six Crises* (Garden City, NY: Doubleday, 1962), which features the inclusion of the "Checkers Speech" as one of the formative "crises" of his early career. Nixon uses his chapter "The Fund" to take several thinly veiled slaps at Eisenhower, saving particular vitriol for members of Eisenhower's team (in Nixon's view, if they had only left Eisenhower alone, the crisis would have dissipated—a view shared by the present author in chapter 4). There is nothing in Richard M. Nixon, *The Memoirs of Richard*

Nixon (New York: Grosset & Dunlap, 1978), on 1952 that is not included in *Six Crises.*

While Stevenson wrote no set of memoirs, the closest we have to his memories of the 1952 campaign is the introduction to *Major Campaign Speeches of 1952* (above). However, Edward P. Doyle, ed., *As We Knew Adlai: The Stevenson Story by Twenty-Two Friends* (New York: Harper & Row, 1966), is quite useful, containing the reminiscences of several Stevenson intimates who were important to the 1952 campaign, most notably Jacob Arvey, George Ball, Stephen Mitchell, John Sparkman, and Wilson Wyatt. Harry S. Truman, *Memoirs*, vol. 1, *Year of Decisions* (Garden City, NY: Doubleday, 1955), is a strong read, carefully written, and useful to sketch in the early stages of his presidency. *Memoirs*, vol. 2, *Years of Trial and Hope* (Garden City, NY: Doubleday, 1956), driven by the demands of the publishing world and hastily written, is much less satisfying. Alben Barkley, *That Reminds Me* (Garden City, NY: Doubleday, 1954), blames labor and Truman, in roughly equal amounts, for causing the end of his brief candidacy.

The most revelatory of the other memoirs are George W. Ball, *The Past Has Another Pattern: Memoirs* (New York: Norton, 1982), the closest thing we have to the memoir of the campaign that Stevenson himself might have written; Herbert Brownell, *Advising Ike: The Memoirs of Attorney General Herbert Brownell* (Lawrence: University Press of Kansas, 1993), which offers the best inside look at the Dewey/Lodge Committee; Milton Eisenhower, *The President Is Calling* (Garden City, NY: Doubleday, 1974), a work written by the president's brother that presents him as being both "tormented" and "vulnerable" in 1951; thus, he "yielded to the pressure" from those around him and finally decided to run (246–247); and William Bragg Ewald, *Eisenhower the President: Crucial Days, 1951–1960* (Englewood Cliffs, NJ: Prentice Hall, 1981), a memoir that is interspersed with the interviews and letters to which he had access while working with Eisenhower on his memoirs.

Other memoirs include Sherman Adams, *Firsthand Report: The Story of the Eisenhower Administration* (New York: Popular Library, 1962); Joseph Alsop and Stewart Alsop, *The Reporter's Trade* (New York: Reynal, 1958); Clinton B. Anderson, *Outsider in the Senate: Senator Clinton Anderson's Memoirs* (New York: World, 1970); Clark Clifford, *Counsel to the President: A Memoir* (New York: Random House, 1991); Alistair Cooke, *Six Men* (New York: Knopf, 1977); Jane Dick, *Whistlestopping with Adlai* (Chicago: October House, 1952); Paul H. Douglas, *In the Fullness of Time: The Memoirs of Paul H. Douglas* (New York: Harcourt Brace Jovanovich, 1972); John S. D. Eisenhower, *Strictly Personal* (Garden City, NY: Doubleday, 1974); John Kenneth Galbraith, *A Life in Our Times: Memoirs* (Boston: Houghton Mifflin, 1981); John Kenneth Galbraith, *Annals of an Abiding Liberal* (New York: Plume, 1980); Katherine Graham Howard, *With My Shoes Off* (New York: Vantage Press, 1977); Emmet John Hughes, *The Ordeal of Power: A Political Memoir of the Eisenhower Years* (New York: Atheneum, 1963); Hubert H. Humphrey, *The Education of a Public Man: My Life and Politics* (Garden City, NY: Doubleday, 1976); Walter Johnson, *How We Drafted Adlai Stevenson* (New York: Knopf, 1955); Arthur Krock, *Memoirs: Sixty Years on the Firing Line* (New York:

Funk & Wagnalls, 1968); Henry Cabot Lodge, *The Storm Has Many Eyes* (New York: Norton, 1973); John Bartlow Martin, *It Seems Like Only Yesterday: Memoirs of Writing, Presidential Politics, and the Diplomatic Life* (New York: William Morrow, 1986); James Reston, *Deadline: A Memoir* (New York: Random House, 1991); Stanley M. Rumbough Jr., *Citizens for Eisenhower: The 1952 Presidential Campaign: Lessons for the Future?* (McLean, VA: International Publishers, 2013); Marty Snyder, *My Friend Ike* (New York: Frederick Fell, 1956); Harold Stassen and Marshall Houts, *Eisenhower: Turning the World towards Peace* (St. Paul, MN: Merrill/Magnus, 1990); Roy Wilkins, *Standing Fast: The Autobiography of Roy Wilkins* (New York: Viking Press, 1982); and Wilson W. Wyatt Sr., *Whistle Stops: Adventures in Public Life* (Lexington: University Press of Kentucky, 1985). Of uneven use are the interviews in Merle Miller, *Plain Speaking: An Oral Biography of Harry S. Truman* (New York: Berkeley Books, 1973), and in Kenneth W. Thompson, ed., *The Eisenhower Presidency: Eleven Intimate Perspectives of Dwight D. Eisenhower* (Lanham, MD: University Press of America, 1984).

As with all studies of contemporary America, the *New York Times*, despite its decidedly pro-Eisenhower stance, is the paper of record. *Time* magazine offers the most detailed reporting of all the news weeklies, but its viewpoint, like that of its publisher, Henry Luce, was also pro-Eisenhower. For a more balanced assessment of the election, one that offers the reader extensive, unedited publication of speeches and campaign-related documents and the like, see the pages of *U.S. News & World Report*.

There are several excellent overviews of American society during this period. See Andrew J. Dunar, *America in the Fifties* (Syracuse, NY: Syracuse University Press, 2006); Eric Goldman, *The Crucial Decade and After, 1945–1960* (New York: Vintage Books, 1960); and David Halberstam, *The Fifties* (New York: Villard Books, 1993).

There is, to date, only one scholarly monograph on the election: John Robert Greene, *The Crusade: The Presidential Election of 1952* (Lanham, MD: University Press of America, 1985). For a discussion of this book, and how it relates to and influenced the present volume, see the author's preface to this book. See also Barton J. Bernstein, "Election of 1952," in Arthur M. Schlesinger Jr., ed., *History of American Presidential Elections* (New York: Chelsea House, 1985). Chester J. Pach and Elmo Richardson, *The Presidency of Dwight D. Eisenhower*, rev. ed. (Lawrence: University Press of Kansas, 1991), begins with a useful survey of the election.

Biographies of the major candidates are a decidedly mixed lot. Books on Dwight D. Eisenhower are a cottage industry. The best one-volume biography continues to be Herbert S. Parmet, *Eisenhower and the American Crusades* (New York: Collier Macmillan, 1972). The best short biography is Tom Wicker, *Dwight D. Eisenhower* (New York: Times Books, 2002). Also useful for a study of 1952 are Piers Brendon, *Ike: His Life and Times* (New York: Harper & Row, 1986); Robert F. Burk, *Dwight D. Eisenhower: Hero and Politician* (Boston: G. K. Hall, 1986); Marquis Childs, *Eisenhower: Captive Hero* (New York: Harcourt, Brace & World, 1958); Peter Lyon, *Eisenhower: Portrait of a Hero* (Boston: Little, Brown, 1974); and

Jim Newton, *Eisenhower: The White House Years* (New York: Doubleday, 2011). James T. Patterson, *Mr. Republican: A Biography of Robert A. Taft* (Boston: Houghton Mifflin, 1972), is a clearly written, dispassionate work that is a model of political biography. See also William S. White, *The Taft Story* (New York: Harper, 1954); and Russell Kirk and James McClellan, *The Political Principles of Robert A. Taft* (New York: Fleet Press, 1967). Ed Cray, *Chief Justice: A Biography of Earl Warren* (New York: Simon & Schuster, 1997), and Jack Harrison Pollack, *Earl Warren: The Judge Who Changed America* (New York: Prentice Hall, 1979), are both serviceable biographies of their subject. William Manchester, *American Caesar: Douglas MacArthur, 1880–1964* (Boston: Little, Brown, 1978), includes the briefest of mentions of the general's starcrossed 1952 candidacy. As for Eisenhower, there are countless biographies of Richard Nixon. The best, and most thoughtful, remains Garry Wills, *Nixon Agonistes: The Crisis of the Self-Made Man* (New York: New American Library, 1969). Those that offer the most insightful interpretations on 1952 are Stewart Alsop, *Nixon and Rockefeller: A Double Portrait* (New York: Doubleday, 1960); Irwin F. Gellman, *The President and the Apprentice: Eisenhower and Nixon, 1952–1961* (New Haven, CT: Yale University Press, 2015); and John W. Malsberger, *The General and the Politician: Dwight Eisenhower, Richard Nixon, and American Politics* (New York: Rowman & Littlefield, 2014).

The best biography of Adlai Stevenson is Jeff Broadwater, *Adlai Stevenson and American Politics: The Odyssey of a Cold War Liberal* (New York: Twayne, 1994). It is balanced and impeccably researched and includes the best bibliographical essay on the life of Stevenson presently available. The most insightful view of Stevenson's character is found in Jean Baker, *The Stevensons: A Biography of the American Family* (New York: Norton, 1996). The rest of the biographies of Stevenson are written by friends or acolytes and are usually fawning toward their subject. Of these, the most helpful here were Bert Cochran, *Adlai Stevenson: Patrician among the Politicians* (New York: Funk & Wagnalls, 1969); Kenneth S. Davis, *The Politics of Honor: A Biography of Adlai E. Stevenson* (New York: Putnam, 1967); John Bartlow Martin, *Adlai Stevenson of Illinois* (New York: Anchor Books, 1977); and Porter McKeever, *Adlai Stevenson: His Life and Legacy* (New York: William Morrow, 1989).

A serviceable biography of Estes Kefauver is Charles L. Fontenay, *Estes Kefauver: A Biography* (Knoxville: University of Tennessee Press, 1980). See also Jack Anderson and Fred Blumenthal, *The Kefauver Story* (New York: Dial Press, 1956), and Joseph Bruce Gorman, *Kefauver: A Political Biography* (New York: Oxford University Press, 1981). Also helpful is William Howard Moore, *The Kefauver Committee and the Politics of Crime: 1950–1952* (Columbia: University of Missouri Press, 1974). The very best biography of Richard B. Russell can be found in Robert A. Caro, *The Years of Lyndon Johnson: Master of the Senate* (New York: Knopf, 2002). Caro's masterful prose establishes how Russell came to believe that he could actually win the nomination in 1952. See also Gilbert C. Fite, *Richard B. Russell, Jr., Senator from Georgia* (Chapel Hill: University of North Carolina Press, 1991). Less helpful was Sally Russell, *Richard Brevard Russell, Jr.: A Life of Consequence* (Macon, GA: Mercer University Press, 2011). Rudy Abramson,

Spanning the Century: The Life of W. Averell Harriman, 1891–1986 (New York: William Morrow, 1992), includes one chapter ("Politics") that deals with both Harriman's run for the presidency in 1952 and his run for governor of New York in 1954. For background on Robert S. Kerr, see a biography of his son, written by Ronn Cupp and Bob Burke, *Robert S. Kerr, Jr.: Mr. Water* (Oklahoma City: Oklahoma Heritage Association, 2005). Add to this introduction the analysis of Ann Hodges Morgan, *Robert S. Kerr: The Senate Years* (Norman: University of Oklahoma Press, 1977). James K. Libbey, *Dear Alben: Mr. Barkley of Kentucky* (Lexington: University Press of Kentucky, 2009), offers little on 1952 that cannot be found in Barkley's *That Reminds Me* (above). Harry Truman has been well served by two biographers: Alonzo L. Hamby, *Man of the People: A Life of Harry S. Truman* (New York: Oxford University Press, 1995), and David McCullough, *Truman* (New York: Simon & Schuster, 1992). The best short biography continues to be Robert H. Ferrell, *Harry S. Truman and the Modern American Presidency* (Boston: Little, Brown, 1983).

Other biographies that contributed to this study include James A. Bill, *George Ball: Behind the Scenes in U.S. Foreign Policy* (New Haven, CT: Yale University Press, 1997); Frank Cormier and William J. Eaton, *Reuther* (Englewood Cliffs, NJ: Prentice Hall, 1970); D. B. Hardeman and Donald C. Bacon, *Rayburn: A Biography* (Austin: Texas Monthly Press, 1987); Townsend Hoopes, *The Devil and John Foster Dulles* (Boston: Little, Brown, 1973); Neil MacNeil, *Dirksen: Portrait of a Public Man* (New York: World, 1970); Jean Edward Smith, *Lucius D. Clay: An American Life* (New York: Henry Holt, 1990); Richard Norton Smith, *Thomas E. Dewey and His Times* (New York: Simon & Schuster, 1982); A. M. Sperber, *Murrow: His Life and Times* (New York: Freundlich Books, 1986); and Alfred Steinberg, *Sam Rayburn: A Biography* (New York: Hawthorn Books, 1975).

This essay cannot do justice to the full scope of the work on the presidency of Harry S. Truman, much of which deals in some way—albeit usually in a tertiary fashion—with 1952. David S. Margolies, ed., *A Companion to Harry S. Truman* (Oxford: Blackwell, 2012), is an excellent starting point for essays reviewing the breadth of literature on the Truman administration. The best one-volume treatment of the presidency remains Donald McCoy, *The Presidency of Harry S. Truman* (Lawrence: University Press of Kansas, 1984)—a book that includes a strong but brief analysis of Truman's role in 1952. Other specialty works useful for a study of Truman's role in 1952 are William C. Berman, *The Politics of Civil Rights in the Truman Administration* (Columbus: Ohio State University Press, 1970); Andrew E. Busch, *Truman's Triumphs: The 1948 Election and the Making of Postwar America* (Lawrence: University Press of Kansas, 2012); Robert J. Donovan, *Conflict and Crisis: The Presidency of Harry S. Truman* (New York: Norton, 1977); Robert J. Donovan, *Tumultuous Years: The Presidency of Harry S. Truman, 1949–1953* (New York: Norton, 1982); Andrew J. Dunar, *The Truman Scandals and the Politics of Morality* (Columbia: University of Missouri Press, 1984); Michael R. Gardner, *Harry Truman and Civil Rights: Moral Courage and Political Risks* (Carbondale: Southern Illinois University Press, 2002); Alonzo L. Hamby, *Beyond the New Deal: Harry S. Truman and American Liberalism* (New York: Columbia

University Press, 1973); and Maeva Marcus, *Truman and the Steel Seizure Case: The Limits of Presidential Power* (New York: Columbia University Press, 1977).

Indispensable to an understanding of the fractionalization of the political parties after 1945 are John Fousek, *To Lead the Free World: American Nationalism and the Cultural Roots of the Cold War* (Chapel Hill: University of North Carolina Press, 2000); Lewis L. Gould, *Grand Old Party: A History of the Republicans* (New York: Random House, 2003); Geoffrey Kabaservice, *Rule and Ruin: The Downfall of Moderation and the Destruction of the Republican Party, from Eisenhower to the Tea Party* (New York: Oxford University Press, 2012); and Jules Witcover, *Party of the People: A History of the Democrats* (New York: Random House, 2005).

The beginning of Eisenhower's decision-making process as to whether or not to become a candidate is well told in Travis Beal Jacobs, *Eisenhower at Columbia* (New Brunswick, NJ: Transaction, 2001), and Jacobs, "Eisenhower, the American Assembly, and 1952," *Presidential Studies Quarterly* 22 (Summer 1992): 455–468. Less helpful is Douglas E. Clark, *Eisenhower in Command at Columbia* (Lanham, MD: Lexington Books, 2013). For a fuller treatment of that process, see William B. Pickett, *Eisenhower Decides to Run: Presidential Politics and Cold War Strategy* (Chicago: Ivan R. Dee, 2000).

The most thorough study of the primaries in 1952, albeit one sourced almost exclusively by contemporary newspapers, is Jerome Nashorn, *Choosing the Candidates—1952* (New York: Garland, 1988). Also useful on the primaries are Donald H. Ackerman Jr., "The Write-In Vote for Dwight D. Eisenhower in the Spring 1952 Minnesota Primary: Minnesota Politics on the Grass-Roots Level" (PhD diss., Syracuse University, 1954); Joseph Reuben Churgin, "Anatomy of a Presidential Primary: An Analysis of New Hampshire's Impact on American Politics" (PhD diss., Brown University, 1970); and William Carl Zehnder, "The 1952 Presidential Election in the State of Florida" (master's thesis, Florida Atlantic University, 1973). Leonard Lurie, *The King Makers* (New York: Coward, McCann, and Geoghegan, 1971), is a useful firsthand account of the Republican Convention.

The breaking of the Democratic control of the South is in many ways the most important outcome of the election of 1952. There is a strong literature on the critical role played by the state of Texas in 1952. Sean P. Cunningham, *Cowboy Conservatism: Texas and the Rise of the Modern Right* (Lexington: University Press of Kentucky, 2010), and Ricky F. Dobbs, *Yellow Dogs and Republicans: Allan Shivers and Texas Two-Party Politics* (College Station: Texas A&M University Press, 2005), offer particularly useful observations. See also Don E. Carleton, *Red Scare! Right-Wing Hysteria, Fifties Fanaticism, and Their Legacy in Texas* (Austin: Texas Monthly Press, 1985); Paul Casdorph, *A History of the Republican Party in Texas, 1865–1965* (Austin, TX: Pemberton Press, 1965); and O. Douglas Weeks, *Texas Presidential Politics in 1952* (Washington, DC: Institute of Public Affairs, 1953). An excellent source on the Tidelands oil issue is Lucius Jefferson Barker, "Offshore Oil Politics: A Study in Public Policy Making" (PhD diss., University of Illinois, 1954). For other useful studies of the campaign in the South, see Philip A. Grant, "Eisenhower and the 1952 Invasion of the South: The Case of Virginia,"

Presidential Studies Quarterly 20 (1990): 285–293; and L. Vaughan Howard and David R. Deener, *Presidential Politics in Louisiana, 1952* (New Orleans: Tulane University Press, 1954). On the black vote in the 1950s, see Timothy N. Thurber, *Republicans and Race: The GOP's Frayed Relationship with African-Americans, 1945–1974* (Lawrence: University Press of Kansas, 2013).

On the early development of television as a political weapon, Eric Barnouw, *Tube of Plenty: The Evolution of American Television* (New York: Oxford University Press, 1975), continues to serve as the standard work. *The Influence of Television on the 1952 Election* (Crosby Broadcasting Study, Miami University, 1953); and Charles A. H. Thomson, *Television and Presidential Politics: The Experience in 1952 and the Problems Ahead* (Washington, DC: Brookings Institution, 1956), both offer useful contemporary analyses. Two excellent articles, John E. Hollitz, "Eisenhower and the Admen: The Television 'Spot' Campaign of 1952," *Wisconsin Magazine of History* 66 (1982): 25–39, and Stephen C. Wood, "Television's First Political Spot Ad Campaign: 'Eisenhower Answers America,'" *Presidential Studies Quarterly* 20 (1990): 265–283, offer particularly prescient studies of campaign advertising in 1952. For the bottom line, see Burton A. Abrams and Russel F. Settle, "The Effect of Political Campaign Broadcasting on Political Campaign Spending: An Empirical Investigation," *Journal of Political Economics* 84 (1976): 1095–1108.

The enormous Nixon literature includes many analyses of the Fund Crisis and the "Checkers Speech." Nixon's *Six Crises* (above) is incomplete but indispensable. The most recent monograph is Kevin Mattson, *Just Plain Dick: Richard Nixon's Checkers Speech and the "Rocking, Socking" Election of 1952* (New York: Bloomsbury, 2012). See also David A. Frier, *Conflict of Interest in the Eisenhower Administration* (Ames: Iowa State University Press, 1969); and Robert W. O'Brien and Elizabeth J. Jones, *The Night Nixon Spoke: A Study of Political Effectiveness* (Los Alamitos, CA: Hwong, 1976).

Jeff Broadwater, *Eisenhower and the Anti-Communist Crusade* (Chapel Hill: University of North Carolina Press, 1992), offers the most thoughtful study on the role and influence of Joseph McCarthy in the campaign. Also consult Edwin R. Bayley, *Joe McCarthy and the Press* (Madison: University of Wisconsin Press, 1981); Fred J. Cook, *Nightmare Decade: The Life and Times of Senator Joe McCarthy* (New York: Random House, 1971); Michael O'Brien, *McCarthy and McCarthyism in Wisconsin* (Columbia: University of Missouri Press, 1980); and Richard Rovere, *Senator Joe McCarthy* (New York: Harcourt Brace, 1959).

On foreign policy, particularly the impact of the Korean War on the election, consult Ronald J. Caridi, *The Korean War and American Politics: The Republican Party as a Case Study* (Philadelphia: University of Pennsylvania Press, 1968); Robert A. Divine, *Foreign Policy and U.S. Presidential Elections: 1952–1960* (New York: New Viewpoints, 1974); Joseph C. Goulden, *Korea: The Untold Story of the War* (New York: Times Books, 1982); Walter LaFeber, *America, Russia, and the Cold War, 1945–1980* (New York: Wiley, 1980); and Martin Walker, *The Cold War: A History* (New York: Holt, 1995). John Foster Dulles laid out his policy of "liberation" in "A Policy of Boldness," *Life*, 19 May 1952, 146+. On Eisenhower's most famous speech, see Martin J. Medhurst, "Text and Context in the 1952 Presidential Campaign: Eisenhower's 'I Shall Go to Korea' Speech," *Presidential Studies Quarterly* 30 (September 2000): 464–484.

There are many useful contemporary studies on 1952. The very best—indeed, a five-volume study that would long be the gold standard for contemporary political histories—is Paul T. David, Malcolm Moos, and Ralph Goldman, *Presidential Nominating Politics in 1952*, vol. 1, *The National Story*; vol. 2, *The Northeast*; vol. 3, *The South*; vol. 4, *The Middle West*; vol. 5, *The West* (Baltimore: Johns Hopkins University Press, 1954). Also useful were Nathan Blumberg, *One Party Press? Coverage of the 1952 Presidential Campaign in 35 Daily Newspapers* (Lincoln: University of Nebraska Press, 1954); Angus Campbell, Gerald Gurin, and Warren E. Miller, *The Voter Decides* (Evanston, IL: Row, Peterson, 1954); Alfred deGrazia, *The Western Public: 1952 and Beyond* (Stanford, CA: Stanford University Press, 1954); Heinz Eulau, *Class and Party in the Eisenhower Years* (New York: Free Press of Glencoe, 1962); Louis Harris, *Is There a Republican Majority? Political Trends: 1952–56* (New York: Harper & Bros., 1956); Morris Janowitz and Dwaine Marvick, *Competitive Pressure and Democratic Consent: An Interpretation of the 1952 Presidential Election* (Chicago: Quadrangle Books, 1964); Earl Roger Kruschke, *The Woman Voter: An Analysis from Personal Interviews* (Washington, DC: Public Affairs Press, 1955); Samuel Lubell, *The Future of American Politics* (New York: Harper & Row, 1965); Samuel Lubell, *The Revolt of the Moderates* (New York: Harper, 1956); and Elmo Roper, *You and Your Leaders: Their Actions and Your Reactions* (New York: William Morrow, 1957).

Walter Dean Burnham, "American Politics in the 1970's: Beyond Party?," in William Nisbet Chambers and Walter Dean Burnham, eds., *The American Party System: Stages of Political Development* (New York: Oxford University Press, 1975), is one of the first pieces to identify and define a "realigning election." For the effect of the 1952 election on the party system, see Everett Carl Ladd Jr. and Charles D. Hadley, *Transformations of the American Party System: Political Coalitions from the New Deal to the 1970s* (New York: Norton, 1975). See also John Patrick Clancy, "Adlai Ewing Stevenson and the Bureaucracy of the Democratic Party in the 1950s" (PhD diss., United States International University, 1975).

The best study of Eisenhower's "middle way" as president is Steven Wagner, *Eisenhower Republicanism: Pursuing the Middle Way* (DeKalb: Northern Illinois University Press, 2006). See also Gary W. Reichard, *The Reaffirmation of Republicanism: Eisenhower and the Eighty-Third Congress* (Knoxville: University of Tennessee Press, 1975). On the 1954 off-year elections, Charles A. Moser, "Watershed and Ratifying Elections: A Historical View of the 1934 and 1954 Congressional Elections" (Washington, DC: Free Congress Research and Education Foundation, 1982), is indispensable, concluding that the key to the outcome was "the question of linkage between GOP congressional candidates and the president" (25). Less helpful is the highly quantitative Angus Campbell and Homer C. Cooper, *Group Differences in Attitudes and Votes: A Study of the 1954 Congressional Elections* (Ann Arbor: Institute for Social Research, University of Michigan, 1956). The best book on the presidential election of 1956, setting the election in the context of both Eisenhower's deteriorating health and the international crisis over the Suez Canal, is David A. Nichols, *Eisenhower, 1956* (New York: Simon & Schuster, 2011). Also useful is Robert A. Divine, *Eisenhower and the Cold War* (New York: Oxford University Press, 1981). Charles A. H. Thomson and Frances M. Shattuck, *The 1956 Presidential Campaign* (Washington, DC: Brookings Institution Press, 1960), is a worthy summary of the secondary sources but offers no real depth of analysis.

INDEX

ABC television network, 91
Abilene (Kansas), 54–55
Acheson, Dean, 7, 134
Adams, Sherman, 39, 40, 129, 130, 160, 165
  and Fair Play Amendment, 96
  and New Hampshire primary (Republican), 45–46
  and "Nixon Fund Crisis," 152
Adlai's Almanac (Stevenson, 1952), 65
Adlai Stevenson: Patrician among the Politicians (Cochran, 1969), 65
Advertising, on television in Democratic and Republican National Conventions (1952), 91–92
Africa, 24
Age of Jackson, The (Schlesinger, 1946), 138
Agricultural Adjustment Act (AAA), 62, 63, 178
Agriculture, Department of, 178
Allen, George, 40, 44, 195n83
Alsop, Stewart, 140, 153, 215n49
America First Party, 101
American Airlines, 107
American Assembly (Columbia University), 25–26, 192n28
American Legion, 148
American Occupation Zone (Europe), 32
Americans for Democratic Action, 133, 150
Anderson, Clifford, 60, 76, 139
Anderson and Kerr Drilling Company, 76
Appel, Monte, 94
Army Air Corps, 43
Arvey, Jacob M. ("Jake"), 62–63, 111, 121, 125, 133, 165, 183
"A Serenade for Ike." *See* Madison Square Garden: rally for Eisenhower (8 February 1952)
Aswan Dam (Egypt), 184
Atlanta Constitution, 84, 94
Atlanta Journal, 127
Atlantic Union, 83
Atomic bomb, 13, 20

Bacall, Lauren, 43
Bailey, John, 168
Ball, George, 67–69, 134, 139, 140, 146, 168, 183
Barkley, Alben, xv
  at 1948 Democratic Convention as keynoter, 100
  and age issue, 88
  background of, 87–88
  "farewell address," 208n46
  and labor, 117–118
  loses Democratic nomination for presidency, 124–126
  and Stevenson, 88
  and Truman, 89, 100, 110, 116–118, 122
  on Truman, 117–118
  withdraws from nominating contest, 117
Baruch, Bernard, 29
Battle, John, 123, 143
Beauchamp, Emerson, 117
Bell, David, 139
Belle Springs Creamery (Abilene, KS), 22
Benedict, Stephen, 96
Benson, Ezra Taft, 178
Berlin, Irving, 43
Berlin Blockade, 7
Biffle, Leslie, 89, 117
Bixby, R. Burdell, 36
Blackstone Hotel (Chicago), 103, 108, 182
Black vote, 5
  in 1952, 21, 79, 171
Blair, William McCormack, 133
Blair House (Washington, DC), 57, 67
Bloomington Pantagraph, 62
Bogart, Humphrey, 43
Bonus Army (1932), 23–24
Bowler, James, 179
Boyd, Ralph, 96
Bradley, General Omar, 25, 29
Brannan Plan, 7
Breckinridge, Henry, 203n73
Brendon, Piers, 194n60
Bricker, John, 99, 178

239

Quezon, Manuel, 24

Rawlings, Calvin, 114
Rayburn, Sam, 4, 85, 115, 123, 124, 128,
    145, 174
  on Kefauver, 123
  and Kefauver's attempt to concede
    defeat at convention, 125
Reagan, Ronald, 66, 173
Reciprocal Trade Agreements Act (1934), 178
Reconstruction Finance Corporation, 7, 133
Reeves, Rosser, 145–146
Remington-Rand, 101
Republican Convention, Credentials
    Committee, 101
Republican Finance Committee, 32
Republican National Committee (RNC),
    30, 41, 93, 95, 98, 130, 146
  Chicago, 1912, 96
  Philadelphia, 1940, 38
  Chicago, 1944, 94
  Philadelphia, 1948, 94
  Chicago, 1952, 90–110
  and "Nixon Fund Crisis," 154, 156
Republican party, split between moderate
    and conservative wings, 17–18, 21
Reserve Officers Training Corps (ROTC), 37
Reuther, Walter, 117
Rhode Island Golf Club, 145
Richardson, Elmo, 11
Richardson, Sid, 26, 44, 195n83
Richmond Times-Dispatch, 145
Rizley, Ross, 102
RNC. *See* Republican National Committee
    (RNC)
Robinson, William, 153
Rockefeller, Nelson A., 186, 195n77
Rodgers, Richard, 43
Roosevelt, Eleanor, 3, 79, 143
Roosevelt, Franklin D., xv, 4, 17, 18, 19, 20,
    24, 41, 58, 64, 70, 78, 80, 85, 87, 139,
    143, 170, 173, 178, 203n73
Roosevelt, Franklin D., Jr., 79
Roosevelt, Theodore, 16, 18, 96, 203n73
Roosevelt coalition, 2, 80, 148
Roosevelt Hotel (New York City), 36
Root, Elihu, 96
"Root Rule," 96
Roper, Elmo, 111

Roper Poll, 7
Rosenberg, Ethel, 13
Rosenberg, Julius, 13
Rosenman, Samuel I., 139
ROTC. *See* Reserve Officers Training
    Corps (ROTC)
Rowan, Carl, 69
Royall, Kenneth Claiborne, 26
"Rule 22" (Senate cloture), 112, 113,
    143–144
Rumbough, Stanley M., Jr., 31
Russell, Richard B., Sr., 70
Russell, Richard B., Jr., 113, 173
  announces candidacy for Democratic
    nomination in 1952, 71
  background of, 69–70, 74, 81
  and civil rights, 70–71
  and election of 1948, 71
  and FEPC, 70, 83, 84
  and Florida primary, 82–84
  loses Democratic nomination for
    presidency, 124–126
  and Nebraska primary (Democratic), 77
  and New Hampshire primary
    (Democratic), 71
  and "Northern Coalition," 116
  refuses to campaign for Stevenson, 145
  and Truman's offer of vice presidential
    nomination, 127

Saltonstall, Leverett, 46
Sandburg, Carl, 81
San Francisco Conference, 147
Sasscer, Lansdale, 123
Saturday Evening Post, 65, 139
Sawyer, Tom, 22
Scherer, Ray, x, 198n153
Schlesinger, Arthur M., Jr., 77, 138–139
Schweicker, Henry, 121
Scott, Hugh, 31, 96
Seaton, Fred, 160
Selective Service Act (1948), 12
Selective Service System, 163
Shanley, Bernard, 38
Shannon, Margaret Rutledge, 127
SHAPE. *See* Supreme Headquarters Allied
    Powers Europe (SHAPE)
Shelley v. Kraemer (1948), 199n2
Sherman, William T., 2, 142

and Fair Employment Practices
Commission (FEPC), 63, 143
as governor of Illinois, 63–64
and Harriman, 77–79
and Korean War, 163–166
and labor, 117
and McCarthy, 63, 162
meeting with Truman and Sparkman
(12 August 1952), 134
on the "mess in Washington," 135–136,
158
and myth of indecision, 69
and NAACP, 143–144
and "Nixon Fund Crisis," 152, 155, 156
personal fund of, 152
photo of, 67, 111, 135, 169, 174
seen as a liberal, 64–66
and Shivers, 144
as speaker, 64–65, 66, 81–82, 137–140,
142
and story of offer of Supreme Court
nomination to Warren, 208n45
and Suez Crisis, 184
on the "Surrender at Morningside
Heights," 132
and Tidelands oil, 144
and Truman, 68, 79, 81, 122, 128, 132–
136, 214n24
and vote on seating Virginia delegation,
123–124
wins Democratic nomination for
presidency, 124–126
Stevenson, Adlai E., II, speeches of
17 April 1952 (New York, Democratic
Party fundraiser), 81
23 April 1952 (New York, dinner
honoring Harriman), 81
21 July 1952 (Chicago, welcoming
address at Democratic Convention),
118–119
26 July 1952 (Chicago, acceptance
speech to Democratic Convention),
126, 208n46
27 August 1952 (American Legion), 161
1 September 1952 (Hamtramck, MI,
Labor Day), 148–149
27 September 1952 (Louisville, on
Korea), 163–164

7 October 1952 (Detroit), 161
8 October 1952 (Milwaukee), 161–162
23 October 1952 (Cleveland), 162
3 November 1952 (Chicago), 167
Stevenson, Ellen, 64
St. Lawrence Seaway, 177
St. Louis Post Dispatch, 71, 156
Stockyard Inn (Chicago), 125
Suez Crisis (1956), 183–185
Sulzberger, Cyrus L., II, 48, 57, 101
Summerfield, Arthur, 130, 139, 153, 159
photo of, 108
Superior Oil Company, 53
Supreme Court, 18, 56, 57, 144
and *Colgrove v. Green*, 208n55
story of Eisenhower's offer of Supreme
Court nomination to Warren, 208n45
and Tidelands oil issue, 4
and *Youngstown Sheet and Tube Company
v. Sawyer* (1952), 13
Supreme Headquarters Allied Powers
Europe (SHAPE)
Eisenhower at, 26, 30–31, 34, 36, 38,
40–41, 42, 47, 48, 49, 106, 137, 142,
164
"Surrender at Morningside Heights,"
130–132, 142, 160, 176
Symington, Stuart, 172

Taft, Robert, xi, xii, xv, xvi, 28, 35, 36, 39,
41, 44, 54, 55, 92, 101, 105, 126, 159,
173, 174, 176, 177
on atomic bomb, 20
background of, 18–22
and black vote, 21
and California primary (Republican),
53–54
as campaigner, 21
as conservative, 19, 176–177
and credentials challenge at convention,
93–96
death of, 172
and Dulles, 148
and Eisenhower, 34, 40–42, 194n72
and election of 1940, 17, 21
and election of 1944, 21, 53
and election of 1948, 21, 38, 41
and Fair Play Amendment, 96–100